Germany's Rude Awakening

GERMANY'S RUDE AWAKENING

Censorship in the Land of the Brothers Grimm

FREDERIK OHLES

The Kent State University Press
Kent, Ohio, and London, England

© 1992 by **The Kent State University Press,** Kent, Ohio 44242
All rights reserved
Library of Congress Catalog Card Number 92-826
ISBN 0-87338-460-1
Manufactured in the United States of America

Library of Congress Cataloging-in-Publication Data

Ohles, Frederik, 1953–
    Germany's rude awakening : censorship in the land of the Brothers Grimm / Frederik Ohles.
    p.   cm.
    Includes bibliographical references and index.
    ISBN 0-87338-460-1 (alk.) ∞
    1. Censorship—Germany—Hesse-Kassel (Electorate)—History—19th century. 2. Politics and literature—Germany—Hesse-Kassel (Electorate)—History—19th century. 3. Literature—Censorship—Germany—History—19th century. 4. Grimm, Jacob, 1785–1863—Contemporary Germany. 5. Grimm, Wilhelm, 1786–1859—Contemporary Germany. I. Title.
Z658.G३०35   1992
363.3′1′09434109034—dc20   92-826

British Library Cataloging-in-Publication data are available.

for Rosemary,
who is my inspiration

Contents

Acknowledgments		ix
1	The Challenge of Censorship	1
2	A Still Life: *The Land, the People, and Their Princes*	13
3	The Police State: *Censorship Traditions and Laws*	28
4	This Hated Office: *The Censors and Their Work*	48
5	Dreadful, Tiresome Reading: *Censorship of Lending Libraries and Periodicals*	70
6	The Logic of Censorship	88
7	Scrutiny before Sale: *The Battle between Censorship and the Book Trade*	109
8	Top Secret: *Chasing Conspiracies among Bookmen*	126
9	Friends of a Free Press: *The Readers of Banned Writ*	147
10	The Failure of Censorship	164
Appendix		171
Notes		199
Select Bibliography		215
Index		221

Acknowledgments

Research for this book was made possible by a generous fellowship from the German Academic Exchange Service, an exemplary organization for the support of scholarship and promotion of international understanding. I am grateful also to Brandeis University for a Scharfman Graduate Teaching Fellowship that supported the writing of my doctoral dissertation. Substantial parts of the book are based on the dissertation, although in some of the evidence and much of the writing, structure, and argumentation it is a different work.

To Rudolph Binion I am deeply appreciative for the helpful criticism and encouragement he gave as my dissertation advisor. Others whose readings of the dissertation raised issues addressed in the book include Eugene C. Black, John J. Gagliardo, Robert Aldrich, David G. Troyansky, and Amy Anderson Troyansky. My thanks go also to more recent readers of the manuscript, including Charles W. Ingrao, Gary D. Stark, and Mary Lee Townsend, as well as to Diethelm Prowe and Karl J. Fink who commented on portions of it. Among the staff of the Hessian State Archive at Marburg, I wish particularly to thank Frau Dr. Ute Löwenstein and Herr Wilhelm Göttig for their kind assistance. Professor Dr. Helmut Berding of the University of Gießen provided a very useful forum in his research seminar for reporting on the work-in-progress. Cameron Munter and Peter Müller generously obtained information in the archive on my behalf when I was far away from it. None of these scholars and friends is responsible for any errors that remain.

At the Council for International Exchange of Scholars, where I served as a program officer while completing the book, Cassandra A. Pyle, Executive Director, and Mary Jane Smalley Roberts, Deputy Director, gave indispensable aid, for which I thank them.

ACKNOWLEDGMENTS

I am glad to acknowledge again the debts I owe to the families of Karl and Elisabeth Müller, Bernhard and Brigitte Wolf, and Arthur and Patricia Holliday who were my hosts along the way, and especially to my parents, John and Shirley Ohles, who gave me unwavering encouragement from the beginning.

The dedication bespeaks a debt like no other.

ONE

The Challenge of Censorship

This is the story of a momentous struggle between old and new views of politics and literature set in a fairy-tale land. On one side was a tradition-bound, paternalist family of German princes who wanted to be loved, trusted, and, even more, obeyed. Arrayed against them were many of their educated subjects who wanted representative government, guarantees of intellectual freedom, and even a German nation. The people read and wrote about their aspirations. The rulers banned literature embodying the people's dream from the shelves of local bookshops, libraries, and private homes. Caught between them, at the center of this history, were censors who served their German princes in the period from 1815 to 1848—intelligent, thoughtful men—pastors, professors, librarians, writers, and one of the Brothers Grimm.

When we think of the Brothers Grimm, what comes to mind first is the fairy tales they collected and the characters who fill them. Only then might we remember that Jacob Grimm and his younger brother Wilhelm were librarians, philologists, and folklorists who lived in Germany, not once upon a time, but just a century and a half ago. Making them part of our world is not eased by visiting the land where they lived and the town where they studied, Marburg in Hesse, because it is a perfect place for fairy tales.

Marburg sits along the banks of the Lahn River, whose source is in the Rothaar mountains where a handful of notable streams are born like fingers from a palm: the Sieg, the Ruhr, the Eder, and the Lahn. Of them all, the Lahn alone takes a foolhardy course, due east into the continent, away from one set of hills but headed straight for others. Then about five miles above Marburg, as if realizing its mistake, it makes a tight turn to the south, passes through the town, and flows on southward and westward until it joins the Rhine near Coblenz. With a mountain ridge to the east, a high plateau to the west, and yet more hills to the north, Marburg sits in a trough that shelters it on three sides from the rest of the world, holds in vapors rising from the Lahn, and keeps out most winds, leaving the town lost in a fog many weeks of the year.

If you travel there by train from the south along a rail line laid out in the 1840s, especially on a March or November morning, you will scarcely know you are approaching a town until its buildings surround you. The eye just catches the facades of sixteenth-century houses perched on a hillside swimming in the mist, finds the sharp-peaked roof of the town hall finished in 1524 and the spires of one or two nearby churches. In the background float the twin towers of St. Elizabeth's Church, built in the thirteenth century, one of the earliest in the Gothic style.

On any very foggy day, the scene appears much the same today as it would have to a traveler one hundred, even two hundred, years ago. On days when the sun burns away enough fog, all illusion vanishes and the twentieth century stands before visitors everywhere they go. But on other days, the mist persists, or even grows heavier, hiding more and more from view. When that happens, it is easy to wish away one hundred and sixty years, walk through the timeless haze, and with a magic found only in fairy tales transport oneself back into the early years of the nineteenth century.

Imagine an autumn day in 1833. The streets of the old town are a medley of cobbles and steps running up and down the steep side of the Marburg hill. On the Wettergasse stands Noa Elwert's bookshop, a favorite way station for students and professors between their rooms in houses on the up-side of the incline and the great hall of the university in a former Dominican cloister down below. Inside, Elwert the bookman lends and sells the works of Martin Luther, Heinrich Heine's *Reisebilder* (Travel Sketches), a play entitled *Napoleon, oder die Hundert Tage* (Napoleon, or the Hundred Days) by Christian Dietrich Grabbe, the novels of Wilhelm Hauff, Walter Scott's in translation, a half-dozen German imitations of Robinson Crusoe, medical handbooks, and a *Geschichte von Hessen* (History of Hesse) by Christoph von Rommel. Once a student and then a professor in Marburg, Rommel is now director of the royal archive, court librarian, and chairman of the censorship commission at Cassel, fifty miles northeast of Marburg and capital of the Electoral Principality of Hesse. Two volumes of Rommel's *History* have been published so far, both of them off the presses in Elwert's own print shop.

THE CHALLENGE OF CENSORSHIP

Up the street, around the corner, and several hundred yards along the Barfüßertor stands the Academic Museum, a private club for gentlemen. Professors, merchants, and local government administrators sit in its parlor, smoke their pipes, play billiards in the game room, and pass an evening reading in the library. Their fare is the *Ober-Postamts-Zeitung* (Central Post Office Gazette) from Frankfort on the Main, Marburg's own smaller official gazette, the *Journal des Débats* (Parliamentary Record) from Paris, and a new Hessian newspaper, the *Verfassungsfreund* (Friend of the Constitution), full of speculation now about the principality's liberal constitution and parliament.

Someone speaks of the Brothers Grimm. It is four years since they left their posts at Hesse's royal library for new ones at the University of Göttingen. It is fifteen years since the University of Marburg conferred doctoral degrees on them for their pathbreaking studies of German language and folklore. It is three decades since the Grimms were young students, walking along the Barfüßertor, through the grounds of the castle atop the hill, attending lectures, stopping to buy books.

The hilltop castle is Marburg's emblem. Sections of it still standing were erected in the fourteenth and fifteenth centuries. For many years it was the residence of the counts of Hesse, and in one of its rooms Martin Luther and Huldrych Zwingli met in 1527, invited by Count Philipp the Magnanimous, in a futile effort to bring their two Protestant movements together. By the days of the Brothers Grimm, the counts of Hesse had long since moved their residence to Cassel, however, and the old castle served as a jail. From 1839 to 1841 and from 1843 to 1845 one of its inmates would be Professor Sylvester Jordan, author of Hesse's controversial, very liberal 1831 constitution.

In the late nineteenth century, the castle became an archive for Hessian state papers, including the records of censorship in the principality. Fifty years ago, a new archive building opened at the bottom of the hill; today, the castle is a museum. What follows, drawn from records in the Hessian State Archive at Marburg, is the story of censorship in the land of the Brothers Grimm.

The setting is Hesse during the first half of the nineteenth century. The characters are Jacob Grimm and other censors of the Hessian principality; the rulers, governors, and administrators of that land; its police, judges, diplomats, and legislators; professors, artisans, and writers; rebels and prisoners. The tale told here is of an old institution called censorship challenged by a new idea called freedom.

The history of censorship is a half-sibling of the history of books. If that vast, overgrown, interdisciplinary subdiscipline, as Robert Darnton describes it, shows "how ideas were transmitted through print and how exposure to the printed word affected the thought and behavior of mankind,"[1] the history of censorship casts a mirror image, showing how ideas were kept out of print and how limiting exposure to the printed word also affected human thought and behavior.

The history of censorship, like the history of books, is part of a larger enterprise, "interpreting . . . literary culture in more than merely literary terms."[2] At the same time, it is an avenue for interpreting political culture in more than merely political terms.

In this book, I take a synoptic view of censorship in a rapidly changing literary and political culture. I keep one eye on authors, publishers, printers, shippers, sellers, and readers, the juncture points on Darnton's schematic "communications circuit," and the other eye on governors, jurists, administrators, police, and censors, all of them "outside influences" on the circuit that printed words took from being written to being read.[3] The characters portrayed in this book were more often "middlemen" than great men of literature and politics and their props were more often middling books than great books.[4] What made the struggle over censorship dramatic in the early nineteenth century was not so much a few notable actors or a few memorable lines but the staging—the place and the time.

After the German princes expelled the French and reestablished their rule in 1813–16, each prince in his own way instituted censorship, which in the sum of its many particular forms became a rare national institution, affecting all social groups, all generations, all careers. It struck at all Germans who could read and write, whoever and wherever they were. Many struck back, in their minds, at least, through what they chose to read despite official prohibitions, and some protested more publicly through what they wrote.

Clemens von Metternich, foreign minister of the Habsburg Empire, fathered a German-wide decree in 1819 that established a standard (often unrealized) for strict literary policing without regard to the many borders between the three dozen German states. Metternich meant to strengthen censorship as an institution to curtail discussion of political issues, but in effect, the heightened attention to censorship over the next several decades made the institution itself a key issue, a new divisive issue.

By the mid-1840s in all German lands, censors invested much of their energy in censoring written works whose offense was that they cried out against censorship. And with each new amputation marked out in ink, disfiguring some author's work, came new outcries, which the literary executioner's instrument had to still. By 1848 the pen of the censor, with its bloodred ink, was one of the most hated symbols of an aging generation of paternalist rulers whom German liberals, mostly young, despised. In that year, when there were revolutions all over Germany, as one of their first acts, the rebels abolished censorship.

Censorship did not begin with Germans in the 1810s nor did it end with them in the 1840s. It existed before there were books and newspapers, long before the invention of movable type; it is part of our world today; it will still be around when printer's ink and paper have given way entirely to computer chips and video screens. But in the long history of how human beings have muzzled each other, the early decades of the nineteenth century were a pivotal time, and Germany was a special place.

It was a time when revolutions in technology, politics, and culture erupted all at once. Cheaper paper and faster printing presses lowered the cost of literature until it became affordable to tens of thousands of people whose means were modest but whose enthusiasm for learning and politics was great. The consequences of this rapid expansion of political literacy were much like the consequences of literacy itself,[5] mainly, increased enthusiasm for change and diminished respect for tradition, twin evils that censorship was meant to counter.

Literate, politically interested subjects in the German lands—whom censorship was meant to keep from reading and politicking—were the spiritual grandchildren of the eighteenth-century Enlightenment, when for a time Voltaire had been a guest of King Friedrich II (Frederick the Great) of Prussia, when for a time Habsburg emperors had tried gently to guide literate culture and to improve popular culture,[6] when philosophers had proclaimed that humankind were naturally equal, reasonable, and, probably, educable too. If these ideas were true, and if monarchs could accommodate themselves to them, then everyone should be able to learn the science of government and to share in it, an idea that France's revolutionaries sought to put into practice throughout Europe.

In the first years of the nineteenth century, cheap paper, French revolutionary armies, and republican ideas spread through central Europe with a speed that frightened and angered staunchly conservative rulers such as Wilhelm I, prince-elector of Hesse, who blamed the French for every unwelcome novelty in his lands. At the same time, the people Mack Walker has called "movers and doers" in German society—civil servants, professors, and publicists principally[7]—were far more welcoming, at least toward cheap paper and republican ideas. Even liberal-minded Germans, though, were patriotic, wanted the French oppressors out of their homeland, and rejoiced when they were gone.

When Napoleon's armies lost the Battle of Leipzig in October 1813 and with it the twenty-year campaign to extend the revolution to all Europe, they left behind these two sorts of German patriots, local autocrats of the old style wanting to return to their habits, and protonationalist liberals eager for change, primed for political and literary freedom, ready to take part in the formation of a German "public opinion."[8] On 1 July 1814 a new liberal newspaper, the *Rheinischer Merkur* (Rhenish Mercury), appeared in the western provinces of Prussia, and in an opening address to his readers, Joseph Görres, its editor, connected political upheaval, which the French had brought across the Rhine, with the new climate of opinion in German literature and politics:

> When a people does its part on behalf of the common welfare; when it attempts to understand what is unfolding; when through its deeds and its sacrifices it earns an increased voice and influence in public affairs, then there must be publications to express the ideas which stir and impel every soul. Now the Germans have arrived at that point, and the newspapers have to take account of it. They must be worthy, the people must be able to recognize and respect them as their spokesmen.

Görres addressed himself further to the restored princes, whose "governments too should recognize this beneficial change in the spirit of their peoples, not letting it awaken in them some false fear, out of which they attack and disturb it. No fearful and fearsome censorship should obstruct the circulation of ideas."[9] But governments did fear journalists such as Görres, self-elected spokesmen for the opinions of the newborn "public," and five years after he founded the *Rhenish Mercury* there was censorship in Germany like never before. In the decades that followed, along with the tandem advance of literacy and literature, ever more readers with more to read, came ever more censors with more to censor.

Joseph Görres was so eloquent and so popular that his literary politics could not go unchallenged. He and his newspaper fell victim to censors and magistrates. In January 1816, the king of Prussia ordered the newspaper closed. In 1820, the government of Prussia silenced Görres cleverly by guaranteeing him an annual stipend of 1,800 taler, a generous amount, on one condition, "that he do and write nothing," as an official in the Rhenish Prussian town of Coblenz told a visiting police commissioner from Hesse-Cassel. It was a creative, rather gentle solution to the threat of popular politics in an emerging democratic literary culture. Metternich in Austria failed in a similar attempt to buy off Ludwig Börne, another liberal writer, in 1821 with the offer of a good income and the title, imperial counselor.[10] But even the Prussian muzzle on Görres did not stay put. By the 1830s he was again writing against the regimes, while Börne, exiled in Paris, continued to urge liberal, nationalist reforms back home in Germany.

By then, a free press was constitutionally guaranteed in some southern and central German states, which complicated censorship, frustrated princely regimes, and, at least for the first several years in two tumultuous, changeable decades that led up to the 1848 revolutions, encouraged opponents outside of government and reformers inside to believe that there could be political and literary freedom after all. Some commentators of the 1830s dared to intimate the dawning of a new enlightenment. In Hesse, a moderate publicist, Friedrich Murhard, welcomed the unshackling of the press promised in his land's 1831 constitution with words that echoed Görres seventeen years earlier, calling it "the most uncompromising sign that a people has come of age, the most secure and most powerful citadel of its communal and political freedom, because it generates and preserves public opinion, against whose omnipotence all attempts at arbitrary rule will be wrecked." A jurist in Württemberg, Robert von Mohl, wrote happily in 1834 of "the change which the spirit of the newspapers has brought to all well-mannered states, making the business of governing considerably more difficult, requiring more strength and wisdom now than previously."[11]

Murhard and Mohl both judged too soon. The literary vigor of men such as Görres and Börne coupled with constitutional reforms for a free press did make governments act with more strength but not more wisdom. In the 1830s, official sanctions against free-minded literature became bolder, less well-mannered. Policing in the individual German states began to smother literary liberty in the way envisioned in the Metternichean decrees of the German Confederal Assembly a dozen years earlier.

The decade of the 1830s closed with censorship a principal issue in the politics of factions that was evolving throughout the German states. Censorship and freedom of the press had an importance in public life now that could not have been imagined twenty years earlier. In rather liberal Baden, the foreign minister warned in 1839, "Freedom of the press could only lead to a metamorphosis of all relations, to revolution." The renowned Badenese scholar and constitutionalist Karl von Rotteck, seeking to calm such fears, said of his own political aims, "It is not full freedom of the press that I insist upon, but only some measure of lawfulness [*Rechtszustand*], only a moderation of the press slavery that weighs over us."[12]

By the mid-1840s, positions for and against a free press hardened, with observers painting a bleak picture of the landscape for German writers and readers. Wilhelm Held, native of Hesse, described in 1846 a threefold violence that German governments used against popular writers *(Volksschriftsteller)* such as himself: first censors, then courts, finally police. He lamented too that the German people "come of age" were not all interested in new literature or new politics; among the reading public many were apathetic. Jakob Venedey, Prussian radical, found additional reasons for despair, cataloging in 1839 the sorts of people who might challenge a government—scholars, large merchants, wealthy landlords—and then writing them all off. They had been bought, like Görres twenty years earlier, the scholars with well-paid government appointments, the merchants with laissez-faire politics that assured them continuing profits, the landlords with agricultural tariffs that kept them prosperous too. When so many opinion leaders were comfortable, few protested.[13] Venedey, who had no government appointment, wrote antigovernment tracts, which the Prussian censors banned.

Throughout the period from the conclusion of the foreign French Revolution of 1789–1815 to the beginning of the domestic German revolution of 1848–71, the press was "a sentry standing ready to wake the nation," in the words of the radical south German publicist Johann Georg August Wirth.[14] Such a national awakening was a recurring image in the German public mind, although not always with happy results. Legend told that the emperor Barbarossa, dead for hundreds of years, in fact only was sleeping in the mountains of Saxony and one day would waken the Germans, leading them, united at last, to their glory. An old German tale, made famous by Jacob and Wilhelm Grimm, had a more frightful aspect; Hansel and Gretel wake up in a gingerbread house to the horrific realization that their hostess plans to eat the little boy. The German nationalist poet, Heinrich Heine invoked the awakening too in one of his pained and patriotic verses, "Night Thoughts," written in the 1840s during his exile in Paris:

THE CHALLENGE OF CENSORSHIP

> Denk ich an Deutschland in der Nacht,
> Dann bin ich um den Schlaf gebracht,
> Ich kann nicht mehr die Augen schließen,
> Und meine heißen Tränen fließen.[15]
>
> (Thoughts of Germany in the night
> Awake me from my sleep,
> Eyes won't close hard as I might
> And hot tears sear my cheek.)

Because of the persistence of old regimes[16] and their habits of rule, notably censorship, the political and literary awakening of the German nation in the early nineteenth century was a rude awakening. Its rudest moment came, doubtlessly, with the abortive revolutions of 1848, but much else was rude before that. For Germany's liberal writers and for their many readers, but also for the princes who ruled them and the censors who muzzled them, indeed, for everyone who had to do with literature or politics, the post-Napoleonic era brought new, unwelcome shocks. Those who had formerly been comfortable in their paternal responsibilities discovered among their subjects men who wanted to take their thrones away or reshape them or at least tell them how to sit on them. Those who drank the nectar of revolution at the twilight of the old regime woke to find that it had only been a dream, and as repression of cultural freedom grew harsher and harsher during the next several decades, they lived a nightmare. Those who believed their bravery against France must be rewarded by invitations to join in the business of government saw instead their champions, men such as Joseph Görres and Sylvester Jordan, father of the Hessian constitution, silenced and the promise of a new order broken.

These things happened simultaneously, but in no way identically, in each of the several dozen German states. The central European movement for change that provoked censorship in the early nineteenth century was pan-German, reaching throughout the German-language area of Europe. Resistance to that change was not German, though; it was Bavarian, Saxon, Prussian, Nassauish, Thuringian, Hamburgish, Hessian, Hanoverian, Württembergian, Austrian, Mecklenburgish, and so forth. It bears frequent repeating that Germany was a culture before it was a nation and a nation before it was a state.

However common it is since 1990 to talk about Germany as a single political place, such a thing did not exist before 1871 except in the

The German Confederation 1815–1848

Map by Nancy Smedstad

human imagination. There was not a German central government or a German practice of censorship because there was not a German state. There were three dozen states in central Europe, associated in a loose confederation, where German, largely standardized in writing but not in speech, was the language of literature, political discourse, and administration; where some inhabitants dreamed that one day all German speakers would awaken as citizens together in a place called "Germany," an event heralded notably, although prematurely, by Johann Gottlieb Fichte in his 1807 *Reden an die deutsche Nation* (Lectures to the German Nation). Until that happened though, the states of the German Confederation, in their "not-quite-sovereignty,"[17] all had their own attitudes toward subversive literature, employed their own censors, and did their own policing of books and manuscripts, readers and writers.

An oft-repeated error in writing German history is to exaggerate how much Metternich led and how much the almost-sovereign rulers of the German states followed him between 1815 and 1848,[18] as if presaging fifty years later when Bismarck would lead and the Reichstag would follow, one hundred years later when Hitler would lead and the *Volk* would follow, one hundred and fifty years later when Kohl would lead and East Germans and West Germans would follow. The confederation that Metternich devised, with its assembly of diplomats from the German states meeting at Frankfort on Main, functioned best as a forum for exchanging opinions and information among German princes, but scarcely as well as an ersatz central government guiding their actions. Its Central Investigatory Bureau, which operated from 1833 to 1848, gave Metternich a "bird's eye view" of the press and made reports to the Confederal Assembly that caused periodicals to be banned and editors to be jailed; but most of all it described and detailed a process of increasing political consciousness and boldness,[19] which neither it nor the Austrian foreign minister nor diplomats in Frankfort could police effectively.

It is too often neglected that reunited Germany is still a nation of more than a dozen "lands" *(Länder)*, with their own everyday spoken variants of German, their own political movements, their own principal newspapers, their own persistent cultural identities.

What follows is rooted in the understanding that the battle over censorship and policing of the press before German unification took place in the states of the German Confederation individually and, therefore, the history of that conflict is to be found in them individually. This book is about the battle as it played out in the electoral principality of Hesse-Cassel, a state in the middle of Germany that shared its borders with unusually many states and was buffeted often by their literature and politics. It was a state small enough to allow the historian a look at cultural politics and censorship all up and down the bureaucratic ladder; in towns and villages; in studies, courtrooms, and taverns; and in the streets. It was a rare state, whose records, particularly the ones kept by courts, censors, and local police, have survived the twentieth century intact in the archive and made that sort of study possible today.

Hesse-Cassel was not a typical German state. It was too poor, too diverse in religious confession, too much enraptured of Prussian institutions, too inclined to share Austrian views about German politics. Its atypicality turns out to be an advantage here.

If any German state ever was typical, it would not reveal as much about censorship as this extraordinary land at the heart of German Europe, which a century and a half ago was a caricature of princely despotism in a proud but pauperish land, where all at once in 1831 a constitution, so bold that it might be mistaken for a caricature of liberal republican ideas, became the supreme law. Caricature,[20] with its exaggerated features, emphasizes what is peculiar, in this instance what was peculiar about censorship, what was wrong, troubling, and ineffectual about that old institution in a new setting.

In Hesse-Cassel during the two decades before and the two decades after promulgation of the 1831 constitution, future Germans awakened rudely to a new political and literary condition, and in their awakening they transformed censorship from an institution into an issue.[21]

TWO

A Still Life
The Land, the People, and Their Princes

What travelers noticed about the electoral principality of Hesse-Cassel was the beauty of its countryside, the splendor of its capital, and the poverty of its people. "The whole country is romantic beyond description, lofty precipices, towering woods, and basaltic rocks," wrote William Jacob, an Englishman who visited in 1819. Mrs. Trollope, passing through in 1833, reported "the whole scenery interesting in no common degree."[1] Woods of beech, ash, and chestnut covered hills and long, low ridges; down between them quiet, limpid little streams wandered along the flats. The climate was humid, the drainage poor. Here and there the soil was rich, especially around the town of Hanau and east of Marburg, but mostly it was not. In a region without much manufacture or commerce and lacking natural resources, agriculture was really all that mattered, and it was beggarly. Yields were low.

Hessian peasants grew rye for their bread, barley and oats for their porridge. They planted more acres in potatoes, sustenance of the wretched poor, than in wheat, the stuff of fine white bread. Although in some districts vegetables were plentiful and fruit trees lined many roads, meat was scarce. Bacon on special days was all that a peasant could expect. Around Marburg, they made their coffee from rye and carrots; no wonder Mrs. Trollope, who had stopped there overnight, declared it "of the worst possible fabric" and left right after breakfast.[2]

Throughout the principality, peasants grew flax for linen and hemp that they broke and wove into a rough fabric called *hessian,* which was good for packing. Their livestock, including draft animals, were few and scrawny. The village women reminded one English traveler of "a Thames waterman or Greenwich pensioner coquetting in petticoats," their calves so stout, he imagined that they "worked like any other animal" on their husbands' teams. In the Hessian countryside, people and animals lived at close quarters in "wooden hovels, dark, smoky, patched, and ruinous." With few exceptions it was a land of indigence in good years, hunger in bad. Though there was some weaving of silk and wool, salt springs near Hanau, glassmaking at Cassel, and potteries in several towns, none was significant enough to provide the revenues that could have made up for the most backward agriculture in all Germany.[3]

Hesse was a land of many villages sprinkled up and down narrow valleys, often several within sight of each other. There were only a few substantial towns. Hanau had about ten thousand inhabitants in 1820, making it second in size to Cassel. It was first in prosperity, helped by productive fields in its environs and by its closeness to the economically vigorous city-state of Frankfort on the Main, twenty-five miles downstream. Hanau's population grew to sixteen thousand by 1846, the fastest rate of increase anywhere in Hesse-Cassel. The city had a spirit all its own too. Heinrich König, a liberal civil servant and novelist who moved there from Fulda in the 1830s, wrote in his memoirs, *Ein Stilleben* (A Still Life), that "the atmosphere was warmer and the hearts were lighter" in Hanau than in "old Hesse" to the north. At Hanau's excellent grammar school in 1844, they celebrated the birthday of the crown prince, who despised constitutions, by hearing a lecture from one of the schoolmasters on "The Spirit of the Civil Constitution in Rome."[4]

Yet even Hanau had typically Hessian problems. In its old town was dire poverty. Hanau suffered in the 1820s when the Prussians built roads bypassing it in order also to bypass Hesse's high tariffs and tolls. It suffered again in the 1840s when the regime in Cassel dawdled and other towns outside of Hesse got key railway connections. Its burghers suffered from knowing too well that nearby in the kingdom of Bavaria, the grand duchy of Hesse-Darmstadt, and the free city of Frankfort rulers were more enlightened, and economic as well as political change came sooner.

Fifty miles northeast of Hanau, on the post road between Frankfort and Leipzig, was the city of Fulda, population eight thousand. In this venerable place, St. Boniface, apostle of Germany, converter of the Hessians to Christianity, sponsored an abbey, begun in 744, which grew into a bishopric that governed its own hinterlands, adhering always to Rome, until the French secularized it, then absorbed it into one of their political inventions, the grand duchy of Frankfort, in 1810. Six years later, by an act of the Congress of Vienna, the prince-elector of Hesse took it over. For the first time since Hanau was added to the Cassel domains in the previous century, it became possible to travel from Upper Hesse, in the vicinity of Marburg, north and east across Lower Hesse, then upriver past Fulda into the southernmost corners of the principality without crossing foreign land. After the annexation of Fulda, Hesse-Cassel on the map looked like a warty apostrophe.

It also became more diverse religiously than any other state in Germany. Fifty-five percent of the prince-elector's subjects belonged to the Reformed church, 25 percent to the Lutheran, 15 percent were Roman Catholic, 1.5 percent Jewish, with small numbers in dissenting, pietistic communities. Most of the Catholics lived in the former ecclesiastical principality of Fulda.[5]

To William Jacob in 1819, Fulda looked "antique, the houses large and lofty, the streets narrow and gloomy, containing many old Gothic public buildings." Its sky was filled with spires and towers. Its cathedral seemed quite old, although it had been built little more than one century earlier, designed as a small copy of St. Peter's in Rome, but scarcely as handsome. Although stripped of his worldly office, the bishop there remained powerful, his church so adamant about his prerogatives that it was 1829 before Cassel and Rome signed a concordat. Even after the agreement, the prince-electoral government was unusually cautious in administering Fulda.[6]

Economically, the city was always less notable than it might have been. Busy roads passed through, but there was little commerce. The guilds like the church clung to old ways. Hundreds of tiny family craft shops predominated, making shoes, linen, hosiery, leather, and dyed cloths. When in other parts of Germany machines began to do some of the work of men, almost no manufacturing came to Fulda. When railroads were built, an important intersection of north-south and east-west lines might have been at Fulda, but it was not. As in other Hessian cities there was a lot of poverty and hunger; the nineteenth century brought few blessings.[7]

Fulda and Hanau together with their hinterlands formed the tail on Hesse's apostrophe. Upper Hesse, with the old capital of Marburg, was the southwestern corner of the ball. The rest of it, by far the largest region in the principality, was Lower Hesse around the modern capital of Cassel.

Nearly all of Marburg's six thousand inhabitants still lived on the steep sides of its hill in the 1820s. Only a few houses were scattered across the meadows of the Lahn valley below. The single notable trade was the university, and it was very small, with forty professors, a couple of hundred students, and several thousand books in its

Hesse-Cassel 1815–1848

Map by Nancy Smedstad

library. It could not possibly compete with the University of Göttingen, the brightest star in Germany's educational galaxy, which was only half as far from Cassel. The Hessian princes granted their own university few resources and less attention.

Marburg was "a gloomy old town, with narrow streets, and a wretched pavement."[8] Half-timbered houses with overhanging stories crowded around St. Elizabeth's Church. In the 1840s, travelers still were likely to see a shepherd moving his flock down the street past the new Anatomical Institute of the university. The city changed only very slowly, its troughlike setting isolating it from more than just the winds and weather in other parts of Germany. That its notable buildings were all in the Gothic and early Renaissance styles told its story unmistakably: Marburg's glory, begun in the thirteenth century, had ended in the sixteenth.

Cassel's principal public buildings were baroque and classical in design, built in the seventeenth, eighteenth, and nineteenth centuries.[9] It was a modern city, by far the largest in Hesse, with 20,000 people in 1820. Visitors admired its principal square, Friedrichsplatz, 160 yards wide and nearly 400 yards long, where the winter palace, museum, royal administration, and Catholic church formed one impressive side, handsome houses of three and four stories lined two more sides, and on the fourth side, to the southeast, a ceremonial gate beckoned to meadows along the Fulda riverbank, with a frame of hills beyond. They called its royal estate at Wilhelmshöhe, on the outskirts of town, enrapturing, with its palace, gardens, fountains, and waterfalls, and surmounting it all a tower topped by a gigantic statue of Hercules. Music and painting thrived in this city dubbed "the German Versailles" by those who liked it, "a gilded bauble" by those who did not.[10]

All the splendors of Cassel were owed to the prince-electors' willingness to spend from their large fortune on themselves. Their presence did not just dominate, it overwhelmed the place. Cassel's administrative function drove the local economy, leaving the guilds with little influence. When Jerome, the French usurper, had ruled over the kingdom of Westphalia, a territory much more extensive and populous than the principality, which required a larger administration, Cassel's population had swelled to thirty thousand; but it shrank just as quickly after the rightful prince returned to rule his land.

Visitors who stayed very long came to know other, less delightful aspects of the Hessian capital. "There is an air of military about the whole concern," wrote Arthur Brooke Faulkner who stopped in

October 1829. "You meet soldiers at every turning, marching, or drilling, or on parade." Henry Dwight of New Haven, a student at Göttingen from 1824 to 1828, reported that Wilhelm II who ruled then was "one of the most unpopular princes in Germany, and if one may believe the Germans, cares nothing for the happiness of his subjects." Furthermore, "the [prince-]electors of this state have never been distinguished for their love of literature." And behind the "light, airy, and elegant" new town was an old section that John Russell found "huddled together on the river, at the bottom of the hill; its streets . . . narrow, dark, and confused."[11]

Hesse a century and a half ago was a land full of contrasts, picturesque and poor, diverse in confession, monotonous in its economy; where Mrs. Trollope felt safer than anywhere else in Germany because "the laws are so faithfully administered"; where John Russell remembered "the crowds of begging children that surround you at every stage"; where William Jacob saw "there is far less freedom of all kinds . . . than in any other country of Germany."[12] The principality took its character from the climate and terrain, from the separate histories of the cities and districts that comprised it, and also, significantly, from the prince-electors who ruled.

The prince-electors of Hesse made an odd family. All three were younger sons who inherited the throne because their older brothers died too soon. They all got along badly with their fathers, a good deal better with their mothers. All three preferred liaisons with women of lower, even common, birth instead of with ladies more suited to their princely station. For Wilhelm I (1743–1821) and Wilhelm II (1777–1847), philandering led to early and rancorous estrangements from the princesses they married. Friedrich Wilhelm (1802–75) instead married the commoner he loved, and for that, his children were disinherited from the throne.

When Wilhelm I[13] was born in 1743, Hesse's rulers were counts (the title is Landgraf in German, sometimes rendered as "landgrave" in English). It was a modest sort of nobility, but there was far more dignity and glory in Hessian counts during the eighteenth century than there would be in their high-titled successors, the princes of the nineteenth century. Wilhelm's father, Count Friedrich II, who ruled from 1760 until 1785, was a skillful ruler whose abilities have most often been forgotten because of two notorious things that he did. He converted to Roman Catholicism while governing a Protestant land, and he sold several thousand mercenary soldiers to the British, who sent them to North America to fight against the armies of the colonists. Friedrich II policed his territories carefully, as every prince of his age did, most of all the enlightened ones. He admired the Prussia of King Friedrich II, and modeled many of his own reform programs on Prussian examples. He battled without success against the terrible poverty of his land, a poverty rooted in the poor soil, the unfavorable climate, and the all-too-tiny plots that most peasants worked.[14]

The family into which Friedrich II's second son, Wilhelm, was born was well-connected. Wilhelm's maternal grandfather was King George II of England, a paternal great uncle was King Fredrik I of Sweden, and when he married, his father-in-law was King Frederik V of Denmark. His paternal grandfather, Count Wilhelm VIII, engaged the boy to the Danish princess Caroline in 1756 when he was twelve years old and she was eight. They were wed eight years later, in 1764. He had his first reported affair in 1770, fathered many bastards, and in 1788 took a nineteen-year-old mistress, Caroline von Schlotheim, who remained with him until he died at age seventy-seven in 1821. He ruled the Hessians for thirty-six years from the death of his father in 1785: the first eighteen as count, the last eighteen as prince-elector, a title he had pursued shamelessly from the start of his reign.

Wilhelm was a man of strong prejudices and limited talents. He built a splendid palace at Wilhelmshöhe, named for himself, on the outskirts of Cassel, and endowed his art museum with wondrous paintings by Rembrandt van Rijn and other masters. He spoke German, English, and Danish, but wrote poorly in whatever language. He was not inclined to be educated. He learned to hate the French during the Seven Years' War (1756–63) when they occupied Cassel and forced his grandfather into exile for a time; he hated them even more from the 1790s, when he as count put constables, professors, preachers, and censors all on alert, lest any excretions from the French Revolution should stain his land. Hesse's historian, Karl Demandt, called the grandfather, Count Wilhelm VIII, "the last capable prince of Hesse." After him, in Demandt's lament, the last four rulers in Cassel together "squandered away the reputation of five precious centuries."[15] Count Friedrich II, the father, deserves a better repute; but of the three prince-electors who followed him, it is all true.

Wilhelm II[16] was born in 1777 at Hanau, where his father practiced for the day when he would rule all of Hesse by governing a territory that the family had acquired piecemeal through several decades of inheritance treaties and disputes with rival claimants. The son relived his father's youth. He studied fitfully and got along badly with the older man. He was nineteen years old when in 1796, by

Wilhelm I's arrangement, he married Auguste, the sixteen-year-old daughter of King Friedrich Wilhelm II of Prussia. Both Wilhelms of Hesse were generals in the Prussian army.

Both of them fled their land, initially north to Danish Slesvig, when French armies invaded Hesse in 1806. Wilhelm I settled in Prague for the next half-dozen years. His son, the crown prince, went to Mecklenburg and later joined the campaigns against Napoleon. During those years of exile, Wilhelm II's stormy marriage to Auguste came entirely undone because of his attachment to Emilie Ortlöpp, daughter of a Berlin goldsmith. The mistress stayed with him for the rest of his life, going along to Cassel in 1821 when he succeeded his father on the throne, then to exile in Frankfort in 1831 when the people of Hesse made him choose between them and her. During the decade that Wilhelm II ruled, the hatred his father had had for everything French and modern diminished at court and was replaced by the son's hatred for everyone who sympathized with his wife, the estranged Princess Auguste—which many Hessians did.

The second prince-elector had a good sense for music and drama, so he brought the talented composer and conductor Louis Spohr to Cassel. He had little appreciation of literature and drove the Brothers Grimm away from Cassel. His personal needs always overwhelmed his public duties. He resisted efforts to separate his fortune from the state treasury. He abdicated, in effect although not in law, and became a mere gentleman living in Frankfort, rather than give up his mistress. He bestowed on her the title of countess of Reichenbach with unseemly haste after his father's death in 1821, married her almost as quickly when Auguste died in 1841, then found himself yet another bride only six months after the countess expired in 1843. It bespoke the fractured ways of the Hessian ruling family that Princess Auguste was buried in Cassel; Emilie Ortlöpp, countess of Reichenbach, in Frankfort; Wilhelm II in Hanau.

The third and last prince-elector of Hesse, Friedrich Wilhelm,[17] was born at Hanau in 1802. His father and grandfather had each been over forty years old before they ruled, but he was not yet thirty when his father's exile made him regent and really sole ruler. This unexpectedly robbed him of the opportunity to equal them in all of their faults, but still he was like them in too many ways. He took to learning as reluctantly as his father had and hated the French in the fashion of his grandfather. Like both of them he prized absolutism. He kept a commoner from Bonn, Gertrude Falkenstein Lehmann, wife of a Prussian officer, as his mistress in Fulda where he could be within the boundaries of his fatherland but away from his father, and away from his father's mistress, the countess of Reichenbach. In Fulda he was also away from unidentified enemies who fatally poisoned his manservant at a masked ball in Cassel in 1822, when the crown prince and the manservant exchanged masks.

Friedrich Wilhelm married his mistress, by now divorced from Lieutenant Lehmann, in 1831, only months before he took up the regency. Her father-in-law awarded her the title of baroness of Schaumburg, while later, in the 1850s, her husband made her princess of Hanau. Friedrich Wilhelm failed, though, to get her a more widely recognized title of nobility from the Austrians, one that he had hoped would entitle their children to his political inheritance. It scarcely mattered. Wilhelm II died, and Friedrich Wilhelm took the title of prince-elector at last in November 1847, but only four months later, in March 1848, he suffered the awful humiliation of a popular revolution. For two years after the uprising, he had to share his government with commoners, who, unlike his wife, were not even of his own choosing. Although he got his revenge and restored a regime that suited him in 1850, it was only a temporary rebound. He had won his battle for an old-fashioned cause, princely absolutism, but the cause itself was all but lost by then.

In 1866, when war erupted between the Austrians, whom he admired, and the Prussians, who were his cousins, a sudden paralysis came over his political powers, leaving him hopelessly caught between insistence on the Austrian side for no central authority in Germany, a position that seemed as imposing as a cliff-face but really was as soft as chalk, and on the Prussian side an overwhelming current of opinion that rushed headlong toward an ill-defined German political union. Friedrich Wilhelm sided with the Austrians, whereupon the Prussians captured him and carried him away to a foreign prison. After they had vanquished the Austrians, they allowed him to go home again, but at what a cost. He lost his throne, saw his land and people ruled by his cousin the Prussian king, and was left with nothing but his fortune and his palaces in Hanau.

The former prince-elector could find no peace in the town where he had been born, where his father was buried, where his grandfather once had practiced ruling. Soon he fled into voluntary exile at Prague, where Wilhelm I had gone sixty years earlier when the conquerors were French. By the time Friedrich Wilhelm died in 1875, still in the Bohemian capital, there was one Germany and no Hesse. His eldest son and the son's descendants went on styling themselves, quaintly, the princes of Hanau.

Under the paternal guidance of its three rulers, the electoral-principality of Hesse became a modern state only by fits and starts in the nineteenth century. The French had brought a whole new set of institutions and practices with their puppet kingdom of Westphalia from 1807 until 1813, and although these changes marked the consciousness of the inhabitants, little physical evidence of them remained after Wilhelm I returned from exile late in 1813, promising "to exterminate these strange institutions and restore the old constitution of our land." He voided all measures enacted during the occupation, took back properties the French had sold, and returned officials to their former posts and salaries, reversals that brought widespread resentment in and out of government. Wilhelm also resurrected the traditional privy council, and old-fashioned institution that had neither responsible ministers nor a clear division of their portfolios. One year after his return, he took the usual course of old-style German princes at such important junctures in the political lives of their territories by calling together the estates to advise him.[18]

It was the first general meeting of the estates in Hesse since Wilhelm's accession to the throne twenty-eight years earlier. His dealings with it showed a willingness to reform some aspects of the old regime, but only some. He allowed the peasantry, for example, to send representatives for the first time in centuries, but he also left wholly disenfranchised the territories recently added to his domain by the Congress of Vienna because their traditional constitutional orders were not ones he recognized. To the second session of the Landtag, during the winter and spring of 1815, Wilhelm presented his plan for a written constitution. It would have established a thirty-one-member assembly, elected by estates, to which all of his administrators would be answerable. The assembly would have had the privilege of ratifying laws concerned with taxes and property. Other legislation would have remained the prince's prerogative. Administration and justice would have been separated for the first time, and a civil code would have been written.

But the estates quarreled with each other and with their princely lord, insisting especially that the constitution be subject to debate. Wilhelm would not allow that, and in disappointment he sent them home without the traditional farewell message. The question of a constitution for Hesse was not raised again for fifteen years. During the remaining five years of his reign, the aged prince-elector made only one concession to modern times. He recognized that the union of his territories was not just embodied in his person but that they formed a single political state as well, a circumstance he had conceded anyway by proposing a single written constitution for all of them.

In 1821, Wilhelm II inherited his father's titles, lands, and subjects but quickly made it clear that he did not also want the traditions and forms of administration that had gone with them. His reign was to be more modern. He declined to call the estates as new rulers before him had done; he reduced the size of his army by two-thirds, reorganizing and reoutfitting it after Prussian example and abolishing the much-ridiculed ponytail haircuts of his soldiers; and he remade the government.

Wilhelm II's administrative reorganization edict, promulgated on 19 June 1821, barely four months after his father's death, was a document that the old prince, "likely the last consistent exponent of princely absolutism in Germany," would neither have accepted nor understood. It introduced to the principality an ordered ministerial government in place of the privy council. The old council became a "consolidated ministry of state" with separate departments for interior affairs, finance, justice, foreign relations and the royal household, and war. Each department was to have its own minister in charge of a staff in Cassel. To carry out the vital work of the new interior department, Wilhelm II divided Hesse into four provinces separated by boundaries that were mostly, but not entirely, traditional: Lower Hesse (administration in Cassel), Upper Hesse (Marburg), Fulda (Fulda), and Hanau (Hanau). A small exclave to the north, the county of Schaumburg (Rinteln) in the midst of the grand duchy of Hanover had a similar administration.[19]

The immediate effect of the new division into provinces was profound because it did away with longstanding variations in local administrative practices owing to different political histories in the territories that made up the principality. Now each province was governed in a fashion reminiscent of Prussian ways, with a council of up to six men deciding matters collegially, one holding the title of administrative director, another, police director. The provinces were further divided into counties, each headed by a councilor with a small staff. Numerous independent commissions and bureaus also came under the interior ministry now, including ones responsible for church governance, medical affairs, trade, education, fine arts, and censorship.

But Hesse still had no representative assembly, so it was entirely up to the prince-elector to determine how different the new organization would be from the old form of government. Wilhelm II's behavior turned out to be less modern than his edict. He retained one old-style privy councilor and deliberated most often with him about all government business, leaving responsible ministers ignorant of policy decisions until they had been made. He also did not really separate justice from administration because he appointed one man as minister for both portfolios. And when all of the department heads except Minister of Foreign Affairs Schmincke left the government in 1826, Wilhelm chose not to replace any of them, again undercutting the apparent intentions of his own reorganization. In later years, his son Friedrich Wilhelm frequently would also place the administrative and judicial departments in the hands of a single minister. Despite these weaknesses in its application, the new edict of 1821 did bring a new standard to government practices, especially in the provinces. The reforms were not, however, as far-reaching as ones enacted in other German states, Prussia, for example, a decade earlier, nor did they introduce guarantees of responsibility and consistency in government that had come in the 1810s to several south German states through written constitutions. Hesse waited another ten years for a constitution.[20]

The constitution promulgated in Cassel on 5 January 1831, an extremely liberal document for the times, marked a sharp departure from earlier government principles. It was an unwelcome reward to Wilhelm II for finally calling together the estates in the fall of 1830. But he scarcely had an opportunity to rule under its provisions because disputes with the Cassel citizenry about his mistress, the countess of Reichenbach, sent him in March 1831 into a self-chosen exile in Frankfort. It was Friedrich Wilhelm, the son and coregent, who ruled under the new arrangement.

In Hesse, as elsewhere in Germany, news of the July 1830 revolution in Paris had sparked broadly based political and economic protests that recurred into the fall. Especially in Cassel, in and around Hanau, and in the towns of Upper Hesse, rioters looted bakeries, attacked stamp offices, burned toll houses, and roughed up public officials. But the initial unity of the rebels dissolved quickly as the propertied classes grew wary of a truly popular uprising, organized themselves into civic guards, and with the royal militia brought back some degree of order—not, however, before Wilhelm II had agreed to convene the estates.

The hapless prince-elector was unlucky enough to have gone to Carlsbad at the end of July 1830, where he became very ill, apparently from a stroke, when the first riots broke out at home. His precarious health prevented him from returning to Cassel until the middle of September, when his welcome was a demand that the estates be called. He acquiesced, ordering the traditional estates to gather in Cassel on 16 October. At the same time, he had Carl Michael Eggena, a loyal civil servant, draft a constitution modeled on Wilhelm I's ill-fated proposal of 1816. When the estates met, again, as fourteen years earlier, the assembled delegates insisted on changes in the draft. They appointed a committee headed by Sylvester Jordan, Marburg university delegate and legal scholar, to develop a counterproposal.[21]

Jordan (1792–1861)[22] was a nineteenth-century Rousseau with better manners. He was such an outsider in Hesse that he could imagine a new constitutional order that no one born, raised, and educated there, steeped in local traditions, would have thought possible. Son of an illiterate Tyrolean shoemaker, he had gotten an education by fits and starts because his family could not afford the cost. After schooling under the Jesuits, he decided that he would not become a priest, the common way out of poverty for a talented youth in Catholic Europe. In 1815, the University of Landshut awarded Jordan a doctorate for a prize essay on the nature of philosophy; it was the opening to an academic career. Two years later, he earned a second doctorate there in jurisprudence. Meanwhile, he supported himself by working in a law office in Munich, drafting briefs on parliamentary questions. In 1820, he became an unsalaried instructor at the University of Heidelberg and received there the license to lecture *(Habilitation)* required for anyone aspiring to a professor's chair in Germany. In 1821, the University of Marburg offered him a temporary professorship, made permanent the following year. Less than one decade later, he was in Cassel drafting a constitution for Hesse.

To Jordan goes much of the credit for a remarkable document[23] which, after a few revisions, Wilhelm accepted. It established a single-chambered legislature with fifty members empowered to initiate bills and to approve the budget and taxes before they took effect. It required the prince-elector to call the legislature into session at least once every three years. It preserved his sole power to appoint and dismiss ministers but also made them answerable to the assembly by allowing delegates to submit articles of impeachment to the Hessian Supreme Court. If the prince-elector dismissed the assembly, its members were then entitled to appoint a standing commission from their own ranks to monitor the government's adherence to the laws.

All males at least thirty years old who maintained their own households and had not been convicted of a crime received the right to vote for electors, who selected thirty-two of the fifty legislators. Electoral districts were created, sixteen for the towns, sixteen for the communes, with one representative apiece. The other eighteen members of the assembly were the princes of the royal house (eight) and delegates from the nobility (eight), the University of Marburg (one), and two charitable foundations (one).

The constitution also recognized basic rights of the prince-elector's subjects, some familiar to us, others peculiar to that era. There was to be freedom of thought, religion, and the press, the right to bear arms and the right to be secure in private property. There were also rights to petition the government, to complain to public administrators and to receive a reply, to emigrate, and to resign a government appointment. The constitution required all adult men, including the prince-elector, to swear allegiance to its provisions, something that Crown Prince Friedrich Wilhelm refused to do.

Although long and detailed, with 160 sections, the constitution left important questions to be decided by later legislation. It abolished all feudal ties, for example, but left unsettled how to compensate the former beneficiaries. It allowed the police to search private houses "in instances and manners prescribed by law." It left it for a later law to determine how many judges should sit on each of the courts in Hesse. It left some civil rights vague too; freedom of person and property were subject to restrictions "by law and right," and press freedom to limitations that would "prevent abuses." This practice of constitutional temporizing occurred in Saxony the same year but had been much rarer when Bavaria, Baden, and Württemberg enacted constitutions in the 1810s. The ambiguities that it caused in Hesse would mean a lot of trouble in the years that followed.

The new Hessian constitution was "the most radical of the early German ones" because it created only one legislative chamber in which noblemen were outnumbered and sat as mere equals with commoners. It gave the assembly a rare entitlement to propose new laws. It also was the first constitution in Germany that compounded the guarantee of press freedom with a "freedom to express mere opinions."[24] Despite its radical character and its elaborate safeguards for representative government or, rather, just because these features of it were so alien to the prince-electoral regime, the constitution soon proved unworkable. The host of issues left to be settled sometime in the future was only one indication that to be effective the constitution would depend on cooperation between ruler and ruled that the Hessians never achieved.

"All laws and ordinances of every sort that are contrary to this constitution and the laws that follow from it are hereby void," read its concluding paragraph. Yet its preamble also made the whole constitution a gift from the prince-elector to his subjects, not a contract between the monarch and representatives of the citizenry that Sylvester Jordan had wanted it to be. Although it offered rights never granted to Hessians before, they were compromised in their formulation. The heading to the section on rights in the constitution read "Rights and Responsibilities of Subjects," not "Universal Human Rights of Citizens," which Jordan had wanted.[25] For years afterward, old practices endured, and the royal administration invoked superseded regulations with impunity. Recourse to the courts was possible, but it was costly, time consuming, and often brought no relief anyway. Justice and administration were still not separate enough for the one to check the other.

What the constitution and the new politics embodied in it did accomplish in Hesse was an openness in the process of government that earlier generations there had not known. Openness was written into the text with its requirement that grounds for denying a complaint against a public office be made known to the complainant, that "all judicial verdicts on political and press crimes be published with the reasons for the decision," and that "the proceedings of the legislature should be public, as a rule." But on all these matters the government resisted change; it denied the increasingly public character of its own work and refused to respect the opinions and deeds of its opponents. It was not an accident that when the government built a new hall for the legislative assembly to meet in, it put it at the edge of Cassel, isolated from other public buildings, away from traditional public life.

In the short run under Friedrich Wilhelm, the Hessian administration often was able to circumvent the constitution, but only by means that themselves departed further and further from the values of the old regime. Censorship and related measures employed to thwart the openness inherent in a constitutional transformation from royal administration to parliamentary politics had themselves been politicized by the events of 1830 and 1831. The tension that came with the constitution between new institutions and old habits, openness and repression, would dominate public life in Hesse during the next two decades.

THREE

The Police State
Censorship Traditions and Laws

The principality of Hesse-Cassel was an old-fashioned state where customs mattered more than documents or officials, where far into the nineteenth century the voice of tradition counted for more than the word of law. The Hessian state practiced censorship before it had censors or censorship laws. No prince in Marburg or Cassel ever needed special readers and rules to know what ideas he would not tolerate in print. As long as he was confident and his administration was well organized, all he needed to rid his land of any book or newspaper or song sheet were the ordinary repressive powers of government, what an 1832 Hessian ordinance justifying newspaper licensing called "the police authority of the state."[1]

Of course, rulers seldom were so confident, and governments never were so well organized that they could stop every bad idea from being written, set in type, and distributed. Princes in Hesse and other German lands did employ censors; they did draft laws to guide them; and yet they also failed to eradicate the fast-breeding spiritual vermin born on printing presses.

Censors and censorship laws were convenient for policing the printed word; policemen were essential. In nineteenth-century Germany, there were many varieties of "police." The word has always meant something rather different in central Europe than it has in lands with Anglo-Saxon law, and to people then it meant something quite different from what we mean by it today. In the United States now, it brings to mind the uniformed officers of public safety and order empowered to arrest people who break laws—constables in Britain. In German-speaking lands, 150 or 200 years ago there were not only that sort of "security" police but also forestry police, health police, building police, poor relief police, commercial police, and more. The police protected the community certainly, but as the sum of local agents of government, they also supervised town and village life.

And policing was very paternal. A Prussian administrative order of the 1790s defined its spirit as "not just preventing danger and harm, and maintaining things as they are, but also advancing and increasing the common weal." That was a very satisfying notion to self-proclaimed benevolent rulers such as Wilhelm I of Hesse. He and his son, Wilhelm II, both spoke of government in language that suggested an eternal patriarchal household, where a kind and wise father, aided only by his faithful servants, cared for a brood of contented children who never grew up. The paternal ideal that the Hessian princes cherished was something German liberals came to abhor. They would grow so impatient with all of that policing that by the 1840s, especially in the wake of the 1848 revolutions, they spoke resentfully of "police states" that had smothered German freedoms for too long.[2]

There was always a lot of informal censoring in a state such as Hesse, censoring that the government called something else, that was done by police rather than censors, that was rooted in the habit of paternal supervision more than in law. Traditional values and proscriptions endured while laws were written, rewritten, and rewritten again. When there were long-established expectations that the prince-elector should not suffer any personal insults, that there should be no politicking without his supervision, that there should be no religious deviants in his land, then often there was also some publication that had reported an insult, espoused a politics, or promoted a heresy, and the police, as a matter of course, suppressed it.

The personalities of the two Wilhelms, as well as the foibles of their families, were irresistible targets for malcontents and gossips among their subjects. In 1820, one year before Wilhelm I's death, when he clearly was an old and tired ruler, articles making fun of him appeared in newspapers throughout Germany—in Berlin, Nuremberg, Hamburg, Frankfort on the Main, all with Cassel datelines—reporting that he was fretfully uncertain whether his subjects were going to remember him as a ruler who had loved them. Out went an indignant protest through the Hessian diplomatic corps: a prince's state of mind was no one's business; the newspapers should be censored better.

Two years later Wilhelm was dead, perhaps forgotten already, yet the royal family's troubles lived on in other distressingly public ways.

From the Rhineland province of Prussia came news accounts detailing what the Hessian government liked to call "the return of Her Highness, the Duchess of Anhalt-Bamberg, from Bonn to Hanau," but what in fact had been the kidnapping of the late elector's daughter who, unfortunately, was out of her mind. An overzealous Hessian general, wanting to help the duchess's brother, the new prince-elector, avoid further embarrassment from his sister's behavior, but acting without orders, had taken her from Prussia to Hesse secretly and by force. The incident sparked a diplomatic firestorm because the general both violated the laws and wounded the honor of Prussia. The Hessian government was doubly embarrassed because the duchess was so ill and the general's behavior was so wrong; but, again, it blamed the newspapers. "There are matters whose singularity, for example purely familial ones, makes them least suitable to satisfy the public curiosity," began an Interior Ministry directive aimed at keeping the story out of sight of Hessian readers.[3]

Direct appeals to the people of Hesse, regardless to what end, were not allowed either under the two Wilhelms, lest they usurp the prince's special relationship with his subjects. In 1813 and again in 1816, a joyful merchant in Cassel named Kersting became too explicit and too bizarre in expressions of gratitude over Wilhelm I's homecoming. Kersting believed that the French occupation had been the end of the world as foretold in scripture and that Prince Wilhelm's return was the second coming of Christ. The merchant commissioned an engraving to illustrate the blessed event and distributed copies of it in Cassel. Although Kersting won no following for this exceptional faith, the police arrested him, confiscated his work, and eventually sent him to be treated by doctors.

In the same years that Kersting was joyful at Wilhelm's return, other Hessians were vexed by it and expressed their feelings just as publicly. One reason was that Jerome, king of Westphalia, had sold royal and ecclesiastical domains, which Wilhelm I took back without compensating their chagrined, temporary owners. Another reason was that in the process of reestablishing the German territories under their rightful rulers in 1815 and 1816, a number of petty nobles in Hesse lost the immediate rights of sovereignty over their properties; their authority was "mediated" through the prince-elector. These sudden reversals, which the Hessian regime handled roughly, led to a public commotion. The injured parties circulated petitions and pamphlets, which the government quashed, because in the words of the privy council, they "could easily lead His subjects astray—His subjects whose well-being is always uppermost among the paternal concerns of His Royal Majesty."[4]

What role did the censors of Hesse-Cassel play in these episodes of policing the press? Never more than a minor one. In a paternal regime, the folly and indignity of allowing public discussion about the ruler's family or his policies were so obvious that expert opinions from learned men were beside the point. Merchant Kersting's unsettling, albeit pious, engraving did go from the police in Cassel to Justus Rommel, who chaired the Censorship Commission in the principality. But it was because Rommel was general superintendent in the Reformed Church Consistory, not because he was chief censor, that Police Director Ludwig von Manger turned it over to him as a matter "properly left to the judgement of spiritual authority."

Censorship laws? The police did not need them any more than they needed the censors.

The laws, although often ignored, were elaborate and thorough. Two sorts of laws existed in Germany then: some promulgated in each of the three dozen states that belonged to the German Confederation, which often were quite different from one state to another, and some that were agreed to by all of the states at meetings of the confederation.

Prince-elector Wilhelm I had had a Book Censorship Commission until the French occupied Hesse in 1807, and after his 1813 return from exile, he restored it just as it had been. By an order of 10 February 1815, he named to it the same men who had served before its abolition by Napoleon's brother Jerome. A press ordinance and an instruction to the commission followed on 14 June 1816. According to the ordinance, the censors had to approve all books and other written materials before anyone could print them in the principality, and they also had to approve all imported works before they could be sold if the publications dealt with the Hessian state. The instruction told the censors in detail how to enforce the ordinance.

In its conclusion, it reminded them, in the fatherly tone favored by Hessian princes, "It is Our paternal intent, through suitable restrictions on the unhindered traffic in printed works, to preserve the state from the anxieties that, at the present time, the dangerous and illegal undertakings of evil-thinking men could excite," and it also warned them not to interfere in "the free pursuit of intellectual improvement and the spread of scholarly and useful knowledge, which for the most part help to further the common weal of the state."[5] These nods to safekeeping and enlightenment were, no doubt, earnestly meant, but they must have seemed like formulaic afterthoughts to the censors, coming as they did after the long list of duties that the instruction assigned to them.

The censors were to hinder distribution of writings that could injure the state, religion, morals, or relations with other governments. They were to report offending writers, printers, and booksellers to the royal treasury and local administrators for policing. They were to examine the printed catalog of the semiannual book trade fair in Leipzig and to investigate all books listed in it with titles that made them suspect a violation of the law. When they spotted offensive books, they were to forbid them and to confiscate copies from bookshops and lending libraries. They were to keep watchful eyes on the hundreds of journals and newspapers published in Germany. These tasks would have been an enormous amount of work for an office of full-time censors. They were impossible for three part-time officials, all there ever were for censorship in Hesse.

Five years after the reestablishment of the Censorship Commission, Wilhelm II reorganized the government that he had just inherited from his father and reduced the scope of the censors' work somewhat. His administrative reorganization edict of 1821 put the commission under the supervision of the new Interior Ministry. The edict also charged the councilors who now directed local administration in each of the four new counties of Hesse-Cassel with "maintaining a watchful eye against the spread of forbidden or politically dangerous periodicals and other written works," and with "carrying out an adequate supervision of public celebrations, exhibitions, pamphlets and other publications, lending libraries, and bookshops."[6]

Under these rules, the Censorship Commission's principal task became quasi-judicial, to judge publications, whereas the county councilors were made the executives for censorship, empowered to execute the censors' judgments. But this neat, American-style separation of their powers should not be taken too seriously; it belies the slowness of change from a government organized according to the personal whims of a paternal autocrat toward a government organized according to departments, functions, and rules. Even more, it belies the fact that men's attitudes and practices changed more slowly than the rules they were meant to follow. When Hessian princes and ministers changed their policing or their laws, it was often only because someone else prodded them, not because they had changed their own views.

A steady influence on Hessian censorship came from the German Confederation. The first time that a press law enacted by the confederation modified the censorship laws of Hesse was in September

1819. The previous spring outbreaks of political unrest had centered around clubs of patriotic German students *(Burschenschaften)*, which prompted ten of the states belonging to the confederation to meet secretly at Carlsbad in the Habsburg Empire. There they agreed that new German-wide laws were needed, one to clamp down on politics in the universities, another to control what Germans were reading, and a third to establish an investigatory commission that could coordinate the pursuit of "demagogues" across central Europe. In these ways the Austrian and Prussian governments especially hoped to counter the triple threat that university students, writers, and liberal governments in the southwest German states seemed to pose to the established order.

Hesse-Cassel had not taken part in the Carlsbad Conference. Wilhelm I, in fact, objected in principle to the laws drafted at Carlsbad that the German Confederation passed afterward, "1. because the police is solely my concern in my land; 2. because there are no traitors in my land; 3. because I predict that only suspicions and denunciations will result, and I abhor that." These sentiments were all part of his fatherly practice of government. Word went out to local officials that they should continue to follow the 1816 Hessian press ordinance. At the same time, nonetheless, because Hesse was a loyal member of the German Confederation, the privy council approved the Confederal Press Law, which was adopted for a five-year trial period at Frankfort on 20 September that year. It appeared in royal proclamations in Hesse on 22 November.[7]

The new confederal law divided everything that was printed into two groups. One group comprised all newspapers, journals, and books that consisted of twenty or fewer printer's sheets (when folded three times into the common octavo format, they produced a 320-page book). All these publications had to be submitted to censors for approval in the state where they were going to be printed—preventive (prepublication) censorship. All other books, longer than 20 sheets or 320 standard-sized pages, were free from prior review because, judged by length, they were probably scholarly, not popular. Every sort of printed work, in both groups, could still end up being banned, confiscated, and destroyed after publication even if it had been cleared before—repressive (postpublication) censorship.

The new German-wide law made each state answerable to the confederation for its censorship practices. If one state complained to another about inadequate censoring and received no satisfactory answer, it could appeal to the Confederal Assembly, where the delegates might forbid a publication even though censors in its state of origin had said it was passable. The new law also gave the Confederal Assembly power to ban writings without previous complaint from anyone if they threatened the honor of the confederation, the well-being of a member-state, or the maintenance of law and order in Germany. It left the states responsible for prosecuting authors, editors, and publishers who trespassed the law. Just to be sure that they would be identifiable, the law made it mandatory to give the name of the publisher on every book and the name of the editor on every journal and newspaper.

By enacting this law, the confederation altered censorship law in Hesse-Cassel, asserting "a standardization such as there never had been before."[8] Wilhelm I's claims notwithstanding, the police and the press in his land were indeed other people's business now. Especially after the delegates to the Confederal Assembly extended the law indefinitely in 1824, it became an additional authority, alongside the 1816 Hessian ordinance, cited not only by police and the ministries as they tried to enforce censorship but also by censors as they quarreled with police officials and government ministers about the proper extent of censorship; and by authors, publishers, and booksellers as they disputed the validity of individual instances of censorship.

At the time of its enactment, the new confedal press law did not alter the practices of German censors—the ones in Cassel were not very busy yet anyway. Even in the 1830s, with the growth of a German-wide oppositional press, its chief importance would be as a legal ground for the German governments to complain about each other's faulty censorship. The Hessians would complain a lot. Not yet a "bench mark" for censorship as an institution, it was, however, an early signal that censorship was becoming an issue as it had not been before.

The Confederal Press Law of 1819 also became the basis for further German-wide legislation designed to keep the press unfree, legislation that conservative regimes such as the Habsburg monarchy thought constructive, while in more progressive states such as the grand duchy of Baden it seemed coercive instead. Using the 1819 law, the confederation banned many publications in the early 1830s, and it pressured Baden into repealing a new liberal press law in 1832.

Censorship was woven into other repressive laws of the confederation too. In June 1832, the Confederal Assembly issued an infamous set of "Six Articles" designed to rein back popular legislative assemblies (including one in Cassel) that had grown more and more unruly during the preceding two years. The fifth article censored legislators, forbidding them from attacking the confederation in print. One week later, the Frankfort assembly passed a law against public displays of German nationalism, prohibiting not only public speeches about politics and the unauthorized sale of foreign publications written in German, but also all display of the black, red, and gold German nationalist banner and the planting of "freedom trees."[9] In an age of so much press censorship, liberals had begun investing visual symbols, a piece of cloth or a tree, with political messages that they dared not express in words.

In June 1834 at another secret conference, held like the 1819 Carlsbad meeting on Habsburg territory, in Vienna this time, the members of the confederation drafted a further "Sixty Articles," to which they bound themselves as if they were published laws. The articles on censorship directed the German governments to watch over their censors more carefully. Only men of "tested conscience and competence" were to hold the office. And censors were now to forbid the frequent editorial trick of leaving blank spaces or dashed lines to let readers know where they had excised parts of the text. They were also instructed to keep down the number of political periodicals by requiring special licenses to start new ones.[10] Through these measures the confederation went beyond the general, coordinating role that it had taken for itself in the early 1820s, and busied itself more and more with the details of censorship.

In a narrow sense, the German Confederation put censorship back on its agenda in the 1830s because the institution, as reestablished after the Napoleonic wars, was faltering, becoming less and less effective while ever more people despised and evaded it. Viewed broadly, though, much more was at stake than just censorship. A political watershed had been reached in the German states that threatened to capsize the entire confederation—the very invention of politics, factions built by popular representatives in legislative chambers debating on behalf of public opinions. Throughout the Western world, in America with the realignment of parties that accompanied Andrew Jackson's election in 1828, in France when newspaper editors and their allies toppled an autocratic king and his coterie in 1830, in Britain through the redistribution of parliamentary seats by the Reform Act of 1832, traditional governing elites were threatened, challenged, and displaced. In Germany, as elsewhere, a new political generation was coming of age, impatient with tyrannical regimes and their censors who tried to hold in check its private opinions on public issues.

Hesse, although a backwater, felt the new currents. Political conditions in Cassel and the provinces changed dramatically under Wilhelm II and Friedrich Wilhelm from what they had been in the days of Wilhelm I, and, consequently, censorship in Hesse changed too. A written constitution and a representative assembly made some politicking inevitable. Censors and police, unable to extinguish popular politics, had to try all the harder to control it.

After 1830, the Hessian prince governed his subjects more through ministers, somewhat less personally than before. Crown Prince Friedrich Wilhelm, ruling on behalf of his father, was not as obviously paternal as either the father or the grandfather had been. Nonetheless, the family's wish to cradle the Hessian people, to nurture their spirit and discipline their behavior, all this government-as-child-rearing endured. And censorship in Hesse remained a consequence of other policing, often going on, as it had before, without the official censors involved at all.

The forms changed, the issues were new, but at the heart of the regime that guardian spirit of old lived on. The two Wilhelms had behaved as if their personal affairs were all that was political in Hesse; Friedrich Wilhelm only reversed the equation, insisting that all politics in the electorate were his personal affair. None of the three ever wanted other Hessians or other Germans meddling in his monopoly on the business of governance or commenting on it.

When Hessians revolted, along with many other Europeans, in 1830, Wilhelm II blamed two common scapegoats of spurned paternal princes: local maligners and foreign agents. "The excesses and disturbances of the peace that have recurred time and again," he proclaimed, "are only the work of ill-willed individuals" who should not be confused with "the overwhelming majority of the townsmen and subjects, law-abiding and orderly." All of Germany's current troubles were simply importations from abroad, he assured the Prussian ambassador in Cassel.[11] Neither formula could explain, however, why in the next several years a parliament of leading Hessians, assembled according to a constitution written by Hessians, would be continually at odds with the Hessian regime. Nor did maligners and foreigners begin to describe all the people in Wilhelm's land who developed an infectious enthusiasm for the novelty of public politics, for frequent elections, and for the partisan discussions that went on now in the local press.

Friedrich Wilhelm as regent seemed unaware that his father's diagnosis of the 1830 troubles was wrong; certainly it was not apparent in the behavior of his government, whose ministers continued to apply the old princely remedy for political discomfort: large doses of police discipline with a sugar coating of solicitude. Because neither the ministers nor their new young master understood the etiology of discontent, their medicines were ineffective. The princely government tried repeatedly to police Hesse's constitution; but the people only paid it more attention than ever. And as they became more devoted to this one printed document that Friedrich Wilhelm could not censor, although he had refused to swear it his allegiance, the people became less devoted to him as their paternal lord.

It was constitutional guarantees of free opinions and a free press that the Hessian public treasured most and that the regime found most unbearable. "Few men are so evil that they would consider doing injustices in the bright sunlight of public opinion," wrote the Hessian liberal Friedrich Murhard in a commentary on the new constitution.[12] Autocratic regimes knew as well as anyone that without a free press other liberties were insecure.

Freedom of the press was written into the 1831 Hessian constitution in a way—absolute and conditional all at once—to be expected from a document that was supposed to meld the customs of an old paternal regime with the aspirations of its freedom-loving subjects. "There will be complete freedom of the press and the book trade," it began. Then came a curiously phrased qualification: "First, however, a special law against press abuses will have to be issued forthwith." And in conclusion, "Censorship is permissible only in cases specified in the laws of the German Confederation." In this final version the article on the press was several words longer than in its initial draft, where the second sentence had read simply, "A special law against press abuses will have to be issued." Wilhelm II made one of his few changes to the constitution here, adding the crucial phrase, "first, however"; and then the drafters insisted that "forthwith" also be appended.[13] This initial sparring about words did not bode well for the future of press affairs in Hesse.

As written, the article probably came as close to an unqualified freedom of the press as was possible, given the limitations that the German Confederation had set for all member-states. It seemed to meet the requirements that Friedrich Murhard gave for a free press to lead to responsible government. But that was only an illusion, because until the summer of 1848, the government and the legislature in Hesse found it impossible to agree on the law against abuses of the press that they were supposed to settle on "forthwith." As a consequence, from the government's point of view the constitutional article guaranteeing press freedom never took effect at all. Murhard had written that the establishment of a free press would let public light shine in on government, but throughout the 1830s and 1840s the Hessian regime answered him and others who prized this new, essential freedom by trying to keep the shutters closed on the chambers of government, to enshroud local politics in darkness, by any possible means.[14]

It was not long after the tumult of 1830 and 1831 that the Interior Ministry in Cassel went to war against people, parliament, and press with a campaign that opened in May 1832 when an earnest conservative, Ludwig Hassenpflug (1794–1862), became minister of both the Interior and Justice departments. Carl Eggena already had led skirmishes on the government side, first as drafter of the constitutional proposal from the prince-elector, then as royal commissioner to the assembly, and finally as interior minister, but Eggena's handling of the legislature was weak. Hassenpflug's by contrast was strong, forceful, overpowering. Hassenpflug would take the leading role in dramatic scenes that followed as Crown Prince Friedrich Wilhelm, more authoritarian than benevolent, tried to reimpose his family's will on an awkwardly liberal political system.

The new interior minister had studied law at the University of Göttingen interrupted by voluntary service in the last campaign against the French, then had begun his career in the Hessian administration as a junior official at the Cassel law courts. In those early post-Napoleonic years, he befriended the Brothers Grimm, librarians in the Hessian capital, and he shared with them an enthusiasm for old romantic German values. In 1822, he married their younger sister.

During the 1820s, Hassenpflug found intellectual and political company in a group of young Hessians who gathered around Princess Auguste, the estranged consort of Wilhelm II, and the sundered couple's son, Friedrich Wilhelm. The Grimms were in this circle too, as was Joseph Maria von Radowitz, then a precocious Hessian military officer, later a confidante of King Friedrich Wilhelm IV of Prussia.

Hassenpflug, like Radowitz, profoundly distrusted modern institutions, remembering bitterly the tempest that had been loosed on Europe in his youth by the modern general turned modern emperor, Napoleon. It was not lost on the generation of Hassenpflug, Radowitz, and the Brothers Grimm that Napoleon had been both a revolutionary and a tyrant. They committed themselves, in Radowitz's words, "to fight against the false freedom of revolution through the new freedom of law, but never through absolutism."[15] In middle age, however, their paths and views would diverge, the Grimms opposing lawless absolutism and censorship in Hanover until it cost them their state appointments there, Radowitz advising a lawful moderation of both absolute rule and censorship in Prussia, while Hassenpflug promoted a harsh, absolute, even lawless program of censorship in Hesse.

As long as Wilhelm II ruled, there was scarcely space for these thoughtful men with their carefully balanced youthful German ideals in Hesse-Cassel. Prince Wilhelm admired absolutists, including his father-in-law the Prussian king, and within the limitations of his own land he tried to be one too. More important to him than differences of principle, though, were personal issues. Throughout his reign he blocked the careers of government servants who dared to take his wife's side in the family feud. He exiled Radowitz in the early 1820s. Jacob and Wilhelm Grimm took their leave, after years of ill treatment, in 1829. But Hassenpflug stayed on.

In 1831, Friedrich Wilhelm, the son who had sided with his mother, became regent, and then Hassenpflug's career fortunes improved rapidly. He rose to be a councilor in the Hessian Supreme Court that year and the next year to deputy in the ministries. Only weeks after that promotion he received both the justice and interior portfolios. For the next five years, Minister Hassenpflug's aggressive administration and his well-known disdain for the most modern forms of government together would make him fiercely hated by liberals throughout Hesse. It was he who directed the paternal assault against the people's political maturity that had appeared so suddenly and so unwelcomely in 1830.

When the first constitutional legislature assembled, the government showed good faith by submitting a proposal for the mandated press law. In forty-four paragraphs, the proposal outlined the many things that would not be allowed the free press.[16] As before, anyone wanting to open a print shop, bookshop, lending library, newspaper reporting current events ("political" in the usage of the day), or magazine, or who wanted to sell printed matter door-to-door, would have to obtain a license first. A written work that made charges against the government, or against any person, could only be printed if the editor knew for certain who was the author, and the government or individual attacked was entitled to space in the same issue to reply. There were also the usual prohibitions against writings that insulted religious faith and practice, or morals. Then came eleven paragraphs detailing unallowable political topics: incitements to treason or other disturbance, false rumors, attacks on the law, the crown, the royal family, the government, the legislative assembly, public authority, the constitutions and governments of the German Confederation and all states belonging to it, crowned heads of the world, their diplomats, and other foreign authorities.

To be sure that Hessians would obey these strictures on press freedom, the royal proposal called for all publications to be submitted to the police at least one hour and sometimes as much as three days before printing began. It also defined libel, gave the order by which persons involved with publications would be answerable for the contents (first authors and editors, then publishers, lastly printers), and established procedures for legal prosecution and appeal.

Sylvester Jordan chaired the legislative committee that considered the draft law. His own views on censorship were complex, although altogether more liberal than what the government proposed. Jordan called freedom of speech and of the press more important than any other rights except the right to receive moral and intellectual training, and he called censorship in any form "contrary to law." Yet as prorector of the University of Marburg in 1826, he had also endorsed the dean of philosophy's refusal of the imprimatur for a pamphlet on Jewish education written by a rural schoolmaster, which contained "insupportable attacks against the Jewish and Christian religions." It was Jordan who wrote to the Marburg bookseller Christian Dietrich Garthe informing him that his request for permission to print the pamphlet was denied. Like almost every educated man of his age, Jordan believed that press misconduct *(Unfug)* should be defined and punished, even if the press were otherwise to be free.[17]

The changes that Jordan's committee made to the government's draft of a press law were not many, but they all harked back to the need to prevent a government from abusing its legitimate powers, a theme that also permeated the constitution that Jordan had largely written. The committee added a section at the beginning, which declared that only through the application of laws could the government restrict printed works, a clear challenge to its traditional extralegal policing. They called for justification when the government withheld permission to establish a print shop, bookshop, or lending library, or to peddle books and pamphlets. They would have shifted supervision of libraries and peddlers away from the central government to the provinces. They wanted to delete the clause requiring prior approval to edit "political" newspapers, proposing instead three general requirements: editors must be citizens, at least twenty-four years old, and able to put up a security deposit of between one hundred and one thousand taler. They also wrote an amendment to a clause that compelled bookshops to have handy a current catalog of everything on sale, limiting the rule to periodicals and pamphlets of not more than five sheets (eighty octavo pages), which exempted most books. When they were done, the draft law on the press was three times longer than when they had begun.

Jordan and his committee stopped short of trying to unfetter the press altogether; they tried, though, to make the fetters visible and lawful. Through their additions and deletions to the government's proposal, they struck hard at its presumption that every printed work was government business, an expression of the paternal tradition. In fact, Jordan reported to the legislative assembly in April 1832 that "the committee, if it had had nothing else to consider but its own view, would have banished every one of the preventive measures against possible press abuses, declared the press free without qualification, and limited the . . . law to press crimes and their punishment."[18] If they had had their way, there would have been no more prepublication censorship, and the result would have been much like the press law enacted in Baden on 28 December 1831, the most liberal anywhere in the confederation and the shortest lived.

The timing of this tussle that Jordan and his committee picked with Hassenpflug over the press law was horrendously bad. It fell amidst the radical action of Baden's legislature on behalf of a free press, the formation two months later of a Press and Fatherland Society sponsored by the liberal Bavarian publicist August Wirth, and, then, in June 1832 a public demonstration at Hambach endorsing liberal, nationalist principles, all events that drew attention in the confederation to opponents of the existing political order and their dangerous free press ideas.

Hassenpflug declined in 1832 to discuss revisions to the pending Hessian press law at all. The assembly, however, called publicly for more talks, making the case to him in one especially naive brief that "the promulgation of this law becomes more pressing every day, because every day concern grows that the Confederal Assembly will enact further restrictions. Meanwhile, the state administration is still in a position to enact, unhindered, a law upon which the improvement of the constitution and constitutional life are so dependent." It was scarcely the sort of argument to persuade a minister who was quite happy about restrictions on the press, who, in fact, designed them, who would rather kill constitutional life than nourish it. Nor did Hassenpflug, the executioner of Hesse's free press, take notice of the legislature's warnings that under existing circumstances the press was going to end up entirely unfettered; nor did he answer their follow-up questions about the status of the press law. Irate that he ignored them, the delegates initiated impeachment proceedings against him, for "excessive, unconstitutional extension of the police powers of the state, and an uncontrolled coercion in press and censorship affairs."[19] The government dismissed the legislature for that action, sending the delegates home early with no press law at all.

Infuriated even more, they looked to the Hessian people for support. Hassenpflug ordered that none of the legislators' protests get past the censors and into print. His directive had no basis in law (there was still no law), and it violated rights of reporting and petition expressly guaranteed to the assembly in the new constitution.

Unfortunately for Hassenpflug, what the delegates could not write themselves, other Hessians quickly wrote and printed on their behalf. Out came a new directive from his office requiring all newspapers reporting on current events to seek licenses from the police. The basis for this order was also not in written Hessian law nor in the new constitution. The Interior Ministry instruction even admitted "that editing political newspapers in the principality has been a business entirely free from the requirements of official consent, endorsement, or concession."[20]

But that could not continue, Hassenpflug's ministry insisted: "The periodical press is . . . enormously important for the peace and security of all states. Dangers can arise from the confusion and misdirection of a large and unrestricted public through irresponsible publication of false reports, through thoughtless or malicious broadcast of corrupting doctrines, and through the excitements brought on by these or other means to dissatisfaction and insubordination." It was the paternalism of old returning, joined by the new fear since 1830 of rebellious crowds. And the legal basis that Ludwig Hassenpflug gave now for shackling the free press was traditional too: "According to the general rules of police law, the political newspaper is and must be among those businesses and trades for which the police authority of the state can grant or deny permission."[21]

In September 1832, Hassenpflug extended his anticonstitutional policing to elections for the assembly, again imposing a censorship unrestrained by either censors or censorship laws. His Interior Ministry sent a note to the Censorship Commission in Cassel, warning that "the election of delegates to the legislature is to be conducted with unrestricted freedom, out of the personal convictions of authorized voters, without encouragement or intrusion. Yet there have been attempts to exert influence—with some success—on that naivete that characterizes the common man especially. Namely, specific persons are identified and recommended for election." To keep the elections free, the censors were not to permit any more endorsements of candidates in the newspapers.

Now it was the censors who objected, as they would frequently to the orders their masters gave them, insisting that campaign announcements were only expressions of opinion protected by the new constitution. They pointed out that there was a new Election Commission, which was itself forbidden from tampering with the vote. They could find no legal basis for reviewing election materials either.[22] But here, as in so many of Hassenpflug's activities during the 1830s, although laws could be debated, it was power that decided the issue, and the government, through its many police, monopolized power.

When the legislature reconvened for two further sessions, the press law impasse continued. A liberal parliamentary majority found the government's proposals contrary to the spirit of the constitution, whereas the government saw in the legislative attitude nothing more than an evasion of confederal laws. The parliamentarians' worst fears had come true in the spring and summer of 1832 when the confederation outlawed the Press and Fatherland Society, issued the repressive "Six Articles," and voided Baden's liberal press law. Under Hassenpflug's stern leadership, Friedrich Wilhelm's government would never be budged into compromise now, not with the obvious, reactionary change of mood at Frankfort. Instructions to the legislative commissioner in October 1833 alluded pointedly to Baden and "embarrassing difficulties that a liberal press law would cause."[23] Censorship went on in Hesse without a censorship law.

There would be other moments when the Hessian regime was less sure and less angry than in Ludwig Hassenpflug's first years as minister. For a time, parliamentary politics was gentler after 1837, when Hassenpflug left office and left Hesse following a series of disputes with Crown Prince Friedrich Wilhelm. But the paternal policing that the minister and his prince cherished did not fade away just because Hassenpflug was gone from the royal court in Cassel. It found other expressions during the late 1830s and early 1840s, mostly through the courts of law, most pointedly in the prosecution for treason of Sylvester Jordan, under circumstances so extreme that it can only be called a persecution.

Jordan, more than any other Hessian legislator, had dared to stand up to the government and criticize its lack of respect for the spirit of written law. His insistence that the constitution he had drafted must be observed made him unpopular at the royal court but very popular among the people. In March 1832, Jordan's landlord,

Friedrich Döring, proprietor of the Swan apothecary in Marburg, organized a committee of townspeople to create a memorial in honor of Jordan. Another committee member was the local bookseller Christian Dietrich Garthe, who would become entangled in the investigation of Jordan's alleged crimes. The committee collected eight hundred taler, considered making it a trust for the education of Jordan's children, invested it, then in 1837 presented it and the interest on it to Jordan so that he could buy a house. In the summer of 1832 large public celebrations in Marburg welcomed Jordan home from a trip to Göttingen.

All of this attention to the professor-turned-constitutionalist-turned-politician-turned-hero upset Ludwig Hassenpflug, who collected names of the Marburgers who had welcomed Jordan and launched a case against them in criminal court. The court informed the minister that he had no legal grounds. When Jordan won a seat in the legislature again in the next elections, Hassenpflug refused him leave from the university and held both the university budget and an increase in Jordan's modest salary hostage until Jordan decided in 1833 to retire from politics altogether.[24]

Six years later, early in the morning on 17 June 1839, Sylvester Jordan awakened to the rude sight of police surrounding his house. They searched it while he stood by, still in his night clothes. Six weeks later, the police arrested him and his alleged co-conspirators. There would be other convictions besides his in the trial that followed eventually, but it was Sylvester Jordan whom the Hessian government wanted to punish, Sylvester Jordan whose treatment was worst, and Sylvester Jordan whose plight caused an uproar in the columns of German newspapers. The early morning house search was the beginning of a six-year-long nightmare for the man who personified the freedoms of the Hessian people.

The police in Marburg had first shadowed Jordan in 1833, after the Central Investigatory Bureau of the confederation in Frankfort reported rumors that he had revolutionary connections; but Jordan's habits were so harmless, the surveillance ended soon. The rumors, however, persisted. Among investigators it was alleged that Jordan's landlord through the early 1830s, Döring, was the Marburg contact for a German-wide revolutionary conspiracy. It was Döring's blatantly self-serving incriminations that landed Jordan in so much trouble.

After 1834, when Döring moved away from Marburg, he had repeated difficulties with the law for his purported political activities but also for killing a man. While under investigation in Berlin and hoping for lenient treatment, Döring incriminated Jordan. So did other, equally unreliable persons. All through the second half of 1838 and the first half of 1839 the Confederal Investigatory Bureau pressed the Hessian government to arrest Jordan.

Once arrested, Jordan was a difficult prisoner for Marburg's police director, W. H. Wangemann, his interrogator, because he would not admit to crimes he had not committed, although Wangemann believed entirely in Jordan's guilt. Held in the Marburg castle for more than two years of investigatory arrest, Jordan's health worsened. In the fall of 1841, the Marburg Superior Court allowed him to go home under a strict house arrest while it tried his case. On Bastille Day 1843 came the verdict. Unable to prove that he was a traitor, the court convicted him anyway "for assistance in attempted treason through failure to hinder treasonous undertakings." In a long, 160-page justification, the judges argued that through his associations Jordan must have known the things that other men were alleged to have plotted. Being a professor and a civil servant made him particularly guilty, they added.[25]

"In my situation, publicity is my only means to justice," Jordan wrote after his conviction. Put behind bars on 2 August 1843 while he appealed his sentence, he became the subject of sympathetic, outraged articles and books throughout the German states. Everywhere there was support for him—everywhere except in Marburg, his adopted hometown, where from the start of his troubles, he noted bitterly, no one had dared to defend this man without local roots. The wave of publicity in Jordan's defense, which the Hessian government could neither stop at its sources nor block at the borders, brought to the government its own rude awakening that the police-driven exercise of state authority no longer went unnoticed by Germans devoted to the rule of law.

Even in Hesse, despotism had its limits. The Hessian Supreme Court, long known for its independence, released Jordan on bond on 3 March 1845, then seven and one-half months later, on 17 October, reversed his conviction with an opinion that did not allow a single one of the arguments used to convict him. Jordan's public life, even after winning in the courts, was practically over.[26] He was elected to the Frankfort Assembly in 1848 that conceived a stillborn constitution for all of Germany, but he scarcely played a role in its deliberations. The Cassel regime never lifted his suspension from the university. Once acquitted, his martyrdom became just a memory. He lived in Cassel, futilely seeking an appointment in the administration, from 1850 until his death in 1861.

Hessian liberals had seemed extremely fortunate when Ludwig Hassenpflug departed Cassel, but Sylvester Jordan's torment showed the truth, that Hassenpflug was not the inventor of the police state but only a very effective agent of it. He left behind a protégé who marched to the same anticonstitutional beat.

Friedrich Scheffer (1800–79),[27] educated at the University of Marburg, had been an efficient, apolitical junior civil servant in the provincial town of Treysa in the 1820s. Then came the months of unrest, the creation of civic militias, and the new constitution. As a member of Treysa's civic militia, Scheffer impressed his liberal townsmen so much with his vigor that they elected him to the first constitutional assembly in 1831. As he immersed himself in politics for the first time, however, he drew away from his sponsors, and before long his defenses of Ludwig Hassenpflug were a nasty irritation to many legislators who had hated the minister from the start. In 1834, Hassenpflug took his young defender into the government. When that cost Scheffer reelection to his parliamentary seat two years later, Hassenpflug made him royal commissioner to the assembly. Five years after his entry into politics through a popular revolt, one year before his mentor would fall, civic militiaman Friedrich Scheffer of Treysa became spokesman for the crown in the chamber of the people.

He stayed in government service after Hassenpflug's departure, becoming de facto head of the Interior Ministry in 1845 and minister in 1847. He was well suited to carry forward Hassenpflug's work, being outspoken to the point of tactlessness. Scheffer insisted that royal proclamations were nearly as good a basis for law as parliamentary acts. And in religious quarrels that began during the 1830s, then grew fierce in the 1840s, between conservative mystical factions in the German churches and their progressive rationalist foes, he too advanced the regime's cause by putting tradition before law.

In 1845, Scheffer forbade the Censorship Commission to review any writings about German Catholicism, one of the liberal rationalist movements, telling them to send all such works directly to the ministry. At the same time, he informed the legislative assembly that whatever he did to discipline religious dissidents was none of its business. When the delegates, thinking differently, prepared to debate the government's harsh stance toward the new sects, Scheffer followed his mentor's example of a dozen years earlier and dissolved the assembly.

What had been paternal in 1816 when Prince Wilhelm I sent home delegates of the estates that he had summoned was tyrannical in 1845 when Scheffer, on behalf of Crown Prince Friedrich Wilhelm, dismissed an elected legislative assembly. What had been despotic, though imaginable, under the personal regime that still existed in 1813, when Wilhelm I took back every office and land that the French had given away or sold, was despotic, unimaginable, and intolerable under constitutional government in 1841 when Crown Prince Friedrich Wilhelm had policemen accompany Sylvester Jordan to the toilet and stand at his open bedroom door while he slept during his house arrest. Thirty years of writing and reading, of uprisings, constitutions, and compromises had changed the rules of politics in Germany. Yet the regime in Cassel held to its familiar course. Through its legislative commissioner, its censors, and especially its police, it often paralyzed and always infuriated the legislature, which tried for one and a half decades to fashion a new, orderly, responsible code for press freedom and censorship. Friedrich Scheffer's attitude toward free discussion of free opinions did not soften. Only a revolution could move him, and when the next one came to Hesse in 1848, he fled Cassel immediately. Within weeks of his removal, Hesse received its long-awaited press law, a very liberal one, respectful of the constitution and indifferent to tradition.

FOUR

This Hated Office
The Censors and Their Work

It is difficult to imagine anyone made happy by censorship. People whose writings were censored hated it, of course, and so did people who wanted to read what they had written. But it also discomfited the rulers who sponsored it, who then frequently took out their discomfort on the censors. As much as anyone, censors hated censorship.

Men did not choose to be censors in the nineteenth century; they were chosen. Who would have volunteered for a task that brought abuse rather than respect, earned fines as often as salaries, and was not intellectually rewarding? It is possible that in earlier times, when both learning and dissent traveled in smaller orbits, the censor's lot had been better. The university professors and churchmen who censored manuscripts would have judged materials that they knew something about, and often the authors would have been their colleagues, friends, and neighbors. In the nineteenth century, however, censors read the words of innumerable faceless men, some known by reputation, but many entirely unknown, and what they were required to censor was so diverse that no man could pretend to know it all. Censors in that age of progress were meant increasingly to be technicians, applying policies that other people formulated, scarcely participants any more in the preservation of a shared system of cultural values. It was a tasteless business.

The censor was a hated, vilified public figure, lampooned in prose, in verse, in drawings, in every way that creative men could imagine. A Badenese newspaper editor wrote from the safety of exile in France about his former censor: "He has no soul in his body, which is why he strikes them out of other beings; he has no warm blood, no beating heart, because only the cold-blooded murder out of conviction, and murder is his business. To spit in the face of this sort of fellow may be naughty, but it is not murder." A popular German poet, Georg Herwegh, called the censors eunuchs in princely harems of intellectual conformity. Another poet, a democrat, Adolph Glaßbrenner, attacked them in insulting lines with an ominous meter:

> Du Censor, du Henker, du Mörder, du Dieb!
> Kein Mensch mag dich achten,
> kein Mensch hat dich lieb,
> Für die sechshundert Taler!

> (You censor, you hangman, you murderer, you thief!
> You'll have no respect,
> You'll be without friends,
> For your six hundred taler!)

Six hundred taler, the salary of a Berlin censor in the 1840s, a respectable amount for a public official then, was also paid to censors in Hamburg, and was, perhaps, a just adequate salve for the verbal wounds that came with the job.[1]

Any censor who became tolerable to the public was only likely to embitter his master. The censors' masters, the governments, handled them as roughly as the public did, often putting them to work against their will, then fining them when they did it imperfectly. In 1835, for allowing the sale of Friedrich Clemens [Gerke's] anti-Christian *Manifest der Vernunft* (Manifesto on Reason), a censor in Saxony earned a twenty-taler fine and a dismissal from his post. (For a sense of the scale, imagine an assistant professor today fined one thousand dollars for assigning the wrong book to a class.) At Hamburg four years later, a lax censor allowed one of the local journals to publish a letter from Giuseppe Mazzini, the notorious Italian nationalist, and was fined fifty taler, one month's pay. Another Hamburg censor thought that perhaps the city council could "find a pardoned criminal and entrust censorship to him—although he would certainly have to have a very precise acquaintance with the daily press, a reliable, conservative attitude, and the wisdom of the ages."[2]

In Cassel the story was told in later years that a citizen of the 1830s had named his dog "Censor." Even if apocryphal, it shows the notoriety that enveloped censors in Hesse as well, to their dismay. Christoph von Rommel wrote a letter to his superiors in October 1831 in which he lamented "the struggle and vexation that this office brings with it every day, hated as it is by the general public."[3] Even he who was born to be a censor—his father had served as chief censor before him—despaired of the work after only sixteen months of what would be eighteen years in office.

It was always difficult to find and keep good censors. The Hamburg censor who wanted the job reserved for criminals was right about its qualifications. Censors had to know a lot about the press, newspapers especially, and they also had to be generally acquainted with the dozens of journals and hundreds of books published in German every year. They had to be well and broadly educated because in most states there were only a few censors with a lot of topics to censor. And if these requirements were not enough, it did help censors and rulers both if their politics were similar, which usually meant quite conservative. A censor who met these requirements could expect a very long tenure in office, far longer than most would have liked. When the president of the Prussian province of Posen feared he was about to lose a censor in 1825 because the man's eyesight was failing, the master declared his servant's work to be a *munus publicum* that no one, once entrusted with it, could relinquish. On that basis, the half-blind censor had to stay on the job until he found his own successor.[4]

In Hesse too, the regime held men captive in public service, at least up to promulgation of the 1831 constitution that enshrined a right to resign government appointments. In practice though, even that new guarantee was useless for men who seldom had alternatives to working for the state. However much the Hessian censors disliked their work, they could not do without it because it was an obligatory second job. No one in Cassel was a full-time censor. Their principal responsibilities, the duties they were paid for, were in other parts of the administration.

Being a censor in Hesse was unpleasant work, especially after 1830. There were plenty of reasons for distress, not only the parsimony of the administration but also a continual lack of clarity in its instructions and the censors' own unfortunate ability to see that they were not fulfilling, never could fulfill, the enormous task given to them. The perceived need for censorship grew rapidly as new publications and new readers appeared like mushrooms in the morning, but the government adhered to old attitudes and relied on old institutions that could not keep pace with the changes going on all around. The prince-elector of Hesse and his ministers, in their old-fashioned way, chose public servants from just two branches of the state service to be censors. All but one man who did that work came from the staffs of the Reformed church and the Royal Library, the best places to find people who were broadly educated and knew a lot about books. The exception was Karl Hermann Pfaff, a finance councilor in the Rural Mortgage Bank and censor from 1836 to 1841. Beginning in 1838, the Hessian government also assigned to the Censorship Commission an army officer responsible for military writings, but none of the four men who successively filled this post ever participated in the deliberations of the civilian censors. For all practical purposes, career cultural administrators served as censors, most of them for long terms, and usually three at a time.[5]

In February 1815, Prince Wilhelm I appointed Justus Rommel (1753–1837) to be chairman of the restored Censorship Commission. As a high official of the state church, Rommel was already well-known and respected in Cassel, and he had been chief censor in Cassel before the disruptions brought by the French Revolution. During more than forty years as court preacher he gave the holy blessing at all great state occasions: the awarding of the prince-electoral title that came so belatedly in 1803; the laying of the cornerstone in 1820 for a royal palace that, alas, never was finished or occupied; the laying of another cornerstone in 1834 for a parliament building that was finished two years later and occupied most notably by the regime's opponents. Rommel was a faithful servant of Hesse's princes, unobtrusive as a censor, and head of the commission for fifteen and one-half years.[6]

Serving with him for most of that time were Johann Ludwig Völkel and Jacob Grimm, both accomplished scholars who worked in the Royal Library. Völkel (1762–1829), like the chairman, was at the height of his career in the 1810s. Educated in classical philology and ancient Roman studies, he had served for two years as a temporary professor at the University of Marburg before moving to Cassel in 1789. There initially he worked in the Royal Museum and tutored the crown prince. From 1795 he was an assistant librarian at the court. During the French occupation he stayed in Cassel and got along badly with the occupiers. The prince-elector rewarded this evidence of his patriotism in 1815 by putting Völkel in charge of the Royal Library, although he waited until 1821 to award him the title of director and its salary. Völkel was a modest man. Even after he finally received the promotion he had long deserved, one of his assistants, Wilhelm Grimm, said of him "our . . . chief is good-natured . . . and it never occurs to him to play the role of director."[7] On the Censorship Commission, Völkel was cooperative, liberal, but, most of all, reserved.

The third censor was Jacob Grimm (1785–1863). He was quite a different person from Rommel and Völkel. A generation younger than either of them, his politics were more liberal than Rommel's and more pronounced than Völkel's. He was the pest of the commission but also had to do most of its work.

In 1808, at the age of twenty-three, with five orphaned brothers and sisters to support, Grimm had gone to work as private librarian to Jerome Bonaparte, then living in the prince-elector's palace as king of Westphalia. When Prince Wilhelm I moved back home five years later, he appointed this talented young librarian to be secretary of the Hessian diplomatic mission to Vienna, where Clemens von Metternich was orchestrating the creation of a post-Napoleonic international order. Grimm spent two years commuting between Vienna and Paris, helping Ludwig Völkel to retrieve from the French capital books that Napoleon's minions had stolen from the Hessian library.

It was 1816 before Grimm could return to Cassel and join his brother and Völkel at the library. Years later Jacob Grimm would write of the satisfaction he had felt in the decade that followed, having a chance once more to work on his treasured philological and folkloric studies "disturbed only through small additional duties, such as censorship which usually was left to me; but the disturbance was not significant." "In a way befitting the nature of the task," he told his friend and teacher Friedrich Karl von Savigny in 1823, "I am not quite scrupulous in my handling of it."[8] Although there were frequent complaints that he and his brother, with nine hundred taler between them, were underpaid, Grimm stayed on as assistant librarian and junior censor, mollified by his own lack of censorious scruples, his family's strong ties to Hesse, that precious time he had to continue his own studies, and the knowledge that his colleague Völkel was getting to be an old man.

In 1829, Ludwig Völkel died, but to their dismay, neither Jacob nor Wilhelm Grimm was promoted to director of the library. Instead the post went to Christoph von Rommel, royal archivist. Jacob Grimm's disappointment was profound and predictable, but most of all it was very naive. In 1808, when only twenty-three, he had been miffed that the library directorship under Jerome Bonaparte went to Friedrich Murhard, editor of the Francophile newspaper, the *Moniteur Westfalien* (Westphalian Monitor), instead of to him. In 1819, Rommel's appointment as royal archivist had piqued him too. Yet the Grimm brothers knew all along that they were not royal favorites. When the newly crowned Prince-Elector Wilhelm II reorganized the government in 1821, virtually all public servants received increases in salary; but they did not. Their well-known sympathy for the estranged Princess Auguste was reason enough to keep from them the favors of her husband, a ruler who even more than his father rewarded loyalty above talent.

Jacob and Wilhelm Grimm resigned their public offices in 1829. With Wilhelm's young family they moved to Göttingen in the neighboring kingdom of Hanover, site of a renowned university where they both received appointments. There the brothers would meet new difficulties. Eight years after their arrival, when the last Hanoverian ruler in Britain, Wilhelm IV, died and his niece Victoria acceded to the Anglo-Saxon throne, the medieval Salic Law still mandated succession only through the male line in Hanover. So another of Victoria's uncles, the duke of Cumberland, became the next king of Hanover, Ernst Augustus. He was a tyrant who promptly abrogated the liberal constitution of his dead brother, an act that brought forth eloquent public protests from members of the Göttingen faculty including Jacob and Wilhelm Grimm. King Ernst Augustus dismissed and exiled all of these detractors, the "Göttingen Seven." The Brothers Grimm then returned to Cassel where they worked privately for several years only to leave their homeland again and take appointments in Berlin at the Prussian Academy of Arts and Sciences in 1841. All this was a better fate for Jacob Grimm, though, than staying on as a censor in Cassel.

After Ludwig Völkel's death and Jacob Grimm's resignation, the seventy-six-year-old Evangelical church superintendent Justus Rommel was all that remained of the Censorship Commission, to his dismay. It stayed that way for a year, until the early summer of 1830 when the Interior Ministry allowed him to retire, as he had requested, and appointed two new censors.[9]

For the next eighteen years the chairman of the Censorship Commission was to be Christoph von Rommel (1781–1859),[10] son of the retiring chairman, a historian of his native land, and the man whose appointment as librarian had been the immediate cause of Jacob and Wilhelm Grimm's departure. The younger Rommel was scarcely as accomplished in scholarship as the Brothers Grimm; nonetheless, he was quite a learned man, and by 1830 he had made an outstanding career. Two years earlier his services to the Hessian state had won him a hereditary title of nobility.

Meant to follow his father into the church, he had studied theology at Marburg at first but liked other subjects better. He earned a doctorate in classical studies instead at Göttingen, returned to Marburg in 1804, and one year later at the age of twenty-three became professor of oratory and Greek there. Then came the armies of the French, and the patriotic Rommel family suffered under Jerome Bonaparte's regime. Christoph Rommel went into exile, taking a professorial chair at the newly founded University of Kharkhov, far away in the eastern Ukraine. He stayed there several years, long enough for a brief, unhappy marriage to the seventeen-year-old widow of a Russian major, then returned home without her soon after Wilhelm I repossessed Hesse-Cassel. From then on, Rommel was married to his work.

In 1815, he became a professor of history at Marburg, marking a shift in his interests from the classical age to the modern era. The next year his fellow professors entrusted to him the sending of a petition to Cassel to ask that the university be exempt from censorship by his father's commission. The answer was no.[11] Christoph Rommel gladly resigned his chair in history after only four years, in 1819, and became royal archivist in Cassel. At the same time, he began writing a multivolume history of Hesse-Cassel that would occupy him during much of the remaining forty years of his life.

Rommel knew better than his princes what Hesse lost when the Brothers Grimm departed, for it was he who insisted in 1819 that their scholarly work deserved doctorates from the University of Marburg. As a censor, initially he was very frustrated and sought reforms too, but after several fruitless years of objecting, he just did what was required.

Assisting him as censor was his new deputy in the library, Karl Bernhardi (1799–1874), the son of an Evangelical pastor at Ziegenhain in the province of Upper Hesse, who had also begun his education at Marburg. Bernhardi's activities as a German nationalist in Marburg attracted such attention in the government that he prudently left Hesse in 1821. He went to Belgium, where he found employment as a tutor and continued his studies at the University of Louvain, earning a doctorate there in 1826 and becoming university librarian. But to the regret of his Belgian friends, Bernhardi left after only three years and returned home to take the more modest position and smaller salary of an assistant librarian in Cassel. "I cannot deny," he would recall a quarter-century later, "that for me, who had found a second home in hospitable Belgium, the offer unleashed a hard struggle. But in the end, the pull of the fatherland won out." Because Christoph von Rommel was not a librarian and did not care for that part of his duties, except as a way to increase his standing and income, Bernhardi was de facto director from the start. As for censoring, like Grimm before him he thought poorly of it.[12]

Bernhardi's pronounced liberalism did not fit well with his responsibilities as a censor. Secretly, he was the "soul" of the *Verfassungsfreund* (Friend of the Constitution), leading newspaper of the political opposition in Cassel from 1831 to 1834. In 1848, he would be elected a delegate to the Frankfort Parliament meant to create a German nation.

Christoph von Rommel and Karl Bernhardi inherited the work of the Censorship Commission on the eve of disturbances that would lead to constitutional reform in 1831. A wave of new political reportage arose then too, across central Europe, and continued for several years. This boom in writing, a lot of it tendentious, meant, in turn, that the censors' work increased suddenly several fold. The new appointees in Cassel had a difficult time, especially because there were only two of them now, instead of the three men who had sat on the commission in much quieter years. Repeatedly, Rommel and Bernhardi protested against the unreasonableness of their situation, but it was only in 1836 that finally, on the recommendation of the Justice Ministry, the Interior Ministry appointed Karl Hermann Pfaff (dates unknown) as a third censor.

The route that the search for the right man took this time, from the Interior Ministry to the Justice Ministry to the Finance Ministry to the Rural Mortgage Bank where Pfaff worked as a finance councilor, was unusual because cultural and religious institutions had always furnished censors before. However, after 1830 most men who were learned enough for the job were also adherents of the new constitution. Many of them featured in the new partisan politics that appeared even before there were political parties, and some were delegates to the new legislature. The crown prince and regent, Friedrich Wilhelm, objected to every one of these novelties. As his subjects who embraced them became unlikely candidates for such a sensitive role, the pool of would-be censors was both more shallow and more dispersed through the state service than it had been before.

But for all the care taken to select Pfaff, it was a mistake. During his five-year tenure on the Censorship Commission, both he and Karl Bernhardi had serious differences with the Interior Ministry about the principles and practice of censorship. Relations between them and the ministry worsened steadily until the crown prince dismissed the two troublemakers in the spring of 1841. To replace them, his government returned to its traditional sources, the Royal Library where J. H. Christian Schubart was now secretary and the Reformed Church Consistory in which Franz Carl Theodor Piderit served as a councilor.[13] These two men were at least compliant, although not complacent, at the job and would serve with Christoph von Rommel until the Censorship Commission was dissolved in 1848.

Theodor Piderit (1790–1848) was an accomplished amateur historian who wrote books about Hersfeld, Rinteln, and Cassel, the three towns where he spent his adult life. He had studied theology at Marburg, then preached and taught at Hersfeld during the 1820s. He was Dr. Piderit by the time he went to Rinteln in 1831 as principal pastor of the Reformed church there. Several years later he moved to Cassel where for a half-dozen years he was Justus Rommel's successor as court preacher, an appointment that ended abruptly when Crown Prince Friedrich Wilhelm dismissed him for neglecting to wear the prescribed surplice in the royal presence. He lived only several years more, dying in 1848 at age fifty-nine. From his dismissal as court preacher until his death he worked under Christoph von Rommel in the royal archives.

Piderit's history of Cassel shows that he had a great enthusiasm for recreating the past tempered by good sense about what could not be said; he had good practice censoring himself while he censored others. With laconic irony he wrote of how Count Moritz had ordered a printing press for Cassel sometime around the turn of the sixteenth century, "installed namely in his pavilion on the green, where he could keep his eyes on it." Piderit's lengthy account of a futile effort to ban coffee in the eighteenth century must also have brought smiles to the faces of readers who knew about his duties as censor.[14] On the Censorship Commission he was more critical than Christoph von Rommel but more subdued than Schubart.

Christian Schubart (1800–85) was a native of Marburg where he enrolled for university study of philology and theology in 1816. There he earned a doctorate for his profane studies—an 1832 work by him in Latin on the heroes of ancient Greece, published at Elwert's university bookshop in Marburg, has the look of a thesis. With Christoph von Rommel and Karl Bernhardi in 1834, he founded the Hessian Historical Association (*Hessischer Geschichtsverein*). In his mature years, he translated Pausanius's *Description of Greece* from Latin into German. It appeared in six volumes between 1855 and 1892 and in four more editions later. His career developed slowly and surely too. During the 1830s he had been gone from Hesse, tutoring privately in Württemberg and Austria. He returned to be library secretary in 1839, then moved up to assistant librarian in 1850, and, finally, to librarian in 1874, retiring seven years later at the age of eighty-one. Schubart had one great advantage over all other censors in Cassel: from about the time of his appointment he was very deaf.[15] Although that might have spared him insults on the streets of Cassel, he still had to read and judge according to standards that he, like most of the censors, thought were indefensible.

Most German censors got few rewards for their work; Hessian censors got none. In Cassel censoring paid nothing like the six hundred taler that salved the wounds caused by an irate citizenry in Berlin or Hamburg. Each Hessian censor as a government servant was expected to manage on the salary provided for his other, full-time duties. That should not have been a problem for Christoph von Rommel, who drew a different salary for each of his several titles and in the 1830s was earning about four times the three hundred taler that he had gotten by on as a young professor thirty years earlier. Still, he thought it was unjust to receive nothing more for being a censor, especially when the work busied him for several hours every day. The nine hundred taler that the Brothers Grimm earned between them in Cassel was perhaps adequate to support them and Wilhelm's family, but it was also less than the one thousand taler that had been Jacob's salary during the French occupation. And censors whose principal jobs were more junior that Christoph von Rommel's or Jacob Grimm's had to live in Cassel throughout the early nineteenth century on sums as meager as the couple of hundred taler that professors frequently were paid.[16]

In fairness to the Hessian government, it is also true that it was a common practice throughout central Europe then to pay apprentice state servants nothing at all for some half-dozen years and then to give them only modest sums for an additional time as if they were journeymen in their trades. Only the masters in state service could truly afford the lifestyle that everyone in the cultural and administrative elite was expected and wanted to keep.

Even at that, evidence is abundant of an unusual stinginess toward censors, particularly in Hesse-Cassel. As early as 1824 Justus Rommel had complained that he and his colleagues had no funds even to purchase writing materials. Christoph von Rommel and Karl Bernhardi got an extraordinary one-time payment of one hundred taler to offset their office expenses in 1831, but for the next decade the government refused to do anything more for them. They had no budget to purchase published works, even though it was essential to see them in order to censor them. Nor were they able to buy newspapers, which contained useful notices about what new books and periodicals were in the bookshops. In the 1840s, when the censors sought once more to be paid for their work, they discovered another opponent besides the miserly government, the legislative assembly, which refused to authorize any funds for censorship as long as there was no press law. In fact, the delegates averred that under a future press law there would be no need for censors at all.[17]

Through this extreme, public opposition to the entire effort to control the spread of ideas, the Hessian legislators, despite themselves, finally achieved what the censors had not been able to do in more than twenty-five years of trying. If the assembly was against paying censors, then the government began to be for it. In 1842, the censors (two of them recently appointed) renewed their request for money. When the delegates met the following year, they refused again to budget anything for the commission, but the ministry granted each censor thirty taler anyway, to cover pressing office expenses, it was said. Then Christoph von Rommel insisted that the ministry ignore the unfriendly assembly entirely and petition the prince regent to put his censors on salaries. In slow stages, the government went along, finally granting each censor a one-hundred-taler annual stipend. Even after this long-awaited, halting concession, the Hessian government treated its Censorship Commission worse than other government agencies. As late as 1846 its members did not have the common privilege of franking their official correspondence.[18]

It is a wonderful irony that the censors finally got the funds that would help them fulfill their legal duties only because the Interior Ministry unconstitutionally circumvented the budgetary rights of the legislature. For if anyone wanted laws clarified, harmonized with the constitution, and observed faithfully and consistently, it was the censors. These concerns recur all through the circular notes that they used to conduct most of their business—the commission seldom actually met. Not all of the censors took equal part in the philosophical and practical controversies that would erupt in their triangular correspondence, and that sometimes also rebounded between them as a group and the Interior Ministry. In the early years, Justus Rommel and Ludwig Völkel wrote sparingly, wanting to get the work out of the way quickly, whereas Jacob Grimm expounded at length on the logical and spiritual defects of it all. From 1830 on, it was Christoph von Rommel who kept a low profile in commission discussions while his successive partners bemoaned the inconsistencies and decried the injustices.

There was always a self-appointed conscience in the group. After Grimm's departure, Karl Bernhardi from 1830 to 1841 and then J. H. Christian Schubart from 1841 to 1848 each mused and fussed over the censor's mission. Is it just a coincidence that all three of these men were subordinate officials in the Royal Library, full of ideas, impatient, all possessed of great but unfulfilled ambitions? They who could least afford it demonstrated the greatest independence of mind. Most remarkable of the three was Karl Bernhardi, who for a time was both a censor and the guiding force, although anonymously, of the *Friend of the Constitution,* which the government viewed as anything but a friend and soon quashed.[19]

Jacob Grimm objected to censorship in general. He was especially troubled by the boundless scope of work assigned to the censors through their instruction of 1816. Censoring ought to be selective, he thought. Concern might be legitimate, for instance, about written works that attacked the prince-elector's government and would be published and consumed in Hesse but not about the same sorts of materials if they were published somewhere else or aimed at some other government. Grimm wanted the Confederal Press Law of 1819 to be the sole standard for censorship in Hesse-Cassel. The local instruction of 1816 went far beyond what was needed, he said, because the Confederal Assembly had acted on behalf of all German states.

Along with legitimate concerns and criticisms, Grimm introduced mischief too. He must have enjoyed raising difficult questions as a sort of intellectual sabotage, a distraction from the censors' true work. In 1823, he tried to persuade the other censors that their commission did not exist anymore:

> Without reference . . . to any particular case, it is perhaps . . . obvious that we should petition to superior authority: that the commission must consider itself superseded, because it is nowhere mentioned in the reorganization edict, probably because superiors realize that censorship is unworkable as it is now organized. Then, this unworkability should be clarified and a proposal made: to establish censorship solely for works to be printed in the electoral principality.

And so Grimm logically found his way to a new plan for strictly limiting censorship, always his preference. But his reading of the reorganization edict was entirely wrong. The commission was included in it and made subordinate to the new Interior Ministry. His "error" almost certainly was deliberate because Grimm had already written a detailed account of the important new law to his friend Friedrich Karl von Savigny only two months after it was promulgated, well before he revealed his incredible discovery to the other censors. This clever scheme got no further than Grimm's many other attempts to limit censorship.[20]

Karl Bernhardi was less expressive than Grimm as a dissenting censor, as he had to be, given the political editing he did on the side. His secret journalism also gave him a vent for his personal opinions that was not available to every disgruntled censor. Bernhardi's thoughts on censorship as a part of his own professional life were evident in an autobiographical essay in which he did not even mention that he had been a censor for eleven years. In notes to the other censors, he argued that there was no need for repressive censorship of works already published if only the government would be more efficient in policing the book trade. The Censorship Commission had no business doing anything about published works except perhaps writing some advisory opinions, he said. His proposals, like Grimm's, aimed to reduce the censors' authority, their work load, and especially their responsibility for executing government policies that he abhorred.

Bernhardi's wit at least got him farther with Christoph von Rommel and Pfaff than Grimm's had ever gotten him with Justus Rommel and Völkel. Once, in 1837, when the Interior Ministry sent an especially confusing and self-contradictory directive, Rommel and Pfaff wanted to ask for a clarification, until Bernhardi suggested that they just acknowledge the directive. They did so and heard nothing more about it.[21]

Christian Schubart, like Grimm and Bernhardi before him, wanted to limit the censors' duties, especially by getting them out of the onerous business of reviewing long books. His plan was simple: ignore local censorship laws and just follow the Confederal Law of 1819, Grimm's plan of years before, and one that both Piderit and Christoph von Rommel might have liked, but Rommel knew it would not work. Schubart, like Grimm, was expert at misreading or misunderstanding the law in ways that harmonized it with his own opinions.[22]

Most of the debating and complaining that went on in the notes among the censors was not meant for the eyes of their masters at the Interior Ministry. When occasionally they did gripe there, the responses were not generous. To an 1844 assertion that their work was futile, the ministry told its censors curtly,

> They are not responsible for its success. And even if they should be of the opinion on future occasions that the dutiful exercise of their profession is pointless, or even counterproductive, oversights would be even less excusable. While the actual success of actions against printed materials remains uncertain under all circumstances, nonetheless, the commandments of appointed authority exercise a healing power.[23]

It is doubtful that censorship, always and at all costs, had "a healing power." Certainly, it was no balm for the censors, who fought long and hard just to be paid, who knew that they were unpopular, and who often felt overworked. The later censors could only be glad that in the years after 1816, with its sweeping instruction to the censors, the government relieved them of many of their original duties.

Again and again during the early nineteenth century the Interior Ministry reshuffled censorship arrangements, trying to sort out responsibilities of the Censorship Commission and other policing agencies. There were two, often contradictory impulses behind these changes. One was an interest in making the work of government more orderly, something found all across central Europe then, which had begun under enlightened rulers even before the far-reaching administrative changes of the Napoleonic era. Against that desire worked a new phenomenon, the enormous growth in the world of reading and writing, which seemed to call for much more censoring by many more censors than there had been in the eighteenth century. Principles dictated that the administrative centralization and rationalization started earlier be continued, even hastened. In practice though, that became less and less possible.

During the eighteenth century there had been various local arrangements for censorship in the territories of the count (from 1803, prince-elector) of Hesse. Where there were universities, at Marburg in the province of Upper Hesse and at Rinteln in the county of Schaumburg, their faculties did the job. In the duchy of Hanau two representatives of the Reformed Church Consistory served as censors. In the bishopric of Fulda, which would become a Hessian province in 1816, the ecclesiastical government employed censors for both religious and secular writings. In Cassel, a handful of government servants reviewed local publications, as they had at least since the beginning of the eighteenth century. Cassel's Book Censorship Commission replaced them in 1780 during a general reorganization of local governments, also apparent in the numerous police commissions founded throughout Hesse-Cassel about then. It was then, too, that Bavaria and Baden established censorship commissions for the first time. All established censorship arrangements in Hesse disappeared during the French administration that began in 1807—the occupiers brought along their own institutions.[24]

After the 1813 liberation, while Prince Wilhelm I reestablished his government to be much as it had been before, he also looked for new ways to rationalize the makeshift bureaucracy. By 1818, in place of the old plethora of police commissions, he had appointed four provincial directors under the command of a director general of police in Cassel. And, for the first time, the prince-elector made the Censorship Commission in Cassel responsible throughout his lands. His decree of 1815 that reconstituted the commission defined its duties much more broadly than they ever had been before. In principle, it would now administer all censorship and press monitoring in the principality.

Originally, the Cassel censors had only been commissioned to examine manuscripts readied for printing in the capital. From the 1790s on, they had to supervise lending libraries there too. In 1816 their duties became the wide-ranging ones described in chapter 3.

The new assignment was impossible, as both the censors and the local administration in Cassel tried to explain to Prince Wilhelm I through his privy council. A small, ill-equipped, part-time, unbudgeted commission in one of the poorer German states could scarcely monitor all German-language publications that appeared in Europe every year, and just might end up in Hesse. In the entire German Confederation, only Austria had a similarly broad concept of censorship—but there was also a paid staff of full-time censors at police headquarters in Vienna.[25] Formally, no one in Cassel ever changed this unwieldy instruction, but informally, everyone found ways to cope with it. Some of the Censorship Commission's duties went eventually to other authorities, and others were simply ignored.

The government assigned some local censorship to people outside the commission who had been doing it before. In Marburg, professors continued to screen manuscripts set for printing, a privilege that dated back to the founding of the university by Count Philipp the Magnanimous in 1527. After issuance of the 1816 Instruction to the Censors, which the professors had petitioned unsuccessfully to be exempted from, the government considered the university a "special censorship authority." Its prorector and deans censored some ninety publications before printing in the years from 1816 to 1832. When the Censorship Commission in Cassel took care to notify the university in August 1818 that it had fined the Marburg bookseller Krieger twenty taler for publishing a nonacademic book—*Bemerkungen auf einer Reise in Amerika* (Remarks on a Journey Through America)—without precensorship, this notice was more than a courtesy. It acknowledged the university's role in censorship.[26]

After the unrest of the early 1830s, Cassel authorities took political censoring away from the professors, but they protested and continued to censor with their accustomed independence anyway. Noa Gottfried Elwert, successor to Krieger in the book business, defied the Censorship Commission right up to 1848, citing his privilege, never suspended by any new law, he claimed, to publish the writings of professors on any subject without censorship except by their deans.

In Fulda, the Roman Catholic church also kept its traditional role. Although the Censorship Commission and other civil officials now examined many manuscripts and all of the contents of bookshops there, ecclesiastical censors still read anything written by Roman Catholic clergy, and the bishop's office made sure to tell the Cassel censors about lots of other offensive material.[27]

Hesse-Cassel's other two regional centers, Hanau and Rinteln (where the university closed permanently in 1803), did not have higher institutions of education or religion and so lacked the readily identifiable people who were competent to censor in Marburg and Fulda. Because they were farther from Cassel than the other two towns, though, there was even more need to have censors on the spot. To solve these problems, the government appointed provincial deputies to the Censorship Commission—in Rinteln in the fall of 1818, when a local printer asked for a committee to review the work done in his shop. From the start, the two-man deputation there (one ecclesiastical, one civil censor) had only limited powers. They could not act independently but always had to consult Cassel officials—the censors about manuscripts, the Minister of the Interior about local political periodicals. They were neither paid for their work nor burdened by it. In September 1830, they reported to the Cassel commission that in twelve years they had never banned a single publication.[28]

In Hanau, censors were needed because of the town's liberal politics and its proximity to the free city of Frankfort, seat of the German Confederal Assembly. But the government established no deputation there until 1827, when the Hanau printer and publisher Kittsteiner asked that someone go over the manuscripts in his print shop. (It might seem odd that printers asked for censorship, but there was a good reason for it: without censorship, what they printed the police might confiscate, with no compensation to the printers; with censorship, they hoped that would not happen.)

In Hanau as in Rinteln, the Interior Ministry appointed one deputy censor from the local administration and one from the Reformed Church Consistory. Unlike their northern cousins, the Hanau deputies were busy and often in trouble. Especially in 1832 and 1833, they had to answer repeatedly for allowing local journalists and pamphleteers to publish things that outraged officials in Cassel, in Frankfort, and in the neighboring grand duchy of Hesse-Darmstadt. The Hanau censors did not enjoy their work either. In May 1832, even before their liberality began to concern officials in Cassel, both men asked to be relieved of the job, but to no avail. Three years later the ministry dismissed them. Their successors encountered fewer difficulties; they were lucky to serve at a time when there was less political tension in Hanau.[29] In 1840, as part of a broader effort to tighten up censorship practices, the government abolished the deputy committees at both Hanau and Rinteln.

The Censorship Commission was relieved of some work also by the appointment of special censors for newspapers and journals. Usually, the Interior Ministry co-opted local police officers to read periodicals before they were printed. The police directors in Marburg, Fulda, Hanau, and Rinteln and an administrative councilor in Cassel tended to get important—that is, political—publications, but some went to ordinary policemen and other government servants.

In the 1830s, the Interior Minister also named special censors to supervise the collections of lending libraries, which were appearing and growing quickly then, in the principality and everywhere else in Germany. As with periodicals, there was no effective way to monitor these libraries from a central place. Appointing local clergymen to be library censors in each community circumvented that problem; but it also had the unwelcome effect, from the government's point of view, of broadening awareness among the cultural elite that the state faced enormous difficulties if it really meant to control libraries, short of closing them altogether.[30]

Farming out censorship of newspapers, journals, and library collections eased the Cassel censors' task without, however, making it any more clear or more sensible. How should they behave toward one sort of book or another? they often wanted to know. A manual, even a compendium of current regulations, might have helped them, but there was nothing like that in Cassel.

The government almost never issued directives or clarifications to the commission before 1831 because until then most people, in government and out of it, were indifferent about censorship. The commission, or rather Jacob Grimm on his own, allowed the publication and sale of free-minded works that stopped short of insulting the home government—exactly the standard that Grimm wanted adopted officially. The number of works banned in those years was quite small, and Grimm and the other censors were never overworked. They did not bother themselves with the demanding requirements of their instruction, nor did they have to. The government dealt with major disruptions of the literary status quo as they occurred, one at a time, calling censors and local police into action when it needed them.

After 1831, directives on censorship came more frequently. There were new orders on how to scrutinize periodicals better, and a lot more about lending libraries. Twice, in 1835 and in 1841, the government asked the commission to suggest how to improve censorship generally, prompting enthusiastic, costly proposals that it did not adopt. There would have been little to gain from changing how censorship was done, certainly not in ways that the reading public might notice, which could only have exacerbated conflicts with the legislature over the law that was forever pending and never enacted on censorship and the press. Change would have encouraged even more lawsuits on the obscure interrelations of Confederal law, old Hessian law, new Hessian constitutional law, and official behavior toward the press, all of them different and inconsistent with each other. As it was, too many cases about censorship and the press were pending in the courts by the 1840s.

The prince-elector of Hesse and his chief functionaries could afford to leave censorship as confused as it was because they had other police measures to control print. And they were not bashful about distorting or ignoring difficult parts of the new constitution when it suited them. The Interior Ministry was confident that a constitutional exemption of long publications from prepublication censorship would never take effect. It ignored the constitution's guarantee of "the free expression of mere opinions." Even after twelve years of constitutional government, it was sure that its coercive powers over the press would prevail "so long as the right of the executive remains intact, to hinder traffic in works that are constitutionally exempt from censorship."[31]

None of this helped the censors. While trying to understand the constitution and obey it, they were caught in more and more misunderstandings with the public and with their masters. Who was at fault? Their masters were, they said, for never clarifying questions of jurisdiction, procedure, and standards that, by the 1840s, censors had raised for more than twenty years. In these difficulties, all of the censors became alienated from the government they served. Jacob Grimm, Karl Bernhardi, and Christian Schubart spoke out more vigorously than the others on questions about the censors' task; but they were not alone. On one or another of many sore points, every member of the commission complained about the arrangements for their work. What troubled Jacob Grimm in the 1820s were the same issues that would bother other censors ten and twenty years later. Even Christoph von Rommel, although less political and more politic than other censors, regretted decisions that he was compelled to make because of his official position. "Professional duty is often so much at odds with personal conviction," he, the government's favorite and most faithful censor, lamented in 1831.[32]

Thoughtful men, and all of the censors were that, knew far better than suspicious rulers and high civil servants the difference between serious dangers and the specious ones that printer's ink allegedly posed. "What are punishable are demagogic works that poison and insult the existing political system," Jacob Grimm wrote in 1822, "but not those that bravely and necessarily uncover the failings of individual governments, of which none can be entirely free."[33]

"Every intellectual viewpoint should be permitted, especially on domestic politics," Christian Schubart echoed almost twenty years later, "so long as the discussion remains within the bounds of propriety."

> Censorship should not muzzle literature. It should not fault the perceptions and opinions of others according to the idiosyncracies of one man's point of view; nor should it snoop about nervously like the police, wondering whether this or that might conceivably meet with displeasure from someone or other. It should not inhibit the independent development of the mind, but rather promote it—not cut away every new sprout, but rather purge the poisonous fungi that are deadly to spiritual, moral, and civil life. Neither liberty of thought in matters political nor a self-deprecating wit has ever overthrown a state, nor will they in the future. The Christian Church is strong enough that it does not need to shy away from serious examination.[34]

The censors knew equally well the practical difficulties of their work. They knew that much of what they did was transparently ineffective and had been for a long time. For example, they tried to pay attention to what booksellers were selling, even though it was naive to imagine that these tradesmen were the only, or even the most important, conduits for getting every sort of undesirable literature from authors to readers. In 1797, two of the early Cassel censors had written: "There are always other ways than bookshops by which almanacs and other scandalous writings come in from those lands where boundless press freedom reigns, and reach the hands of the people." Grimm, in 1822, concurred: "Our sphere of influence is largely illusory, at most covering domestic dealers. We can only forbid [them] from selling written works; we cannot prevent anyone from procuring them somewhere else and reading them."

Even news that Hessian journalists could not print locally was easily exported for publication elsewhere and then reimported for local residents to read. "So many articles are sent from here to the papers in neighboring states which still have no constitutions," said Christoph von Rommel. Controlling the borders was difficult, usually impossible. Karl Bernhardi wished that the Hessian government would recognize that and distinguish as in Austria between an outright ban on possession, usually placed on domestic publications that had evaded prior censorship or foreign publications about Austria, and simpler prohibitions of public sale that were placed on other, objectionable but less dangerous, publications from abroad.[35] Such a refinement, which would have eased the censor's burden, never found a place in Hessian censorship rules.

But even had the censors, aided by the police, been able and willing to control the borders, if they had been able to monitor the circulation of literature outside the bookshops, and if they had also been able to see a copy of each work that was banned, there would still have been difficulties. How, for instance, were uniform and agreeable standards to be found? Jacob Grimm reported that he wanted to let some works pass that should be banned if he followed the 1816 instruction rigorously. "His distinguished colleagues," he added, "were of another opinion," so the books often did get banned. Christoph von Rommel, explaining why the task was so unpleasant, pointed to the problem of "maintaining consistent standards in the practice of censorship . . . with the great divergence of *powers* and *opinions*."

Should it matter whether a work was in manuscript or already in print? The censors of 1837 thought so: "In all [published] works there are individual passages, more in some and fewer in others, that could not be permitted—in part on moral and in part on political grounds—if the work in question were being submitted for permission to print." Were political and moral transgressions equally damnable? Again in 1837, the censors argued that distinguishing between them, condemning political failings sooner than moral ones, warped censorship; yet they found it difficult to avoid the distinction. In the censors' view, some publications got through even though they were morally far more repugnant than others that the ministry insisted be banned on political grounds.[36]

Jacob Grimm had offered a simple solution: apply censorship only to political works. But even then, who was to say what was political and what was not? The censor's definition of politics seldom matched the government's. Years after Grimm's modest proposal, that bothered Franz Piderit:

> With only a few exceptions, just about all literature today is political, and nearly everything that is printed in a periodical can be labeled "political news" or described as "having a political tendency." Even religion serves politics now, so that every confessional work is at the same time political. Every biography, every statistical footnote, yes, even every innocent story can take on a political character. Where should the limits be set? Should . . . [a] journal not report any news of Russia, America, or Egypt, or about the present? Every mention of a prince is political.[37]

Piderit meant it as an argument for less censorship; but to Germans who approved of modern censorship he was simply stating the obvious—everything written had to be scrutinized.

The censors wanted less tedious work and more autonomy. What they got, especially in the last years of the commission's existence, was less creative work and less autonomy. The original 1816 instruction that set out their job always had been deceptive because it seemed to make them responsible for executing their own decisions. *"Are we censors or policemen?"* Christian Schubart asked shortly after he and Franz Piderit became censors in 1841. Piderit had been going through old commission files, trying to understand their charge without success. "As a general rule," Christoph von Rommel told them, "the Censorship Commission is not responsible for books that have not been presented to it, because it is not an *executive* authority."[38]

Indeed, it was far less than that. By the 1840s the censors often seemed condemned to ignorance as well as impotence. They wanted to know when new print shops and bookshops opened, but no one would tell them. They asked for lists of publications banned in neighboring states, but no one would get them. Unsure of their proper role, they blundered about, writing directly to publishers when they should not have, being rebuked by the Interior Ministry for conduct "improper, unsuitable, and contrary to the rules."[39]

These last years before the 1848 revolution were especially unhappy ones for the Cassel censors. The discretion that once had seemed their entitlement vanished altogether. One decade earlier, during the summer of 1837, the commission had dared to refuse two ministerial requests for bans on published works. In one case, the censors insisted that a few undesirable excerpts from a forbidden novel, Karl Gutzkow's *Wally,* imbedded in a book that was an attack on Gutzkow, was not reason enough to prohibit the entire book. In the other case, they agreed that there were offensive passages in *Ost und West: Reisen in Polen und Frankreich* (East and West: Travels in Poland and France) by Otto Spazier (a pseudonym), but the book was not particularly dangerous and no other German state had banned it, so they would not either.[40] The timing of these audacious stands was fortunate. In Cassel the government was in turmoil right then, the vigorously illiberal Interior Minister of the past five years, Ludwig Hassenpflug, had just resigned his post and would soon leave Hesse.

In later years, rather than getting their own way, the censors obeyed direct orders to issue bans and answered contritely when the ministry scolded them about works that they should not have approved. By the end of 1844, a tone of resignation was in their notes to each other. "There is certainly nothing to do but take the steps ordered" was Piderit's reaction to one of many ministerial demands for a ban. "The Censorship Commission is no longer asked to judge, but simply—to comply!" The following summer when he and the other two censors hesitated over a dictated ban, the ministry's reaction was swift and sure: "The Censorship Commission is . . . to take the required decision on prohibition of the book in the Principality *immediately* and to report accordingly."[41]

It was too bad for the prince-elector that his censors were necessarily intelligent men. His good fortune was that his government could ignore most of their complaints. The censors rarely acted on their deviant beliefs anyway, instead exercising the sort of caution to be expected from men who depended on the state for their livelihood. When it needed to, the government simply forced their actions or bypassed them. Why then did the Censorship Commission last so long as an institution? Because once it had worked reasonably well and now there was no imaginable substitute.

FIVE

Dreadful, Tiresome Reading
Censorship of Lending Libraries and Periodicals

The censors in Cassel tried hard to avoid two sorts of literary policing—censorship of lending libraries and domestic periodicals—that between them contained, by the 1840s, the principal reading matter of a rapidly growing literate public. Monitoring their contents was not much like the work of the Censorship Commission anyway and fell naturally to other, specially appointed, local censors. It was easier because most of the material was predictable and safe, but it was also more taxing because the volume of work was enormous. For both of these reasons it was better done individually than collegially.

The men assigned to police libraries and periodicals had a task that was more private than the work of the Censorship Commission, less likely to earn them public hatred, but no more satisfying. It was monotonous to comb through the pages of an unimaginative newspaper week after week, day after day, or when the editors had their way, sometimes night after night. It was vexing to decide what could stay and what could not in a newspaper that was imaginative. It was no better to sit in a library thumbing through thousands upon thousands of volumes, mostly cheap novels, one hardly distinguishable from the next.

"The number of novels and plays is so vast, reading most of them so dreadful and tiresome," Jacob Grimm wrote in 1823, "that even for a simple man of letters it would be a burden to acquaint himself with such books, not to mention actually reading them."[1] Yet the Hessian princes insisted that what was in libraries, newspapers, and journals all had to be read and censored. They insisted, even though what Hessians found there did not often treat politics or faith, the principal worries of censors and police. If it offended most likely it was scandalous, and scandal was only the third concern of governments that instituted censorship.

There was also not the stealth, sleuthing, and uncertainty about this work that there was with book censorship. Libraries and periodicals were open to view, not hidden as easily as single copies of a book or, especially, a pamphlet. Each of these literary institutions had a regular domicile and a known proprietor, who announced publicly his rates and schedules. For all of these reasons they were easier to police, if only enough of the right police could be found. What made the task difficult for the Hessian government was that there were too many periodicals of every sort and lending libraries filled to overflowing with books. It never found a good way to monitor them.

Lending libraries posed an insolvable problem. The men made to censor them, like many of their educated countrymen, like the government that appointed them, found what was in the libraries lamentable at best. Even more than other varieties of censorship, however, adequate supervision cost more trouble and time than it was worth, especially from the 1830s when many new libraries appeared and their collections grew quickly.

The first ones in Germany were founded in Berlin early in the eighteenth century, about the same time that newspapers first appeared. A few more appeared in the Prussian provinces of Pomerania and Brandenburg and in the kingdom of Saxony by midcentury, but only from the 1770s were they found all over Germany. And like bookshops, to which most were attached, there were never many of them until the 1830s.[2]

At the end of the eighteenth century, several libraries did business in Cassel, where the old Book Censorship Commission inspected them. Through its instruction of 1816, the revived commission again was charged with keeping unsuitable books off library shelves, now not only in Cassel but throughout the principality. The censors, however, did nothing about them. In 1821, the reorganization edict made it the county councilors' task to watch over them; the Interior Ministry instructed councilors to keep complete sets of the catalogs of local library collections and to apply the same general standards that applied to book censorship. Only approved books could be listed; any that insulted or undermined good morals, encouraged superstition, or were politically dangerous could not be allowed. Administrators who found the wrong sorts of books in a library were to remove them and to see that the proprietor crossed them out of his catalog. The government threatened to close libraries that did not cooperate.[3] This system had a thorough appearance, but it never worked.

Every few years afterward, officials in Cassel tried to repair it, with little success. In 1823, in the first of these efforts, the Interior Ministry invited the Censorship Commission to draft a new instruction as the basis for lending library review. Jacob Grimm, characteristically taking up the challenge, wrote a long, shrewd report on the philosophical, juridical, and practical reasons why the government should leave the libraries alone, and why if it would not leave them alone, at least it should leave the Censorship Commission alone about them.

Grimm did not like the libraries. They "spread harm among the people," full as they were of "vacuous books"; their very existence was "dangerous," he agreed. But the prospect of improving them was bleak. "They are simply an evil of the age, a product of some of its better aspects, and will not be overcome except through an inner, spiritual improvement of humankind." The crux of the problem was not what library proprietors had to give but what their customers insisted on getting. "People do not gladly take instructions from a government bureau on what they should or should not read. There are good books in every lending library, but they are unprofitable. . . . True scholarship and history may be listed, but typically go unread. . . . If someone wants to spend his time reading vacuous books, who is to stop him? Perhaps he cannot digest healthier fare."

Grimm sought, as he always did, to separate politics, which he considered the proper and legal concern of censors, from religion and morality, which were not their business:

> Through the formal establishment of censorship organs since the Peace of Paris and the decrees of the German Confederation . . . governments have sought to hinder print and broadcast of free, unrestrained opinions on defects in the political system and to snuff out what they fear is their harmful influence. Religion and morals are mentioned simply in passing, being in fact camouflage. It goes against Protestant teachings to inhibit discussion of theological issues, especially through partly or wholly secular agencies. Blasphemous and obscene books are unknown in German literature or appear so seldom that even without state intervention they would reap public condemnation. The censor's task is purely political.

If he were right, then there would be no reason to confuse policing of libraries with censors' work. "From a political standpoint they are harmless. People do not borrow political pamphlets from them, just enormous numbers of novels and plays. . . . What the censors ban would never find their way into lending libraries anyway."

All this arguing served Grimm's most immediate concern that he and the other Cassel censors not be "further burdened, by having to supervise lending libraries." Why not, he asked, just tell the ministry that "the undersigned office, since its establishment, has never had the least to do with lending libraries and reading rooms here, far less with any of them elsewhere in the land." It was true, they had not, even if they should have. Grimm urged the state to "limit itself to removing from circulation, now and then, more or less lascivious, immoral writings." But who should do even that? Local administrators?

> There may be no one among the county councilors big enough for the job, even less their subordinates, who would get it. We cannot expect them to read and judge all of the new popular books that appear, in ever greater numbers, at each book fair. A central office to do this work for the whole state, even if not impossible, is wholly inadvisable. Its establishment, the effort that would go with it, the paperwork, the resulting costs are wholly out of proportion to the minimal gain it could bring.[4]

Grimm thought "it would be far more useful to hand over this policing to ecclesiastical authorities, who employ means that work more slowly but are also more effective morally. Besides, the preacher in a rural town usually has more literary tact than the county councilor." It was the only one of his many suggestions that the Interior Ministry adopted—thirteen years later.

The ministry would have done well to pay more attention to Grimm's objections because what happened with lending library supervision showed that what he said was true. By and large the libraries had no political books, harboring instead the sorts that he described. No one in state service wanted to read them, numerous and vapid as they were. Yet the government was not wise; it never abandoned the attempt to control all printed works wherever they appeared.

The guide for censoring lending libraries that one of Grimm's colleagues wrote in 1823, submitted by the commission instead of Grimm's draft, was far more cautious. It admitted that no one seemed to pay attention to libraries. It did not even mention the Censorship Commission, lest it get the assignment. In conclusion it urged that "the opening of new libraries . . . be hindered, and forbidden entirely in smaller country towns."[5] That would have been one logical way to diminish all of the difficulties that Jacob Grimm had identified.

Despite the censors' wish though, by the 1840s there would be many more lending libraries in Hesse-Cassel than twenty years earlier, including some in country towns. The book trade was very prosperous after 1830, when the number of works published in Germany was growing more than 10 percent annually; it continued at almost that rate for another dozen years. New shops sprouted to cater the growing trade in books and magazines, and most had a library attached.[6] But it was not only booksellers who opened lending libraries. Other merchants, book binders, even a preacher, a town chamberlain, a stationer, and an art dealer ran them in Hesse.

About one dozen libraries were in the principality by 1830. Cassel had three, and elsewhere in the province of Lower Hesse were four more. Two were in Upper Hesse, both at Marburg, and one was at Fulda. For a time Hanau had three but two closed. Through the 1830s and 1840s requests came frequently to the Interior Ministry for permission to open new libraries, which it often granted. There were at least twenty-two libraries in the four provinces by 1840, much of the increase coming in towns where there had not been any one decade earlier. In Lower Hesse outside of Cassel, there were six in 1840 and at least eight, probably eleven, five years later. Some had small, insignificant collections; some appeared and then vanished quickly; others endured for decades and eventually stocked tens of thousands of volumes.[7]

As lending libraries became more common, so did calls to control them better. Educated men, in and out of government, believed they were an evil influence on common people. The dean of the Fulda cathedral complained to the local police in 1830 "that most of the books in this sort of lending library are very indecent and immoral. . . . They make a dangerous, corrupting impression on the imagination, temperament, morals, and life. At the very least," he believed, "the tastes that such disreputable reading fosters will spoil the appetite for serious literature and more substantial spiritual nourishment."[8]

At Melsungen, south of Cassel in Lower Hesse, the county councilor urged in 1837 that a local bookbinder, Karl Moritz, be refused his petition to open a bookshop with lending library attached because "lending libraries are just another sort of book business with the one crucial difference that they are intended solely to gain money and waste time. They allow the public easy access to every sort of literary excretion. They are the secret reservoirs and circulators for all bad products of the printing press." Moritz did not receive permission.[9]

Metaphors linking mind with body, books with food, learning with nourishment, but lending libraries with filth and poison were common then in discussions of the people's reading. Witness the lurid indignation of a school inspector named Collmann, writing to the Cassel police in 1845.

> As far as I know apothecaries may not dispense poisons to just anyone, although they only bring death to the body. It is my sorry lot to learn, however, that even today that poison which is deadly to the soul is being dispensed in lending libraries, and yes, even into the hands of children. . . . Enclosed is a book, *Der Hundsattler* (The Man Who Saddled Dogs), which for the benefit of the reading public is already in its fourth printing. It belongs among the abominable abortions of the human imagination, . . . damnation, blasphemy, lust, seduction, abduction.
> A young boy, . . . a confirmation pupil at that, brought it with him to school.
> Now what use is all of the instruction in school and in confirmation class? . . .
> Once before I had the sad case of a pupil who got a similar book, or maybe the same one, . . . a youth who by such reading went astray. . . .
> Let there be established here for us soon a public library where the people are offered healthy fare for mind and body.[10]

Whatever Inspector Collmann might have thought, through the years the government had not been indifferent to the libraries and their filth. It had tried again and again to clean them up but always without lasting success. In 1836, at the height of Ludwig Hassenpflug's powers as minister, the government came upon what seemed a workable method for reviewing them. That year, when the Interior Ministry raised the issue, the Cassel censors and local officials both claimed that it was the other's responsibility. The censors did not want the task any more than they had before, although it seemed that the instruction of 1816 made them responsible. Police directors and county councilors did not want it either, although the reorganization edict of 1821 seemed to make it their job as well. Karl Pfaff, just appointed to the Censorship Commission, asked whether county councilors could not enlist clergy to examine the catalogs and then have them forward objectionable or questionable books to the Cassel censors. That way censors and local officials would share responsibility without either really having to do the work.[11]

This time, for once, the Interior Ministry followed its censors' advice. Soon it asked leaders of the Evangelical and Roman Catholic churches to recommend pastors for library review committees to advise the county councilors, just as Pfaff had suggested. Usually following church recommendations, through the summer and early fall of 1836 the ministry named one or two men to be lending library censors in seven communities: Eschwege and Witzenhausen in Lower Hesse; Marburg in Upper Hesse; Fulda, Hersfeld, and Schmalkalden in Fulda Province; Hanau in Hanau Province. Here were toilers to do that awful spadework in the libraries, taking out weeds such as *Ferdinand und Karoline, oder Wiedererscheinung eines betrogenen Mädchens* (Ferdinand and Caroline, or the Return of a Girl Who Was Deceived [Berlin, 1805])—"an immoral book so badly written that one can hardly read it"—and *Auguste, oder Geständnisse einer Braut vor ihrer Trauung* (Auguste, or What the Bride Confessed Before Her Wedding [no place, no date]).[12]

The new plan, whatever its administrative merits, did not make the gardens of popular literature any smaller or give them a better smell; it only left their weeding in new hands. When the clergymen-turned-censors complained, as they often would, the Censorship Commission, county officials, and the Interior Ministry all were dragged back into the problem again. And it only took a few months for the complaints to begin. In January 1837, the Marburg library censors, Evangelical Pastor Klöffler and Roman Catholic Auxiliary Dr. Malkmus asked for permission to go directly to the two local proprietors of lending libraries, Christian Dietrich Garthe and Noa Elwert, instead of having the police act as their intermediaries. Even then, Malkmus warned, reading all of the books thoroughly was going to be impossible. Klöffler wrote, more warily, "The completion of this task will take considerable time."[13]

At the end of the year, Malkmus reported on his progress. Censoring Garthe's lending library, he had gotten through the first one thousand volumes that were listed in the nine-year-old catalog of 1828. "Through this work I have had the occasion to acquaint myself with many writings whose wretched contents have made me regret that there still is a ravenous reading public for books that, although containing nothing obviously immoral, nonetheless through their racy contents and sentimental character, encourage sensual and imaginative excesses." He asked for and got permission to resign. His replacement was a Pastor Schmidt, who worked on the catalog for two months then turned it over to Klöffler again.[14]

In Hanau, Pastor Trinthammer drew a library of nearly nine thousand volumes, two hundred of which he knew were harmless, which left about eighty-eight hundred for him to examine. Four years and several thousand books later, he too asked for permission to resign.

His petition worked its way slowly up to the Interior Ministry, then over to the Censorship Commission. The ministry asked the commission what guidelines it had given reviewers of lending libraries. The censors answered with an evasive statement that dwelt on the satisfactory work being done by censors in Fulda and Witzenhausen, who "have sent in several objectionable books from the lending libraries in those places, the greater part of them retained here [being unsuitable for return]." Local censors did not have to read cover-to-cover all of the books in library collections, said the commission, but they should pay attention to novels, tales of robbers, and the like. None of this really told the ministry what it wanted to know or offered much help to Trinthammer, who still had to contend with thousands of wretched books.[15]

Trinthammer's attempt to resign, and the Cassel censors' casual attitude about it, set off a general housecleaning of censorship only weeks later in December 1840. The government abolished the long-standing censorship deputations in Hanau and Rinteln and reassigned their duties to the commission in Cassel. At the same time it had local administrators gather lending library catalogs in their towns and compile from them surveys on the number of volumes in each library, its location, the name of its proprietor, how he had permission to do business, how many catalogs he had issued, which had been reviewed and approved, and what censorship remained.[16]

The Censorship Commission was ordered to report too. In February 1841, it submitted an accounting of all the catalogs it had received since the 1836 reform of library policing. As they were wont, the censors appended an unsolicited commentary on the conditions of their work:

> To date our other official duties have not allowed us time to review the books found in lending libraries, and that will go on being the case. Unless we can be freed from other obligations for the time that it will take, then either the role of the Censorship Commission, pursuant to these catalogs, must be limited to checking whether novels and other books are listed that we already know are unsuitable for a lending library and all other review is the responsibility of police authorities, or else this review will have to be transferred to some other agency that has the free time and can do the job.

There was, however, another option that the censors had not considered. On 27 March 1841, Crown Prince Friedrich Wilhelm asked the Interior Ministry to recommend changes in the staffing of the

Censorship Commission. Within the week, Karl Bernhardi had been dismissed, and Karl Hermann Pfaff followed soon after.[17]

Whatever its other merits from the government's point of view, replacing two censors in Cassel did not change the character or size of lending library collections. It also did not ease the resentments between the Cassel censors and police officials, based on their different values and backgrounds, which came out when they had to work together on libraries. In 1847, a particularly bitter exchange between the Cassel police and the Censorship Commission followed a police complaint that in the sixteenth supplement of Bohné's lending library catalog, volumes 16,593 and 16,594 were politically suspect, and volumes 16,846 through 16,849 and 16,885 through 16,887 were by authors whose other works had already been banned.

The censors went along in part and banned volumes 16,593 and 16,594. But they also insisted that their responsibility for lending libraries only covered publications that they had banned before, the same argument that the commission had made in 1841 just before two of its members were dismissed. Now the censors added a bitter, sarcastic denunciation of the police, who through the years had often steered extra work to them:

> It should be obvious that men who live every day in the midst of literature must have a different, perhaps a more reasonable, understanding of it, in its entirety and in the effect of particular writings on literature and the public, than other men whose profession only permits them a superficial awareness of published literature.
>
> Furthermore, what we were to do here was to establish a principle and a procedure that at least *might* be applied consistently. Banning all books in which there are offensive passages, or even whose presentation is dangerous, simply does not work. One would have to destroy at least half of all literature to be consistent. Moser and Möser, Schlözer, Spittler, Goethe and Schiller, the best that our literature has to offer . . . would be hopelessly lost.
>
> In closing, we are obliged to commend the Bohné lending library, which has exercised commendable caution in building its collection, by doing all that it can to keep out novels about robbers, rogues, and gore, which are the truly dangerous poison of lending libraries.[18]

In less than three months, a revolution would overthrow the government, and a new ministry would abolish the Censorship Commission. Nearly three decades had passed since Jacob Grimm first expressed doubts about the wisdom and practicability of lending library censorship. What had changed in the meantime?—the names of the censors, some of their procedures, and the pace of their work. Their attitudes however had scarcely altered, including their disdain for the opinions of less-lettered men and their futile hope that censorship could be a rational enterprise conducted according to principles, rather than random, capricious policing.

Unfortunately for the censors, the government's attitude never changed either; its enthusiasm for all forms of literary policing persisted. In 1840, the government of Baden asked for a report on Hessian library censorship. The reply that the Hessians sent summarized their relevant laws and emphasized the roles of local authorities and the clergy. "To date," it concluded triumphantly, "there has been no instance in which the manifest obstinacy of a proprietor required that a lending library be closed."[19] That happy statement left unsaid almost everything about library censorship that mattered to the men who had to do the work.

One thing made periodicals censorship less troublesome than library censorship, and that was that successful, enduring periodicals were always rare in Hesse. During the 1820s there were political newspapers only in Cassel and Hanau, which both filled their few pages by lifting most of the news from more substantial German papers. The editor of the *Kassel'sche Allgemeine Zeitung* (Cassel General Gazette), Jacob Pinhas, was a master at reconciling his own interests with the regime's, something he demonstrated through his leadership in relations between the Jewish community and the Christian state, and through his very endurance as a journalist in the residence city of the Francophobe, Prince-elector Wilhelm I, after having edited the *Moniteur Westphalien* (Westphalian Monitor) during the French occupation. The monopoly that the government granted him ensured the survival of his newspaper as well as its harmlessness. The *Hanauer Zeitung* (Hanau Gazette) circulated fewer than one hundred copies during the 1820s and was lucky just to survive. Eight regional, weekly newspapers existed primarily to publish government decrees and other official news. They ran advertisements and offered some entertainment (*Unterhaltung*) but had little opportunity to offend anyone's political, moral, or religious sensibilities.[20]

Censorship of periodicals was haphazard and left mostly to the police before 1830. Of course, the general guidelines for censorship, embodied in the instruction to the Censorship Commission, could be applied, but mostly, the police dealt with difficulties individually, as they arose.

In 1818, the editor of the *Hanau Gazette* disputed the local police director's claim that the newspaper should be censored. Why was he publishing articles without submitting them for approval? the police director wanted to know. Because they were exempt, the editor replied, exempt because he had lifted them from other newspapers. Censorship was impossible anyway, he added; it would prevent him from mailing the sheet on time to his out-of-town subscribers. The police director, unpersuaded, imposed a fine of twenty gulden, a serious penalty for a marginal publication. He urged the editor to be more careful.

About one year later, in the fall of 1819, just after the German Confederation passed its famous press law, the Hanau police director instructed the editor to include his name and the printer's name on every issue, as the law required, to send copies regularly to the Censorship Commission in Cassel, and to adopt a clearer, blacker typeface. Such individualized treatment was easy for the police then, and a newspaper editor had little choice but to obey. At any time, the government could have imposed new requirements for free advertising space or cost-free copies to local administrators, or security deposits that would have driven the sheet, with its eight- or nine-hundred word issues, out of business immediately.[21]

One decade later came rapid changes in the periodical press and its readership that, like so many other changes in German public life, began about 1830. Fast steam-driven printing presses arrived. The price of newspapers fell relative to the cost of essential goods such as food, and for the first time it became possible to buy single issues. Few Germans had been able to afford the annual subscriptions that were required before, but many could manage to buy a newspaper now and then, and, as a result, circulation rates went up rapidly. The number of periodicals in Germany also rose from about eight hundred in 1833 to more than eighteen hundred in 1846.[22]

These changes even touched Hesse-Cassel. Article thirty-six of the 1831 constitution abolished the government's absolute authority to grant or deny concessions for all businesses, including the press. With the rise of political interest that the constitution stimulated came a new wave of publications. Many were short-lived, but a few became popular, especially when they offered a political point of view opposed to the regime.

As the number of periodicals and their popularity grew, the Hessian government sought to limit what could be published, to prescribe review procedures, and to plug all of the administrative leaks that diluted the effectiveness of its vigilance over the press. Despite the Censorship Commission's ten-year-old disclaimer of any responsibility for periodicals, its members were drawn in intermittently because policy questions on periodicals as on censorship of books and lending libraries were bound to involve them. But the actual work of examining newspapers and journals could not all be put on the Cassel censors, even if they had been more willing to take that responsibility. In the constitutional state there were too many publications in too many places too far away from Cassel for a three-man censorship commission to deal with them effectively. Before 1830, responsibility for censorship of periodicals had gone to diverse officials because the censors made themselves unavailable. After 1830, it still did because there was more censoring to do.

Police chiefs were the overseers of many periodicals, and political newspapers were their exclusive terrain. In Cassel, the director general of police, Ludwig von Manger, censored the *Cassel General Gazette* until he was fired for not solving the murder-by-poison of the crown prince's lackey in 1824. After that, it was done at the police directorate of Lower Hesse, where the government also recruited censors for two newspapers begun during the 1830s, the *Friend of the Constitution* and *Blätter für Geist und Herz* (Review for Head and Heart). Throughout the period, the *Hanau Gazette* remained under the watch of the Hanau police director. In Fulda as well, it was the police director who reviewed two newspapers born of the freedom that came in 1830, the *Fuldaer Zeitung* (Fulda Gazette) and *Teutsches Volksblatt* (German National News). In Marburg, bookseller Garthe's stillborn plan announced in September 1831 for a daily newspaper, the *Marburger Zeitung* (Marburg Gazette), "on one-quarter sheet, to discuss in concise summary form the most recent political events of importance" would also have had the police director as censor.[23]

All sorts of government officials censored nonpolitical publications. The *Bote aus Kassel* (Cassel Courier), an entertainment sheet, went to officials in the Lower Hessian provincial administration for review, while a pastor named Kraushaar censored the *Kasselsches Schulblatt* (Cassel School Press), and the director of a seminary in Homberg censored the *Musikalische Zeitschrift für Kirche und Schule* (Music Journal for Church and School) edited by one of his staff. At Marburg, professors did duty as periodicals censors, and at Bockenheim near Hanau a bailiff did.[24]

Just as with book censorship, the government had to have men of some education and discernment who were mostly in public service anyway. But recruiting people already on the payroll was doubly advantageous for the parsimonious Hessian regime because it made the work inexpensive and ensured easy policing of the policers. Only in one instance did anyone outside state employ censor periodicals, and that was unavoidable. No Jews were in public office, so the government had to entrust censorship of the Hebrew-language press, calendars in particular, to the elders of the Jewish community.[25]

Despite their aversion to it, members of the Cassel commission censored some periodicals too, especially ones likely to be challenging, controversial, or very scholarly. Christoph von Rommel had responsibility for the *Friend of the Constitution* during the first months of its publication in 1831 before it went to the police directorate. Three years later he and his colleagues were censoring *Christliche Kirche* (The Christian Church), a quarterly, and during the 1840s, they supervised publication of a local German-language Jewish weekly, *Der Israelit* (The Israelite), as well as several specialized publications, *Staatswirtschaftszeitung* (Political Economy Report), *Zeitschrift für Alterthumswissenschaft* (Journal of Classical Studies), and *Monatliche Berichte der Deutsch-Chinesischen Stiftung* (Monthly Reports of the German-Chinese Foundation).[26]

The government also enlisted Christoph von Rommel, just appointed to the Censorship Commission, to write an instruction for all newspaper censors in 1830. Gone, it seemed, was to be the old-fashioned policing of the periodical press. In its place was to come regulation, devised by a man of culture and learning, based on the written code of law, orderly and constitutional, a standard that could be applied uniformly. In his draft, which the Interior Ministry soon issued substantially unchanged, Rommel presented a very liberal interpretation of both the Confederal Press Law of 1819 and the new Hessian constitution. Certainly the way he applied them to the periodical press, abounding as his text did in words such as "discrete," "considerate," "moderate," "proper," and "illuminating," was gentler than what could have been expected if the guidelines had come from the ministry. Rommel instructed whoever would censor the periodical press not to hinder most commentary on the government, either its structure or its conduct, even if the opinions expressed were incompatible with the censor's own or the state's. Only written opinions that threatened to undermine faith in the governors or to incite rebellion should be disallowed.[27]

This final qualification had to be interpreted, and it soon became clear that the government would include much more under serious breaches of press freedom than Rommel had in mind. Pressures that he could not have anticipated soon led to a hardening of the government's treatment of the periodical press. But for about the first year of constitutional life in Hesse, the newspapers had few shackles. In the fall of 1831, when Rommel was lamenting the public hatred of his office, asking for and getting release from his odious duty as overseer of the *Friend of the Constitution,* the police director in Hanau was writing to Cassel of how he had "to struggle every day in order to restrain the editor of the local newspaper, whose censorship . . . is especially assigned to me." He "wished nothing more ardently than that the press law cited in our constitution might appear soon." The year ended with the Interior Ministry trying to bring two journals that were appearing in Hanau without formal authorization, *Volks- und Anzeigeblatt für Mitteldeutschland* (People's Herald and Advertiser for Central Germany) and *Zeitbilder* (Timely Sketches), under better control.[28]

The next year, 1832, was worse for the government. Police Councilor Bernhardi, in his second attempt to resign as censor of the *Friend of the Constitution* and *Review for Head and Heart,* complained that their staffs had been submitting very liberal copy. His alterations angered them and alienated the public. The items were appearing elsewhere in any case, some of them in *Zeitschwingen* (Signs of the Times), published in Hanau. And now the Confederal Assembly stepped in, demanding stronger censorship of that and other Hanau publications. In 1831 and 1832, newspaper censorship was failing quickly.[29]

The Fulda press was also constant trouble in these years. Jakob Förster inserted uncensored articles into his *German National News* but only to fill spaces left by the censor's excision of other articles, he explained. Police Director Scheffer submitted his seventh resignation as censor there on 1 July, but the ministry rejected it two weeks later, as it had the earlier six. After the government suppressed the *German National News,* Förster brought out uncensored "pamphlets" that looked a lot like it. The police director and the Censorship Commission both shied away from responsibility for them.[30]

In September 1832, responding to these problems, dissatisfied with the progress of periodicals censorship generally, and compelled by unwelcome attention at the Confederal Assembly to what was going on in Hanau and Fulda the Hessian government reimposed its policing on top of Christoph von Rommel's procedures. Out went a directive to the many officials responsible for censorship of periodicals: "Again and again, the editors and publishers of domestic newspapers and journals have disregarded regulations against abuse of the press, to an extent that cannot be overlooked. To wit, they have published articles and passages without submitting them to the censors for prior approval, sometimes even after expressed denial of approval."

To prevent these abuses in the future, newspaper censors were to mark passages that they disapproved by striking them through with red ink, then keep a copy of the submission and compare it with the published text. Local police were to get copies of publications about to be printed too. Finally, the government threatened criminal penalties for continued offenders.

As the legislative stalemate over a new press law dragged on through the 1830s, the government issued many more directives of the same sort, trying to correct mistakes made by censors of newspapers and periodicals. In 1832, one directive forbade periodicals from commenting at all about censorship while another gave editors only one chance to submit passable new material for the gaps caused by censors' deletions. Other directives prohibited editors from leaving gaps where words or passages had disappeared, insisted that censors not be bothered at all hours, warned about inaccurate reports on the government's activities and intentions, and disallowed comment on proceedings of the legislature. Together with reports of the many new confederal decrees of the 1830s about the press, these directives were compiled into a de facto code of laws and regulations on periodicals censorship that the Interior Ministry sent to provincial officials early in 1841.[31]

Ultimately, it was recourse to police and the courts that settled problems over periodical censorship. Police arrested Dietrich Albrecht Geeh, editor of the *Friend of the Constitution,* in 1834, which ended its publication. The confederation complained about the *Hanau Gazette,* which forced its editor to moderate what he published. Otherwise, his newspaper would have gone the way of *Neue Zeitschwingen* (New Signs of the Times) and *German National News* in Fulda, which both fell victim to bans in 1832, the first by the confederation, the second by Hessian officials.[32]

The government always had these easier, more direct, police methods for controlling the printed word, not so cumbersome as working through the censors, methods that worked just as well on periodicals as on books. The demise of publications in Cassel, Hanau, and Fulda during the early 1830s signaled only the most obvious means at the regime's disposal. It could also refuse permission to begin a new publication or attach conditions to permission that were so stringent the publication would be harmless. The constitution, with its guarantee of freedom to pursue any trade unhindered without the need for a license except where expressly required by law, should have ended these old-fashioned restrictions on publishing. But even with the new fundamental law, the government stuck to its traditional practices, and even when courts rebuffed its claims to police powers not reserved in the constitution, it merely changed its semantics in order to comply superficially, without changing its actions. In 1839, with the constitution in mind, the Interior Ministry informed the editor of the *Cassel Courier* that it no longer granted privileges for journals such as his; however, he was permitted to issue it unconditionally.[33]

Conditional permission was more common. During the 1830s, the Interior Ministry repeatedly admonished persons it allowed to start new publications to steer clear of politics. Heinrich Hotop, a printer in Cassel, got the official okay for his *Gewerbeblätter für Kurhessen* (Commercial News for Hesse-Cassel) on the understanding that it would remain "strictly technical." Meant to appear monthly, printed on two sheets, there is no evidence that it lasted past its first issue of January 1831.[34]

Eighteen months later the Hanau police reacted sharply to the printing without permission of prospectuses for a new periodical, *Conversationsfreund* (Conversational Companion), and a supplement to it, *Spiegel der Geschichte* (Mirror of History), which the would-be editor, J. H. Fiedler, a copper engraver and bookbinder, insisted would not be political and so required no authorization. The police investigated. Sitting as a court of inquiry, the Hanau police commission wanted to know whether the Hanau bookseller, Edler, on whose premises the new journal would be printed, had regularly submitted other publications for approval. Assured that he had, they cleared the new journal with the proviso that it not be political. During the five years that the *Conversational Companion* lasted, the police regularly extended permission for its appearance. In an 1834 report, they informed the Interior Ministry that most of what it printed was plagiarized, which readers did not seem to mind, and it avoided politics entirely.[35]

Of twenty-four requests to start up periodicals during the years 1832 to 1847, officials rejected only six outright. That is not to say that the other eighteen were successful enterprises. It was easy to ask for permission, more difficult to imagine the expense and trouble that regular publication entailed. All that remains of a good half of the periodicals recorded by the police is bureaucratic haggling leading to a grudging grant of permission to publish. And ones that actually appeared often succumbed to the suffocating restraints placed on them or to the indifference of the reading public.[36]

The year 1831 was the best one in a long time to launch a newspaper, just after the Hessians had obtained a new constitution, when censorship was in disarray, and there was an eager audience for news. When Marburg's ambitious but naive bookseller, Garthe, announced his intention that year to publish a daily newspaper, the Marburg administration asked if this meant that Garthe and his cohorts in the enterprise were going to copy items from papers in Cassel and Hanau. Probably it did, but, nevertheless, the Interior Ministry granted Garthe permission. In April 1831, at Hanau, Jakob Förster had received permission to publish his *German National News* with the local police director as its censor. One year later, Förster complained that having to submit his copy three days before publication allowed others, particularly editor Zick of the *Fulda Gazette,* to scoop him on news that had cost him money. He insisted that the review should take only one hour of the police director's time, but the director was a busy man who refused to adapt his schedule to Förster's needs. The three-day routine continued until the *German National News* was banned later the same year.[37]

Garthe and Förster had asked for permission in heady days. Permission came less easily one decade later. Publications bound to compete with existing ones or to be burdensome to the men who would have to censor them were frowned upon most. The problem of competition nixed an 1847 proposal for a "district gazette" in Ziegenhain, judged unnecessary because official announcements appeared nearby already in the Hersfeld *Intelligenzblatt* (Intelligencer).

The Cassel printer, Heinrich Hotop, had been more insistent but no more successful with an application in 1839. Lamenting the sad state of business at a print shop he had inherited from a brother, citing the loss of work it suffered to two other establishments in town, pointing to the expense of supporting a large family, Hotop sought permission to publish a daily newspaper. The existing *Cassel General Gazette* was inadequate, he argued. It had only six hundred subscriptions throughout Hesse, too few he thought when Cassel alone must have thirty thousand residents. Hotop began issuing his newspaper in the expectation that permission would follow soon. It was not a good way to improve his chances, although other more fundamental difficulties would have nixed his plan anyway. The Cassel district commissioner doubted Hotop's ability to come up with original material, and he frowned at the likelihood that Hotop would just reprint what other people had written. More serious in the commissioner's view was that Hotop wanted his newspaper to appear a few hours before the *Cassel General Gazette,* mornings rather than evenings. A censor would have to be available late the previous night, and he would have to be clever because at that hour it would be impossible to consult other officials on troublesome items. Hotop got no permission, and his newspaper ceased.[38]

The political climate in the principality was inhospitable to periodicals from the beginning. When popular interest in them grew and more appeared, the government reacted with new means to control and restrain them, never appreciating but only tolerating them. Sometimes it was fortunate that the government had that paternal good sense, which prospective editors lacked, to ask whether a newspaper or journal stood any chance of surviving, financially or popularly. The government's firmer stand toward new periodicals from about 1840 was not unique because in Prussia, too, the regime concluded that its existing controls over newspapers were no longer working and created a "newspaper bureau" in Berlin to supervise the daily press.[39] But Cassel was not Berlin, and the hottest news stories did not get written in Hesse but in other German states, even when they were about Hesse.

After the journalistic wild times of the early 1830s Cassel officials were more often concerned with journals and newspapers brought in from other German lands, where popular literature, led by the highly successful *Illustrirte Zeitung* (Illustrated Gazette) in Saxony, fared better. The Hessians worried a lot about what came in from neighboring Saxony, just as other reactionaries of that era, the Hanoverians, worried about what sneaked in off the presses in liberal Hamburg.[40] The concern in Hesse about newspapers, foreign or domestic, was overblown by the midforties because at home the growth of literary appetites showed itself less in the consumption of politics offered by the periodical press and more in a gluttonous enthusiasm for the amorous and adventurous volumes that filled the shelves of lending libraries.

SIX

The Logic of Censorship

It would be natural to suppose that officials kept a master list of books banned in Hesse during the early nineteenth century, a list that reflected some uniform standards on what should be banned, and that together the list and the standards would reveal the logic of censorship then. But none of this was so. The fact is that standards were confused, too often made up as they were needed. They were impossible to clarify because the regime's habitual way of governing was so incompatible with the new political demands of the age, and, as a result, the men who governed in Hesse had to resort always to makeshift and make-do.

At one time or another several Hessian offices kept lists of banned books—the Censorship Commission in Cassel, the deputation to the Confederal Assembly in Frankfort, the Hanau administration, the Hünfeld County office—but no office maintained its list for very long, and no list agrees with any other. To know the sum of what Hessian authorities banned, I have compiled my own historical list. The logic of censorship that I draw out of the list is mine, the historian's, not theirs.[1]

The separate lists compiled then did not agree even when they were concurrent because censorship in the early nineteenth century meant several different things, and different list keepers had different sources of information as well as different senses of what was important. Censorship was three activities going on all at once, sometimes interrelated but not always.

First, censorship was the review of manuscripts before publication. In Hesse that meant newspapers most of all, with their special censors, but the Censorship Commission reviewed some books and pamphlets too, before they could legally be printed or published. Second, censorship was policing aimed to preserve local welfare against the dangers to good morals, simple faith, and political innocence that bad writings might bring. Bailiffs, police commissioners, and clergymen were enlisted in battles to keep the devil's smut out of lending libraries, his blasphemies off tavern walls, his occasional incitements to rebellion away from peasant cottages. Third, censorship was a cooperative enterprise of central European princes, acting through their plenipotentiaries at the Frankfort Assembly of the German Confederation, to keep the people in each state from having a hand in politics by keeping political literature out of their hands.

These were censorship's ideal forms. In practice, manuscripts escaped review, devilish threats to local welfare went unchecked, and German princes were uncooperative.

Because the censor's trident aimed three different ways, its catches were varied and unpredictable. Because it was imperfect, trying to do such disparate things, it missed a lot that it aimed at too. At times in Hesse, what it hauled in was so unpredictable and irregular that the better metaphor might be a fishnet of uneven weave. Even without the sum of banned books before us, we have sensed censorship's divided attention, in the 1816 instruction to the censors that had such scattered, impossible objectives, in later censorship legislation that intermingled prevention and repression, in the tortuous wording of the ineffectual 1831 constitutional clause on press freedom, in the frequent debates and misunderstandings about the censors' mission, authority, and achievements, and in the repeated efforts of Hessian administrators to write a manual, staff a deputation, recruit a clergyman, or levy a fine to make the process work better.

There is a further twist to the logic of censorship. All three of its varieties—traditional manuscript review, old-fashioned policing on behalf of public welfare, modern repression of German liberalism—went on at the same time in two sorts of settings, in halls of government but also along the lanes of small communities. "Macrocensorship," the centrally coordinated administrative, legal, and diplomatic defining and processing of damnable writings, or censorship from above, which I have concentrated on up to this point, was accompanied by "microcensorship," local policing of literature and the literate, or censorship from below, to which I will turn more attention soon. Often macrocensorship drove microcensorship, but sometimes it was the other way around.

No sharp edge marked where one level of censorship ended and the other began. Usually they were intertwined. The German Confederation could issue decrees on the proper way to censor manuscripts, which it passed on to its members, including Hesse, yet it was not anyone in Frankfort or Cassel but rather police sergeants and bailiffs in a dozen Hessian communities who had to make the decrees work. The gendarmerie in one province might confiscate a pamphlet, but it was only authorities in the capital who could see that warnings about it reached every corner of the principality where perhaps other copies were being read, as yet undiscovered. The Censorship Commission in Cassel might decide that a book was politically dangerous, but it took police visitations to each bookseller in Hesse to give some assurance that it was not being sold. It took macrocensors and microcensors working together to have any chance of policing literature effectively.

Macrocensors and microcensors in the German states pursued their three aims with varying intensity. In general, the local policing of literate culture, which was ages old, became busier after 1831 simply because the numbers of readers, writers, and bookshops grew rapidly then. More places and people needed supervision. In Hesse, campaigns launched in Cassel against bad books in lending libraries, one in 1837 and another in 1841, brought momentary urgency to censoring popular culture. The level of manuscript censorship depended everywhere on the condition of publishing more than anything else. Hesse was not a publishing center, so there was never much of that variety of censoring to be done. German-wide efforts to control liberal politics had two acute phases, in 1819 and 1832, then became chronic all through the 1840s, a pattern that held in Hesse as much as in other states of the confederation.

In this third, most modern variety of censorship, the regimes of Wilhelm II and Friedrich Wilhelm in Cassel followed eagerly whatever promptings came from the Confederal Assembly in Frankfort. As a result, by about 1845, as members of that German-wide body urged more and more bans on each other, strangling German liberalism seemed to have become the chief purpose of censorship in Hesse and elsewhere in Germany. But the truth was that books and magazines banned in Hesse and kept on lists in Cassel and Frankfort because someone in the confederation willed it did not often have much to do with local policing of literature. The more attention the Hessian government paid to what it wished was a coordinated, German-wide political censorship, the less connection there was between the bulk of macrocensorship in Cassel and microcensorship in the Hessian provinces. Hessian censors pointed out this divergence, as we have seen, objecting to what they knew were pointless bans, then issued them anyway because it was what they were ordered to do.

The striking thing about the whole period of the 1820s, 1830s, and 1840s is the diversity of materials and topics that came before the censors. That such a variety of things was banned—insults to the Hessian prince-elector in yearbook articles of 1824, pamphlets on local politics in 1832, indecent novels in 1837, long juridical tracts defending Sylvester Jordan in 1844, and whatever the Prussians wanted banned in 1845—shows that censorship, at least as it is preserved in lists of prohibited writings, was not a machine set to a straight course but a mirror that reflected the political moment, with all of its odd angles and changes of direction.

The prince-elector's chief censors were occupied most of the time from the beginning with what they called "book censorship," repressive attention to things already published, a macrocensorship conducted at the center of government, with the results relayed as necessary out to the periphery for microcensorship—from Cassel where judgments were rendered to the provinces where decisions had to be executed. Manuscript censorship, which was historically a local, preventive microcensorship, was a much smaller part of the Censorship Commission's work. It always censored some manuscripts, typically reviewing about one item weekly during the 1830s and 1840s, but that was a minuscule share of what Germans wrote, censored, published, and read annually.[2]

The topics of Hessian manuscripts were diverse—annual programs of social clubs, compilations of folk wisdom, sermons, discussions of railway financing—but they were seldom controversial. In a quiet year, 1837, the censors reviewed just ten manuscripts and altered only one of them, a light-hearted collection of sayings called *Denk- und Sittensprüche* (Maxims to Think and Live by), which contained some uncomplimentary remarks about the Hessian sanitation commission that the censors excised. Their busiest year with manuscripts was 1840, when they went through ninety of them. They approved the vast majority outright, struck some passages from a dozen, and wholly disallowed just two.

One of the two was an item from Luckhardt's printing shop in Cassel that the censors called superstitious nonsense. The other was a collection of sarcastic verses on freedom, tyranny, and related universal political themes. Entitled *Lieder eines kosmopolitischen Nachtwächters* (Songs of a Cosmopolitan Night Watchman), it was the work of a Hessian native son named Franz Dingelstedt, who was then a young, well-regarded Cassel schoolteacher.[3]

Dingelstedt's poems, controversial and timely, were exceptional among manuscripts submitted for censorship in Hesse. Even among the few submissions that the censors rejected, politics cropped up only rarely, and when it appeared and was deemed offensive, it was almost always on the narrow grounds that it insulted the prince-elector and the land he ruled. Most manuscripts that Hessian censors banned were not political at all but superstitious or heterodox. It would be wrong to imagine that the censors went about their work deep in thought, conducting long discussions with each other about sophisticated questions of political philosophy. Their work on manuscripts was far more dull. The most protracted discussion they ever had on what to do with one was about whether to allow references to flatulence and women's breasts.

Manuscript censorship was not very important in Hesse because of the peculiar situation of thought and learning in the principality, a land whose poverty extended beyond the countryside economy and into the intellectual and artistic endeavors of its towns and their educated elites. It is true enough that the principality was not altogether without scholarly treasures. It could claim the Brothers Grimm as its own, although the prince-elector had driven them away. Karl Bernhardi created a notable map of the German language, and August Vilmar, who directed the Marburg grammar school, was an accomplished investigator of dialect expressions. For a few years, 1840–48, the pathbreaking economist and statistician, Bruno Hildebrand, was a professor at the University of Marburg. But Hesse-Cassel produced few writers with more than local reputations. The best-known of its learned men were conservative theologians. Its university was among the tiniest in all the German-speaking lands; according to the *Foreign Quarterly Review,* only Groningen (actually Dutch, not German) and Rostock had fewer students. Printers and publishers were also scarce, unable to compete with the more active literary centers of middle Germany, Leipzig and Frankfort.[4]

Most damning to the prospect of getting politically engaged literature past the censors and published in Hesse was the prince-elector's insistence that politics was his personal prerogative. As a penalty for writing the *Songs of a Political Night Watchman,* the government transferred Franz Dingelstedt to Fulda, that relatively remote, arch-Catholic town where civil servants guilty of some liberal trespass routinely found themselves reassigned. Heinrich König— secretary in the royal treasury, a liberal member of the legislative assembly from Hanau during the 1830s, and a popular novelist—also went involuntarily back to Fulda, his hometown, as a penalty for liberal politicking. It was there as well that the government promptly reassigned Chief Judge Arnold of the Marburg Superior Court in

1841, because the court had released Sylvester Jordan from jail pending his trial for treason. Before long, Dingelstedt would move again to exile in Paris.[5]

Franz Dingelstedt did with his manuscript what other creative opponents of the Hessian regime would do; he got it printed elsewhere in Germany where the manuscript censors were more free. The publishing house of Hoffmann and Campe in Hamburg issued his *Songs* anonymously in 1841; then the Cassel censors banned them again.

Most writings that the Censorship Commission judged unsuitable for Hessian readers were already in print, like the *Songs* the second time it prohibited them. From 1817, when the records of the commission begin, until its dissolution in March 1848, it proscribed more than four hundred works already published. Usually that meant a formal ban announced by the censors or the Interior Ministry to officials in the provinces, but it did not always happen that way.

There were works that some authority in Cassel besides the censors or the ministry disallowed or that local authorities banned acting largely on their own. The Censorship Commission might concur in these decisions made elsewhere, but it did not always announce them as widely as it announced its own actions. It omitted even some of its own decisions from reports to local administrators and booksellers because the bans had no immediate effect on them. Hesse banned many publications for diplomatic reasons, although as the censors, at least, knew, they were not significant in the principality. They mattered little to local police and administrators, who had a duty to make bans known widely enough to be effective but not so widely that they would pique the curiosity of townsmen and send them looking for things to read just because they were forbidden. If no one knew, then no one could be too curious. These diverse ways that censors and other officials acted against objectionable writ and announced their actions help to explain why there was never one list of all the works that someone or other in Hesse had disallowed. Who would have compiled it?

For the period before 1831 I know of censors' bans on just forty-four publications, scarcely more than three in an average year. One, two, or three a year was common, six or seven was already a lot in the early years of the post-Napoleonic period. In Hesse, the number of bookshops, lending libraries, and periodicals remained small throughout the 1820s. The number of works published annually in the principality was small too. The printed word did not reach great distances or touch many people.

Three out of every four publications that Hessian censors banned during the 1820s were political, and many of them mentioned Hessian politics, such as the annual *Chronik des 19ten Jahrhunderts* (Chronicle of the Nineteenth Century), edited by Venturini, which attacked the prince-elector in person and so earned prohibition in Cassel five times. *Darstellung des politischen Zustandes von Deutschland* (Depiction of Political Circumstances in Germany), which referred injudiciously to Hessian troops in the previous century, "sold and sent to the colonies to die," also was banned. Forbidden, too, were several works by Johann von Horn, chronicler at great length and with unseemly enthusiasm of the 1823 "Affair of the Threatening Letters" that poisoned public life in Cassel for the remainder of that decade. Other, diverse topics interested the public while they unsettled authorities—emigration, nationalist student clubs, Napoleon Bonaparte, the Greek war of independence. The Hessian regime banned works mentioning them as well.

The censors' other two long-standing areas of concern, religion and morality, did not account for much published literature that was banned before 1830. The Censorship Commission in Cassel deemed just five publications heretical, but two of them were offensive for political reasons too. Only Casanova's memoirs and Althing's stories were too scandalous to be allowed.

Finally, among the bans during these first years were several that did not belong to any of the three usual categories. A treatise on animal magnetism, a collection of outlandish remedies and cures, a recounting of "extraordinary occurrences," they are best labeled popular and fantastic. Theirs was a sort of popular literature that would disappear altogether from the censor's horizon within a few years as it became clouded more and more by politics.

Little was mysterious, or even very interesting, about the origins of most of what the censors banned during the 1810s and 1820s. A few anonymous pamphlets cropped up, but mostly they examined book-length works by known authors. How widely were the ones they banned read in Hesse? There is no way to know, usually, although there was surely a market for local topics. Memoirs of the time make it apparent that the civil servants and burghers of Cassel gobbled up news of the continuing intrigues at court and the foibles of the ruling family.

Once in a while one glimpses the police coming upon something sensational, perhaps even dangerous, in those early, comparatively innocent, unpolitical years. In March 1818, an excited bailiff at the village of Treis an der Lumda in Upper Hesse reported that the

Hildburghauser Dorfzeitung (Hildburghausen Village Gazette) was being distributed without permission. In his terms, with his emphasis, it sought "to stir up the populace—especially the *rural populace* as the overwhelming *majority* of every nation—against its princes and their governments; to inform it of a right to *participation of the estates* in the *government;* and to take hold *enthusiastically* of the sentiments and thereby—prepare the way for revolution!!" Higher authorities did not find it so threatening. They agreed to ban it but allowed it to circulate in Hesse again after a while. The official explanation for its temporary removal in 1818 came in the paternal tone that was common then, altogether different from the rural officer's alarmed report: the newspaper was simply not needed, because the prince-elector's government provided a periodical sheet of its own for his peasants.[6]

In the spring of 1819, one year after the *Village Gazette* alarm, the Hessian censors banned a pamphlet that would have made a simple bailiff apoplectic. The *Frag- und Antwortbüchlein* (Little Book of Questions and Answers), written by a lawyer and publicist named Wilhelm Schulz, from the neighboring grand duchy of Hesse-Darmstadt, was an early revolutionary tract, phrased in the language of common people, interspersed with Biblical citations, distributed quietly through the post and by private courier in Hesse-Cassel as well as other parts of Germany.

When it first turned up in the province of Hanau, it loosed a storm of activity as police and postal officials hurried to determine how the pamphlet had come into the principality and who its recipients were. An investigatory judge, scrutinizing the political activities of students at Marburg, joined the hunt, which led among other places to the home of Karl Bernhardi, at Zierenberg in the province of Lower Hesse. This future censor—and secret sponsor of the *Friend of the Constitution*—was a student at Marburg then, associated with the secret fraternities (Burschenschaften) whose goal was German unity. Officials sought in vain for evidence that Bernhardi and other recipients had some connection to the booklet and had not just gotten it unsolicited.[7]

Schulz's pamphlet had a general theme and it was written in a colloquial way that could attract an audience of common people across all Germany; for both of those reasons it stood apart from most political publications banned as early as 1819. It heralded a dangerous type that remained rare until twelve or fifteen years later and would become common only much later. For the time being, Hessian censors and police seldom had to concern themselves with writings like it that posed broad ideological threats to the existing order of society. They could concentrate instead on more parochial expressions of discontent and ridicule of established authority, found mostly in insulting books and pamphlets that assaulted the prince-elector's regime directly and narrowly.

Beyond the caesura in censoring during 1830 and 1831, through political upheaval and the restaffing of the Censorship Commission with Christoph von Rommel and Karl Bernhardi, a wholly new situation arose. The censors now banned larger numbers of published works, not two or three per year, but two or three every couple of months. In 1832, as the regime reasserted its authority, they issued thirty bans, more than in most years that followed, but only in 1840 and 1842 would the number fall again to the yearly handful that had once been common. Beginning in 1843 there was a steady rise to five, six, and seven bans monthly. In the last few years leading up to the end of the Censorship Commission, it suppressed someone's book or pamphlet about every week.

At first glance, the overall pace between 1831 and 1848 seems modest, not quite two prohibitions monthly. It was a busy rate, though, particularly for a small land. Compared for instance with Prussia (where the only comparable count has been made), during 1835–45 the Hessians banned two works for every four or five the Prussians banned, and Prussia was a vastly larger, more populous land, where the system of censorship was more elaborate.[8]

It was not just the volume of work but its character, too, that made the censors busier in the 1830s and 1840s than before. Three of every four bans were still political in some sense, but it was a very different politics that the censors faced now. The audience for political literature was broadening. Public disturbances, new constitutions, the dismantling of economic particularism through the North German Customs Union, all were making active, interested citizens of the German states out of men who until recently had been burghers with narrower concerns centered on their own towns or just passive subjects of the local prince. The growth of regional commerce brought more trade across old political divides in the form of new political ideas and the books that were their vessels.

Boundaries between states had long been permeable to imported ideas in a region of Europe that shared a common written language. Now the traffic of political men and political creeds into and out of Hesse-Cassel threatened to overwhelm the guarantors of order. As the arena, stage, and cast of politicking expanded, the views that Cassel authorities did not want heard (always quite varied) now were spoken from dozens of places, in hundreds of voices, in ever-changing guises. So much variety meant hard work for censors, police, diplomats, and judges.

Less than half of what Cassel authorities prohibited between 1831 and 1848 had been published in Hesse-Cassel or even in the central German states that bordered it. Much of it came all the way from Zurich and Strasbourg, foreign cities that had been lively publishing centers for centuries, where exiled German democrats congregated most often now. Of works published within the German Confederation that the censors banned in Hesse, many, one in three, came from Saxony, a vexingly liberal center of German literary culture.

Dozens of other places contributed to the Cassel censors' work too. Through two decades, the title pages of condemned works carried the names of towns and cities in fifteen of the confederation's three dozen members. Not only in publishing centers (Leipzig, Hamburg), not only in liberal bastions (Mannheim, Stuttgart), but from as far away as Bremen to the northwest and Vienna to the southeast, written works left the printing presses on their way to damnation in Hesse. Paris, London, Brussels, even New York contributed a few. So did all of the principal towns in Hesse.

Who had written these publications that came from so many different places? The list of their authors is long, a veritable "who's who" of the pre-1848 political battles that Germans waged most fondly and most adeptly on paper. At its head stands Karl Heinzen, whose revolutionary tracts appeared first in central Germany in the mid-1840s, then had to be sneaked in from Switzerland where he, like so many others, had fled. Twelve times the censors in Cassel banned Heinzen's writing, an exceptional record, because no one else earned more than half that many bans, and anything more than two or three was already rare.

Other repeat performers in the censorship drama were the south German constitutionalists Karl von Rotteck and Karl Theodor Welcker, renowned for their *Staatslexikon* (Civic Lexicon); Wilhelm Schulz, still busy writing, years after the *Little Book of Questions and Answers* had made him notorious; Hambach Festival principals Philipp Jakob Siebenpfeiffer and Johann Georg August Wirth, the latter a frequent defendant in criminal trials brought on by his political publications in the Bavarian palatinate, which spilled over into the southernmost parts of Hesse-Cassel, and brainfather of a Press and Fatherland Society. There was also the Marburg law professor and author of the constitution of 1831, Sylvester Jordan; August Boden,

Jordan's principal literary defender when the Hessian state imprisoned him; "young Germans" Heinrich Heine, Ludwig Börne, and Karl Gutzkow; Johann Jacoby, unrelenting proponent of a constitution for Prussia; Robert Blum, publicist in Saxony and martyr of the 1848 revolution in Vienna; and in the last prerevolutionary years, the "left Hegelian" Arnold Ruge, the democrat Gustav von Struve, and the socialist Wilhelm Weitling.

To these came other "professional writers," less well remembered today but notable then: Johann Friedrich Funck, Harro Harring, Hartwig Hundt-Radowsky, Johann Wilhelm Sauerwein, and Jakob Venedey. All interested themselves with politics, and all were widely known in their day.[9] Notable Hessian authors appeared also, not many, though, because most of them were too conservative to write anything that would be banned. The exceptions included Franz Dingelstedt, the schoolteacher and poet who gave up on Hesse and left in the 1840s, and Franz Schell, a Roman Catholic teacher in Fulda until he adopted the controversial "German Catholic" modernist religious cause. Schell set down his differences with the hierarchy of the Roman church in several very unwelcome pamphlets that were published in Frankfort on the Main and Leipzig, found eager buyers back in Fulda, and were banned, pursued, and confiscated from their buyers by the Hessian state.[10]

Far outnumbering all of these literary recidivists, though, were more than one hundred writers, each responsible for a single banned work. And to them one must add another hundred or so anonymous and pseudonymous authors because more than one-third of everything banned in Hesse had been published without an author's or editor's real name on it. Altogether the Hessian censorship machine stamped the writings of hundreds of persons with disapproval; two hundred and fifty is a reasonable estimate.

What forms did the condemned works of these many men take? A lot were books, some clearly stretched and stretched until they were barely longer than twenty printer's sheets, just enough to free them from preventive censorship before publication. Wilhelm Held's *Dem deutschen Volke* (To the German People) was 321 pages, one more than the limit, the last six pages comprising the Latin and German texts of Pope Leo X's *Apostolic Chancellery and Penance Assessment* reprinted. Georg Herwegh trumpeted his evasion of the censors in the title of his *21 Bogen aus der Schweiz* (Twenty-One Sheets from Switzerland) and so did the anonymous author of *21 Bogen für Deutschland* (Twenty-One Sheets for Germany). Dozens of banned books ran between 321 and 350 pages; few were 291 to 320 pages.

More than half of what the censors banned was not books of any length but much smaller pamphlets and periodicals. The German princes had good reason to be concerned about that because in these formats dangerous writings were more easily concealed than in any book of twenty or more sheets. They were less expensive too, which made them more likely to be distributed in ways other than just through bookshops. Their potential audience was larger. It was harder to define than the readers of books. Pamphlets with their modest prices, six to twelve Kreuzer, were literature that a worker could sometimes afford.[11]

Such a welter of objectionable publications meant trouble for a government that wanted to police them all. Because publications that earned the censors' ban came from so many places, were the creations of so many different writers, and took such diverse forms, systematic censorship would have meant examining everything published in the German language. But censorship was capricious, unsystematic, and mostly unplanned: patterned certainly, yet not systematic or planned.

Typically, banned publications showed up in official records first under some agency other than the Censorship Commission or the Interior Ministry. Nearly half arrived in Cassel through diplomatic channels. Another third were passed to the capital from local and provincial offices in Hesse. At most, only about one in five prohibited publications owed its fate from the start to the vigilance of the censors and officials in the Interior Ministry. Local police uncovered writings that the censors would not have found themselves, particularly pamphlets. In August 1832, the Marburg police took from Friedrich Döring a copy of an *Offene Erklärung kurhessischer Bürger* (Public Declaration of Hessian Citizens), a pamphlet protest against the new repressive measures that the German Confederation had just taken to throttle increasingly audacious expressions of liberal sentiment in the press and in the chambers of German legislatures. Five weeks after the Marburg police turned it in to the censors in Cassel, the censors announced that the *Declaration* and similar protests were not to be allowed.

The police in Hanau found another nationalist, anticonfederal pamphlet, *Die Sechs Gebote des Deutschen Bundes* (The Six Commandments of the German Confederation) that same summer of 1832. Soon it turned up in Marburg as well. Sent to the censors for scrutiny, at the end of October they banned it. At Rinteln early in 1836, while searching Osterwald's bookshop for "young German" literature, just banned, the police uncovered a suspicious work entitled

Politische Schriften (Political Essays) by Ernst Grosse and sent word of it to Cassel, where five months later the censors labeled it "revolutionary" and ordered it banned.[12]

Provincial offices also turned up nonpolitical items, generally religious and moral transgressions. Some of these submissions to the censors came after inquiries from Cassel, for example, when provincial police forwarded to the Censorship Commission immoral works of fiction that clergymen found during the crackdowns on lending libraries in 1837 and 1841. Other times what came to Cassel was just the fruits of routine local policing, such as the confiscation of four religious tracts in Marburg from a stranger passing through on a wagon in 1838. The same vigilance led to prohibition of colorful, amusing, and immoral lithographs mocking the Ten Commandments discovered on the walls of numerous taverns in Upper Hesse during the late 1830s.[13]

Bans that came from local prompting were based on lots of information, the pertinent and the extraneous all cast together, then poured from the pens of excited bailiffs and sergeants. Bans based on diplomatic urgings were different, brief and to the point, ignoring questions of why and how, emphasizing what, where, and by whom. They differed also from what was banned through local initiative by being entirely political.

In the 1840s, diplomacy came to have a strong influence on the corpus of literature banned in Hesse. It was a natural development that the German governments should begin working together more against their opponents after the fright of revolution in 1830 and 1831 and after confederal investigations begun in 1832 had uncovered nationalist, republican conspiracies, in which pamphlet literature was a key engine and bookmen were often the engineers.[14] There was also an underlying cultural reason why, in the area called Germany, states should band together in censorship. Because language—and with it literature—defied political boundaries in lands where the people all spoke German dialects and where literate people all read the same written German language, the three dozen states belonging to the German Confederation had to cooperate if they hoped to control the printed word. They had prepared the way for cooperation with the Confederal Press Law of 1819. They acknowledged that it was what they wanted to do in the series of new confederal decrees on press matters that appeared during the mid-1830s.

For a state such as Hesse-Cassel that shared borders with many other states and was rather weak, the need for this cooperation was pressing. The principality's many borders made it vulnerable to political and economic pressures from its larger neighbors and to the influence of their printing presses. The confederation was important to Hesse-Cassel also because as a small state it never maintained more than a handful of embassies nor did it host many.[15] Frankfort was the one place where the prince-elector's government had diplomatic contact with all the other German states.

The Frankfort assembly of the German Confederation, made powerful by participation of all the German states, made weak by the rule that their decisions had to be unanimous, this successor to the institutions of the Holy Roman Empire, served the censorship needs of its members in a number of ways. At the most formal level, the Confederal Assembly promulgated general decrees on censorship that took on the force of law in Hesse-Cassel and elsewhere. It acted also to suppress public discussion of problems that were too transitory or too special to warrant general press legislation but too sensitive to be ignored. For instance, in the late 1830s it forbade discussion in print of the Hanoverian "constitutional issue," a circumlocution for the unilateral abrogation of the fundamental law there by a new, tyrannical king. For more than four years, from 1837 until 1842, it ordered that no writings be allowed about a controversial proposal to build a fortification on the upper Rhine, rescinding the gag order only when its members at last agreed on what to do.[16]

The Confederal Assembly was also an informal meeting place for members to exchange information on their separate policing of the press and on the content of local laws. In 1832 the Hessians, then reestablishing political order at home after the disturbances of the previous two years, obtained from the kingdom of Saxony a copy of its press law, just recently drafted. In 1833 and 1836 the Prussians inquired about new press legislation in Cassel. Requests came from Baden in 1840 for information on supervision of lending libraries and from Austria in 1843 on censorship in general.[17]

When home authorities were uncertain about whether to ban a book or whether to allow a journal in through the post, they could ask through the foreign ministry's delegate at the Confederal Assembly whether other German states had banned it already. The confederation also made it possible to ask a publisher's government how many copies of a forbidden work the firm had sent to booksellers in other states, invaluable information for Hessian police as they made their rounds of bookshops after a ban.[18]

The Hessians, alas, did not use these opportunities well. Every year they bickered with representatives of other German states over whose supervision, whose policing, was faulty or negligent. Abroad as at home, the Hessian government too often took up a sledgehammer in its efforts to improve censorship; in diplomacy, the result was self-injury.

The prince-elector's government protested vehemently about all sorts of discussions of Hessian politics and public life in German newspapers. Whether the topic was something politically important, such as relations between the government and the legislative assembly, or as it often was, just another instance of the peculiarities of the royal court in Cassel, the Hessian regime objected to every comment that was not wholly complimentary. It complained all across Germany because censors had allowed remarks on a loan to Hesse from the Rothschild bank in Frankfort, on the number of retainers the crown prince had, on conditions at the state hospital in Fulda, on the fate of German-Catholic dissenters, and on the number of inhabitants receiving poor relief.

It expected a lot from other states for these transgressions. Anonymous authors should be identified, retractions should be printed, censors should be reprimanded, fined, or dismissed. Other governments were accommodating sometimes, agreeing to remind censors of their duties, or persuading an editor to print a retraction, for example, of a critical article on poverty in Hesse, even though what was in it was true. The grand duchy of Hesse-Darmstadt and the kingdom of Bavaria expressed profound regrets for unsuitable comments on Hessian politics that got past their censors, and once even the liberal administration of Hamburg assured officials in Cassel that it would fine a censor who had allowed unfavorable remarks about Hesse in three local newspapers.[19]

But the typical response to requests for censorship from Cassel was quite different. When the Hessians objected to an 1838 *Frankfurter Journal* (Frankfort Journal) article about goings-on in their legislative assembly, the Frankfort senate sent the editor a warning but also told the Hessians to improve policing of the *Hanau Gazette,* "which for years has repeatedly contained malicious articles that endanger harmony and order in this city; as well as serial reports on the secret sessions of our legislative chamber, which it is impermissible to publish here; and also news on the status of investigations about political prisoners, something banned by confederal law." Bavarian officials agreed that articles that insulted Hessian institutions were inappropriate, but they would not track down the authors. Saxony, Hamburg, and Denmark all simply refused demands to punish offending periodicals in 1845 and 1846.[20]

Hesse was hypersensitive. Especially in the 1840s, egged on by the last two men who served as Cassel police director before 1848, Carl Wilhelm Robert and Wilhelm Morchutt, Hesse-Cassel's diplomats made extreme claims that other German states would not satisfy. They wanted newspapers in Baden, the *Deutscher Zuschauer* (German Spectator) and *Mannheimer Abendzeitung* (Mannheim Evening Gazette), and popular illustrated magazines in Saxony, the *Dorfbarbier* (Village Barber) and *Charivari,* to stop reporting bad news and poking fun. But Baden replied that it would not ban publications when no other German state complained about them, and Saxony said the magazines were harmless.[21]

"Although we cannot know whether the government of the Grand Duchy will find itself able to combat such a wicked press offense," the Hessians began one very testy complaint about the press in Baden, early in 1848, "nonetheless we do not want to fail to humbly inform the Grand Ducal Ministry of Foreign Affairs of the same." The Badenese, predictably, objected to the tone and would not cooperate. The Hessians persisted and turned to the confederation as final arbiter of disputes between its members, but it was too late for that. In one week, revolution would break out in Paris; in one month, a new liberal ministry in Cassel would withdraw the protest.

The confederal presidium had warned the Hessians in a prophetic note during the previous summer of 1847, "The introduction of a proposal for suppression [this time of the *Deutscher Beobachter* (German Observer), also published in Baden]—even if there were still enough time—is inadvisable now, given the crisis in which the press legislation of the Confederation, and in fact the censorship system, now finds itself."[22] The entire basis of German-wide cooperation on controlling the press had recently been thrown into disarray by a Prussian proposal to abandon mandatory preventive censorship.

By 1848, there was another reason to turn back protests from the Hessian government: it had thoroughly discredited itself, most of all through its behavior in the matter of Sylvester Jordan. Cassel took the position that nothing should be published anywhere about the arrest, interrogation, trial, and conviction of Jordan. The German Confederation's own Central Investigatory Bureau had played an important role in developing the incredible case that led to his 1843 conviction. The confederation did forbid public comment on investigations into treason, but the rule was understood to mean that only while investigations were underway nothing ought to be published. Long after Jordan had been brought to trial, though, and even after his conviction, the Hessian government objected to published remarks about his fate.

All over Germany, Jordan's outrageous treatment was a cause célèbre that loosed a flood of words defending him and attacking his persecutors. Any government would have been severely tested to achieve the silence that the Hessian regime wanted. Its diplomats, put to work to complain about articles on Jordan, won a few victories initially; at least, they heard that censors and printers were being reprimanded and fined. But by 1844, they met more and more resistance. Saxony reported that the articles that aroused Hessian ire contained only the facts, about which nothing could be done. An editor in Frankfort argued that his "nonpartisan" newspaper was only counterbalancing earlier articles favorable to the court that had convicted Jordan.[23]

Frankfort officials refused the Hessian suggestion that August Boden, a publicist, be tried criminally because his third volume of arguments dissecting the case against Jordan referred "scornfully and spitefully to the . . . courts and bureaucrats, directly and indirectly accusing them of incompetence, lack of reason, malice, falsehoods, partisanship, corruption, etc., etc." Nor would the Prussians silence Jordan's supporters. The *Vossische Zeitung* (Voss's Gazette) in Berlin, in the midst of Hessian complaints to the Prussian government, reprinted these words from the *Aachener Zeitung* (Aachen Gazette): "Chances for Jordan's acquittal on appeal are getting brighter. Dear Boden, undaunted, has won for himself everlasting gratitude in the matter of this German patriot. Seldom do we celebrate a happy day here without drinking one dry for the liberation of this man so revered throughout Germany."[24]

A censor in Hamburg reacted to yet another Hessian complaint, this one against a general discussion of politics, policing, and culture in Hesse-Cassel, including the Jordan case, months after the professor had won his final appeal. "The principal topics here are social, literary, and artistic conditions," he began.

> And if the author has chosen to include the police, censorship, and the theater, admittedly not without some sarcastic allusions, they as well as artistic institutions in all of the German states, including ours, are permissible topics of criticism, however groundless and frivolous, in the daily press. Many German sheets subject to censorship deal with them in far more arrogant and crass ways.[25]

The Hessian government, to its credit, only was expecting satisfaction from other governments as good as it gave when they complained about what came off its printing presses. When several neighboring states objected to faulty censoring of pamphlets in Hanau, Cassel authorities banned them all. In 1844, when Saxony objected that Dietrich Albrecht Geeh, a printer in Cassel, had published *Censuriana* by Wilhelm Held, employing what by then was a standard trick of assembling enough passages that had been censored out of Held's Leipzig periodical, *Locomotive,* to make a book longer than 320 pages, free from prior censorship, Hesse banned the book immediately.[26]

Beyond accommodating complaints about its own imperfect censorship, the regime in Cassel banned many publications that had no connection at all to Hesse. Dozens of books showed up on the lists of banned writings, not because all German states were suppressing them, not because they were about the principality, not even because Hessians were likely to read them, but just because somewhere else someone had banned them already and asked the Hessians to ban them too. By the mid-1840s there was a steady stream of these bans, mostly prompted by two neighbors, Saxony and Prussia. Nearly without fail, publications brought to Hessian attention found their way to the Censorship Commission, which banned them because that was what it was ordered to do. Hesse went along with the judgments of other states as readily as it had so often, so futilely, assumed they would respect its judgments. A rare exception came late in 1844 when, on order from the prince regent, Prussian requests affecting Prussia alone were processed slowly as revenge for reports in Prussian newspapers about Sylvester Jordan's appeal of his conviction.[27]

The Hessian situation was not unique in its basic outlines, but the extremes of sycophancy and outrage in the Hessian response were unusual. Other states also felt pressed to accommodate more powerful governments' interests. Austria and Prussia pressured Saxony on censorship. The Austrians did the same thing to the Bavarians. Saxony followed its own inclinations anyway. Most states would not be coerced. The Danes complained all the time against news about Slesvig that came off printing presses in Hamburg, but to little effect. In many parts of Germany, a stronger censorship in Württemberg would have been welcome too, but it never came.[28]

It was not exceptional either that the Hessians got awfully upset about books and pamphlets devoted to Sylvester Jordan's case, because every German state was sensitive to attacks on its own institutions and the highlighting of its own problems. Among Austrian bans were Hermann Rollett's poems, *Frühlingsboten aus Oesterreich*

(Spring Heralds from Austria), censored in 1845, the anonymous *Memoiren und Aktenstücke aus Galizien vom Jahre 1846. Gesammelt von einem Mährer* (Memoirs and Documents from Galicia in the Year 1846, Collected by a Moravian), and many other works about Habsburg royalty, politics, and nationalities that never came to the attention of Hessian censors. A *Map of Hungary,* published in Magyar and banned in 1846, had no place on Hessian lists. *Oesterreich und dessen Zukunft* (Austria and Its Future), prohibited in 1843, was quite wicked to the Austrians because it reappeared among their bans as *De l'Autriche et de son avenir* in 1844 and *L'Austria e il suo avvenire* in 1847 yet was never banned in Hesse. The reason was simple. Vienna did not entrust its diplomats with the ludicrous task of imposing local difficulties on other governments.[29]

The same was true of prohibitions by the Prussians. They included Adolph Glaßbrenner's *Berlin wie es ist und trinkt* (Berlin as It Is and Drinks) in 1836, an *Index librorum prohibitorum in Preußen* (Prussian Index of Banned Books) in 1838, and *Die erste christliche apostolische Gemeinde in Danzig freundig begrüsst von Rud. Montanus* (Friendly Greetings from Rud. Montanus to the First Christian Apostolic Congregation in Danzig) in 1845, among many works that insulted the kingdom's political and religious values but did not find their way to the censors in Cassel.[30]

One book caused as much fuss in Prussia as the books about Jordan did in Hesse-Cassel. The reaction to Johann Jacoby's *Vier Fragen beantwortet von einem Ostpreußen* (Four Questions Answered by an East Prussian), published and banned in 1841, points out the universality of the Hessians' complaint but also the extremeness of their behavior. Jacoby's work touched a raw nerve in Prussia because it recalled the long-unfulfilled promise of a constitution. "It is long since any book has excited so great a sensation in Germany," England's *Foreign Quarterly Review* reported, "as the little pamphlet entitled 'Four Questions.' It was ushered mysteriously into the world and has been rigidly suppressed." Prussia banned it on 1 March 1841, banned a second edition the following November, and banned a French translation in July 1842. Through the Confederal Assembly, Prussia also got cooperation from other states. In Hesse-Cassel the censors banned it one month later on 1 April 1841, about as fast as anything administrative got done there.[31]

The Prussian giant, as much as its smaller neighbor, Hesse-Cassel, had trouble controlling unwelcome news and commentary. But the shrill, vindictive tone of the Hessians was not heard from the

Prussians, at least not in what they sent out through their diplomats. In part, that reflected how successful most Prussian diplomacy was. Other states tended to follow Prussian leads. When Prussia banned Heinrich Heine's *Neue Gedichte* (New Verses) and *Deutschland. Ein Wintermärchen* (Germany, A Winter's Tale) in early October 1844, Hamburg (home of the publisher, Hoffmann and Campe) followed suit on 14 October, the grand duchy of Hesse-Darmstadt on the seventeenth, Denmark on the twenty-second, Frankfort on the Main and Bückeburg on the twenty-third, Lübeck on the twenty-fifth, Hesse-Cassel on the thirtieth, Mecklinburg-Strelitz on 4 November, Schwerin and Württemberg on the fifth, Bavaria on the twelfth, Waldeck and Lippe on the fourteenth, and Saxony-Weimar and the kingdom of Saxony during the first months of 1845. Hanover, Bremen, and Oldenburg, however, refused to go along.[32]

For a work that insulted only Prussia, Adolph Glaßbrenner's *Berliner Gewerbe-Ausstellung* (Berlin Industrial Fair), other German governments were less eager, but some still cooperated. Within six months of its banning in Prussia, it had been forbidden as well in Brunswick, Bavaria, Schwerin, Nassau, Lübeck, Oldenburg, Saxony-Weimar, and Austria. Württemberg, Hesse-Darmstadt, Hanover, and Hamburg declined to join in. At Cassel, the censors argued through Christoph von Rommel that the book had no connection with Hesse, so Prussian diplomats must be misinformed about the law "in a constitutional state" if they thought that everything Prussia banned, Hesse would ban too. It was the censors who were misinformed; Hesse would and did ban it, at the Interior Ministry's insistence, only weeks after the Prussians had. Three days after the banning, Krieger's bookshop in Cassel returned the only reported copy to the publisher.[33]

What the Hessians got for banning so many books on behalf of other German states was longer censorship lists than they would have had otherwise by the mid-1840s, but not more practical ones. They were cluttered with literature that did not really matter in Cassel, Marburg, Fulda, or Hanau. The logic of censorship by then was not embodied in what Cassel officials commanded through their laws, instructions, and directives. It was not the systematic, German-wide repression of liberal politics that they aspired to through the cooperation of the German Confederation either. A reactive, flexible policing system, censorship emphasized as it always had the peculiar needs—and peculiarities—of each German state.

If there was something good for the government of Hesse about the frequent bans of the 1840s, it was not that they meant censorship was working or that the German Confederation was an effective institution or that the censors had finally figured out what to do. It was simply that they gave the police many opportunities to visit bookshops to try to keep the bookmen of Hesse honest.

SEVEN

Scrutiny before Sale
The Battle between Censorship and the Book Trade

In 1844, the police commission of Cassel, sitting as a court of first instance, arraigned, tried, and sentenced four local booksellers for selling August Boden's *Dritte Schrift zur Vertheidigung Sylvester Jordans* (Third Volume in Defense of Sylvester Jordan). Although at the time the dealers sold the book it had not been banned, the commission fined each of them ten taler plus administrative costs. On appeal, the fines were halved, but the conviction stood. The case was a rude injury to Hessian bookmen, which changed their behavior and the process of censorship. The *Deutsche Allgemeine Zeitung* (German General Gazette) reported soon after that in Cassel "since the proceeding on Boden's book, the booksellers have not neglected to send all new books they receive, in which the electoral principality of Hesse is mentioned, to the censors for their scrutiny before sale."[1]

What happened to the booksellers of Cassel, because they sold a controversial book without asking for permission first, illustrates the importance of local policing in the success or failure of censorship. It hints as well at the impact of censorship on people who sold, bought, and read books. Legislators might debate changes in the press laws, diplomats might dispatch reports on what other states said and did about the press, and censors might judge the suitability of books and manuscripts for local readers. Reviewing all of these activities tells a great deal about the politics of censorship, but their history reveals next to nothing about its practical consequences across the German lands. Macrocensorship of a publication in Hesse, set in motion when the Censorship Commission in Cassel received it for review, was over when the censors issued their ban. Microcensorship, though, the local policing of literature, often had begun earlier and almost certainly would finish later.

Of August Boden's *Third Volume,* it might be said that microcensorship began when the Cassel police first asked one of the local booksellers whether he carried or had sold the work, and it ended when the four convicted dealers paid their fines. More to the point, microcensorship did not really have beginnings or endings—it did not start and stop with individual censored books—it was an endless series of visits by the police and their surrogates (bailiffs and clergymen) to bookshops, lending libraries, taverns, clubs, and even private residences. Before the censorship and confiscation of Boden's third volume about Jordan, there had been the policing of his second volume, his first volume, and Sylvester Jordan's own earlier writings on the case; afterward came the new submissive behavior of the booksellers in Cassel. All these events were links in the chain of microcensorship.

Sellers of books were the first persons affected by local policing of the press because it was in their shops that political literature, the sort usually banned, came most readily into the hands of the educated book-buying public, the likeliest readers. Booksellers were fewer and easier to reach than book readers, so of course the police went to them first. Moreover, if the police could just reach the sellers soon enough, there would not be any buyers, and, by inference, not any readers. Dealers in books complained that it ruined their business when police confiscated what censors had just banned, or took away volumes for "scrutiny before sale." They had plenty of reason to complain; they were in a trade in which everyone had to invest a good deal of money in inventory, whereas it often took them months to get payment on sales. It only made the trade that much more precarious to have the police unexpectedly take away unsold inventory.

Bookselling was not an enterprise for the timid. The governments of the German states, through their police, commonly required would-be proprietors to show sizable capital before opening for business. In Hesse, the requirement was one thousand taler, rather low, but then it was not the best territory for selling books either. In Saxony and Prussia, two thousand taler were required (in Berlin, much more, five thousand taler). To buy a going business raised the cost even higher. In Fulda, in 1830, Kranz's widow sold her bookshop to Carl Müller for seven thousand gulden, about four thousand taler.[2]

Once in business, a resourceful bookseller in Hesse could make a respectable living, but probably not a grand one. In the 1820s, a correspondent of the *Wochenblatt für Buchhändler* (Bookman's Weekly), the trade newspaper in Germany, published at that time in Marburg, wrote that on a three thousand taler investment a dealer in books might earn six hundred taler annually; but then 10 percent of it would have to be written off as uncollectible, and more was always tied up in accounts. By this reckoning, the actual net would have been about five hundred taler. The antiquarian bookman and lending librarian Jungklaus in Cassel estimated his annual income during the 1850s at seven hundred to eight hundred taler. It was enough, he admitted, to conduct "a bourgeois way of life."[3] The towns of Hesse were so different, one from another, their book-buying populations so dissimilar, that incomes among Hessian booksellers must have varied a lot. Three hundred to nine hundred taler net in a year was likely the range.

The bookseller's living was sufficient then, or even good, but not particularly secure. Creditors were insistent and debtors were slow. Newcomers were always trying to get into the trade, which dealers protested made it more precarious. And there was the state's expensive meddling.

In Hesse the prince-elector's government, ridiculously stingy even about funding its own Censorship Commission, was worse with booksellers: as a creditor when it fined them, always eager to collect; as a debtor when it bought or confiscated their wares, always reluctant to pay. Krieger's bookshop in Cassel had to resort to the law courts to force the royal household to settle an outstanding bill for more than two hundred taler, plus interest, due for forty-one books that Prince-Elector Wilhelm II had purchased, all on account, between 1824 and 1830. In 1836, Krieger's nephew and heir, Karl Kempf, succeeded in collecting this and other outstanding debts by winning a judgment against the larcenous royal family.[4] But Kempf was stonewalled when he tried several years later, again through appeal to the judiciary, to be reimbursed five taler, his cost when the Cassel police confiscated a political pamphlet, *Wahrhaftige Geschichte vom deutschen Michael und seinen Schwestern* (The True Story of German Michael and His Sisters).

Officers took away ten copies of this anonymous pamphlet that they had found in Kempf's shop in March 1843, and soon afterward the Censorship Commission banned it as subversive. Kempf sued for compensation the following summer in Cassel Superior Court, which decided in his favor in March 1844. But the regime continued the case to the Hessian Supreme Court, which overturned the lower court decision in December 1845. What a lot of trouble for plaintiff and defendant both, it would seem, to litigate nearly three years over a sum as small as five taler. In fact, more was at stake than the cost of ten pamphlets. Police confiscations like this one were frequent in Hesse. If all booksellers had to be reimbursed for what the police took from them, then the cost to the government each year would be considerable. Just as important, Kempf argued, and the government agreed, questions of principle were involved.

Bookman Kempf claimed that the police had violated the Hessian constitution of 1831 and the laws of censorship too. How could he have known, he asked the court, that the pamphlet was going to be forbidden? The censors had banned it only after the police confiscated it. The sole allowable ground for taking it from him, Kempf told the Cassel lower court, was expropriation for a public purpose, which article thirty-two of the constitution allowed, but only "with prior just compensation." Kempf claimed further that the constitution had superseded the instruction to the censors of 1816, which the Interior Ministry cited when it refused to reimburse him. And he objected that the police were not even the proper authority in press matters—the censors were. These were points that the censors, too, had argued with the ministry and the police, to no avail.

The Superior Court agreed with Kempf on all points. The judges ruled that the pamphlets were legally his property, even though he only held them on commission. It was true as well, they wrote, that the censors' instruction of 1816 was no longer valid law. Kempf was right that the censors should have come and gotten a copy of the pamphlet themselves, if the reason for the whole episode was that they needed to examine it. Finally, the lower court agreed with Kempf that he could not be liable for violating an ex post facto ban, and it ordered the police to return all ten copies of the *True Story* to him.

The Hessian Supreme Court, also sitting in Cassel, took a different view, far less favorable to Kempf, much more accommodating to the administration, and very traditional. This would happen frequently in court cases involving bookmen. Like the crown prince, the appellate judges of Hesse seemed to place little value in the constitution that they all were sworn to uphold. Hesse's highest judges preferred older legislation, sometimes much older.

Reversing the initial judgment in Kempf's case, the appellate court ruled that the police had not exceeded their lawful authority or trespassed in the affairs of the censors. As an arm of the local administration, the police were carrying out duties given to the administrative council in Cassel, as in each of the provinces, through the 1821 reorganization edict. The appeals judges upheld the lawfulness of police confiscations according to a law of 1762. Removing a publication that was dangerous to the community, they ruled, was not the sort of expropriation meant to be compensated under the new constitution either. The censors' ban proved that the pamphlet was dangerous. Finally, the judges found that the 1816 instruction to the censors had not been voided by the constitution, indeed it was "not in the least touched by it." For his ten pamphlets, what Kempf got in the end was a bill for the court costs.[5]

Meanwhile, Kempf was one of the four booksellers in Cassel who had been convicted in police court and lost again on appeal in the case of August Boden's *Third Volume*. The Supreme Court was consistent in its rulings on censorship, treating this case like the other one and agreeing entirely with the prosecutors. It rejected all of the defendants' arguments against their conviction: that censors in Frankfort, seat of the German Confederation, had passed the book; that it had not been forbidden in Hesse when the police took it from them; that there were so many books published in Germany each year, no dealer could be responsible for knowing what was in all of them; that if their customers always had to wait until the Hessian Censorship Commission reviewed and judged new books, they would go buy them in other, neighboring German states, and then the bookshops of Cassel would close for lack of business.[6]

These cases reached beyond Cassel to affect booksellers in other Hessian towns. In Fulda, after the censors forbade Boden's book, the police found six copies of it at Euler's bookshop and confiscated them. Euler complained "that already on previous occasions banned books have been confiscated from him, . . . which only brought him harm; and the affected bookstores [that is, the publishers or wholesalers who had sent him the books] will not write off anything." Given the recent history of booksellers before the courts, he could do nothing but complain.[7]

During the 1830s, policing of the Hessian book trade had been more lenient. Sometimes local officers had been willing simply to put their seal on contraband to prevent its legal sale, and then allow the dealers to return it to the publisher, so they would not be liable for its wholesale cost. Booksellers took most of their merchandise from publishers on commission. Therefore, they either had to sell it, remitting the wholesale price to the publisher, or return it within an agreed time in good condition. In that age of craft work, when bookbinders folded printer's sheets into pages by hand, "good condition" meant more than anything else that the folded edges of the pages should still be uncut.

After 1841, the year when Cassel officials cracked down on a variety of flaws that they perceived in the censorship system, the police routinely confiscated banned books and pamphlets instead of sealing them for return. To judge the contents of new books not yet scrutinized, police or censors had to cut their pages, and it was well known both in the trade and in government that publishers refused to take them back after that was done. Most of this contraband the police simply deposited in their provincial offices; a few volumes they sent on to the censors or other government agencies for inspection.

When Hessians revolted in 1848 and the new liberal March ministry lifted censorship, booksellers sent in petitions listing what had been taken from them since 1832. Only then did they get some of the books back and belated compensation for the rest. In Fulda, the police returned to Euler his six copies of August Boden's *Third Volume* that they had confiscated three and one-half years earlier. Along with them came sixty-eight other items taken from him over the previous fifteen years.

What was the impact of these confiscations on the book trade? Were they really as ruinous as booksellers alleged? Euler's careful accounting of what he was due from the Hessian state offers some clues. The list he submitted on 13 March 1848 had entries for wares taken on twenty-eight visitations by the police, or about two per year. The earliest confiscation had been in 1833, the most recent just a few weeks before the revolution in the winter of 1848.

During one visit, the police had taken forty-seven copies of a pamphlet from him; another time they had walked off with a twelve-volume work from his lending library. These, the six copies of Boden's book, plus other works taken in ones, twos, and threes, added up to ninety-three volumes with a value of about eighty gulden, or forty-five taler. The Fulda police found in their repository seventy-four of the ninety-three items on Euler's list and returned them to him. Eight more turned up later, but eleven were still outstanding when he sent in a second bill on 22 August 1848.[8]

Euler's bills to the police were written on his ordinary shop stationery, which meant they had printed on them his customary offer of 10 percent discount on books bought at the retail price and paid for within six months. Of course, for most of his books that the police held, it was too late for the discount. Euler's stationery is a reminder of the long intervals that booksellers then were accustomed to waiting between selling a book and receiving payment. Still, Euler and other tradesmen assumed that most debts would eventually be paid. The government of Hesse-Cassel was a very bad customer.

What Euler lost through police confiscations would have permanently damaged only marginal establishments, but it was harmful nonetheless. The fifteen taler's worth of his wares taken during 1836, and another fifteen taler's worth during 1839, represented for each year a real loss of ten taler that he owed to the wholesalers because he could not return the books to them. That would have been as much as one week's income for an average bookseller, more a penalty than an inconvenience, and a penalty that Euler could not have predicted or averted.

This unpredictable, often arbitrary character of censorship and policing of the press harmed booksellers and their relations with the government as much as the revenue that they lost in the process. Of course, if the government had been more efficient, confiscating all of the copies there were of everything that it disallowed before they could be sold, it would have seemed less arbitrary, but the financial cost to the dealers would have been higher as well. So whether censorship was efficient or inefficient, orderly or arbitrary, because it reached into their shops it was bound to hurt the booksellers' trade and their feelings as well.

Censorship was inefficient in Hesse mostly because the procedures for announcing bans were so ponderous that they compromised the whole enterprise. Illicit literature spread quickly, especially among booksellers who knew in many cases what was hot, no matter what innocence they feigned, and whose only choice was to sell it fast or get burned. To work, measures taken by the government against these books and pamphlets needed to be just as speedy, but they were not.

The chain for passing information through Hesse-Cassel's administration was long. The Interior Ministry sent notices about censorship, as about other internal affairs, to each of the four provinces, where administrators informed the local police directorate and county councilors. The county councilors passed the news to minor officials in towns and villages, and there were a great many of them. By the time all of officialdom knew what to look for, even a pamphlet passed hand to hand among semiliterates traveling on foot could have gone a long way and been seen by many eyes.

In the county of Hünfeld alone (one of four counties in the province of Fulda), there were eighty-five community leaders to inform whenever something notable happened, like a censor's ban. In the 1840s, for the county councilor in Hünfeld to distribute six copies of a notice from Cassel, first a scribe in his office had to write out the copies. Each copy, when it was ready, went to ten or twenty places and was carried by horse and runner to each of them in turn. Is it any surprise that three or four weeks would elapse, or six or more sometimes, until everyone in the province who ought to know, did?[9]

This was the routing that almost all administrative news was supposed to take. It was the path that the government in Cassel used to tell civil servants in 1824 to loosen up on the harsh treatment of newspapers and pamphlets that the prince-elector's ministers had ordered some months earlier during the "Affair of the Threatening Letters." It was the same path used later in 1824 to gather reports from local officials on what they were doing about immoral songs and prints that had been showing up all over Hesse and were not to be tolerated any more.[10] Of course, neither of these instances was a political emergency. The welfare of the principality was not going to be harmed by a difference of days or weeks in getting the word around. Twenty years later, when the German press was more active, more political, and less innocent, when the German public was more literate, more political, and less innocent, this was still the way that official news left Cassel and returned from the provinces, and by then its slowness was harmful to the state.

Exceptions to this slow transmission of news in and out of the capital were supposed to exist. In an emergency, local administrators were told to contact the government in Cassel directly. It even supplied them with a list of eleven natural and man-made disasters that qualified for direct reporting. Two of the man-made disasters might have involved the censors. In case of "so-called demagogues and propagandists" inciting the people to riot or in case of "distribution of harmful pamphlets, and so forth," administrative niceties were to yield to rapid action; the news was to be brought straight from its source to the capital.[11]

But written orders did not ensure the right results. To the dismay of leading officials in Cassel, especially during the 1820s as they tried to form a modern administration under Wilhelm II, they repeatedly had to chastise local administrators who would not stop sending all sorts of trivia straight to Cassel. Yet word of emergencies too often went back and forth the long way bogged down with so much else on the provincial and county circuits. It took days and weeks for the censors to hear about discoveries of harmful writings, and once they had heard, deliberated, and acted, news of their bans filtered back very slowly too. These were problems that could not be corrected, owing as they were to the general slowness of communication and the isolation of many communities in the years before railways and telegraphs.

Perhaps the news traveled faster in some provinces or at other times than it did in Hünfeld in the 1840s, but it is unlikely. In 1841, at Ziegenhain in the province of Lower Hesse, the county councilor received an order from Cassel to warn twenty-five rural mayors that they were going to be fined if they did not answer immediately a memorandum from the Interior Ministry asking whether copies of Johann Jacoby's *Four Questions Answered by an East Prussian* had been in their communities.[12] The warning came barely four weeks after the censors' ban had issued from Cassel, too soon for word to have reached every hamlet in Hesse. But for effective censorship it was already too late; two months had passed since the pamphlet was distributed and banned in Prussia.

The government of Hesse-Cassel was fortunate, under these circumstances, that most forbidden publications were not going to turn up outside the larger towns or be distributed very widely except through bookshops, lending libraries, and, sometimes, through clubs. It was also fortunate that in all Hesse there was only a handful of communities large enough to support bookshops, or large libraries, or clubs with a political tendency. It was unfortunate, though, that when books or pamphlets did turn up in numbers, most of them would be about Hesse's own politics and problems that Hessians were eager to read about. It was unfortunate, moreover, because even a few bookshops would be difficult to control.

How many copies of banned books circulated in the principality? Answers are bound to be sketchy because the main source of information is police records, and the police often knew only some of what was going on. The police directorates in Fulda and Marburg did keep careful records about how they followed up the censors' bans between 1832 and 1848. They came upon one or more copies, or their traces at least, for about every fourth ban in Marburg, about every fifth one in Fulda. One in five is a believable ratio for all the major Hessian towns. The university in Marburg and the Catholic Church in Fulda were magnets that attracted contentious literature, but then Cassel and Hanau had their own magnets in the princely government that ruled in Cassel and the German Confederation that assembled in Frankfort near Hanau. If fewer forbidden writ would have circulated in Cassel because the official presence there was so overwhelming, then surely more would have circulated in Hanau, which was notorious for the political liberalism of its citizenry.[13]

The police came upon banned pamphlets and books of every variety with about the same regularity. What did not turn up, though, were publications that Hessians had prohibited because some other

German state had wished it. When the police found large caches of banned writings, the topics were local.

In 1832, Jakob Förster of Hanau issued two pamphlets to evade the banning of his *Teutsches Volksblatt* (German National News). Police learned that the print runs had been five hundred copies of each. They were able to confiscate twenty-eight copies of the first pamphlet and two hundred and ninety-four of the second.[14]

The following year, Dietrich Albrecht Geeh in Cassel printed several hundred copies of *Reisen eines deutschen Freigeistes* (Travels of a German Free Spirit), which led to an Interior Ministry reprimand of the Censorship Commission for approving it, and occasioned hectic police activity. Dozens of copies were confiscated in Cassel, Fulda, and Marburg. In 1834, there was yet another large catch. Nearly seventy copies of an anonymous work, *Der Missionsverein, oder die Jesuiten in Hessen, Stimme eines Kurhessen* (The Missionary Association, or the Jesuits in Hesse: The Voice of a Hessian), found their way into police storerooms.[15]

In 1841, a Dresden journal, *Sächische Vaterlandsblätter* (Saxon Fatherland's News), attacked the Hessian government and for that found a wide audience in Cassel. The bookseller Fischer in Cassel told police that the publisher had forwarded one hundred copies to him, and seventy-seven were already gone from his shop by the time they came to ask. Three years later, when the Sylvester Jordan literary boomlet peaked, the police knew that books, pamphlets, and newspapers with articles on his plight were about, but they had little luck intercepting them. Dozens of copies found buyers before police visits to booksellers could begin. In 1846 came pamphlets by two Hessian religious dissidents, Professor Bayrhoffer in Marburg and Franz Schell, a former priest in Fulda, which also spread quickly to many readers.[16]

Of course, these were only a few of the publications that the Hessian censors had banned. Three-quarters of the time, when the police located any copies, it was four or five at most. In Fulda, half of these times, just one copy turned up. Unless the police were extraordinarily unaware of goings-on in Hesse, for most forbidden literature there was simply no large public.

Banned books most frequently turned up in bookshops. Cassel, by far the most populous town, had the largest number of book establishments, four important ones in the 1840s: Luckhardt's, Bohné's, Krieger's, and Appel's. Elsewhere there were very few. Hanau had two bookshops during the 1840s, those of Edler and König. There were two each also in Marburg and Fulda, smaller towns than Cassel or Hanau, but with a university in the one and an ecclesiastical seminary in the other that brought more book trade than there would have been otherwise. In Fulda, Euler and Müller and in Marburg, Elwert and Garthe were the principal dealers. Most of these businesses had lending libraries and print shops attached to them.[17]

In the provincial capitals and in scattered smaller towns as well were other, more marginal operations. Professor Bayrhoffer ran one in Marburg. Other persons in the professions, clergymen especially, traded in books sometimes as a sideline. In Eschwege, in the province of Lower Hesse along the border with Saxony, the bookbinder Carl Friedrich Hoffmann was periodically in and out of that other, more elevated trade in finished books. Even when he was in it, though, it seems that he made most of his money from lending the books, not selling them.[18]

What Hoffmann tried to do, without much success, was the dream of bookbinders and book printers, to gain money and social status by rising into the more privileged circle of booksellers, or to become editors, for that matter. Either way, they wished to become merchants in the ideas that books and periodicals contained, instead of just purveyors in some of their ingredients—paper, ink, leather, and the string and glue that held them together. Often the government in Cassel allowed these men a bit of that dream, but not more than the proprietors of lesser lending libraries or the editors of minor journals. Neither job did more for their purses than furnish a small supplement to the usual income.

Tradesmen in commodities of every sort petitioned often, but seldom successfully, for permission to enter the book business. In the Marburg archive are some forty requests by men with diverse occupations and social standing seeking official approval for their plans in the years between 1820 and 1848. Barely more than one-half of them ever got it. Adolph Hornthal of Cassel, music shop proprietor and professional singer, asked first in 1832 and again in 1842. Pastor Diedrich of Fritzlar had asked in 1828. Wood engraver Henze of Volkmarsen near Fulda would in 1844. So did Moses Goldschmidt of Fritzlar, also in 1844. He and other Jews residing in Hesse-Cassel were the least likely to get favorable replies to their petitions. Restricting the book trade by keeping these various outsiders out of it was one of the few things that the government and established dealers agreed about as prohibitions of the booksellers' wares by the censors and visits to their shops by the police became more frequent.[19]

The small number of successful booksellers and their concentration in a few towns meant that provincial police did not have many places to visit or far to go when news came in of a new ban. It did not mean that they had an easy time making their rounds or that most repressive bans on books already published were effective. Word of a prohibition rarely arrived in time for police to announce it to booksellers before they had received their half-dozen or so copies, sold them, returned them, or passed them on.

The police could do little except visit individual shopkeepers, tell them about the latest bans and ask them whether they had seen the publication, received it, or sold it. If anyone answered yes, then the police wanted to know who had sent it and who had bought it. Sometimes the police had useful information about distribution of the book because another interested state in the German Confederation had reported, through the Confederal Assembly in Frankfort, where shipments had gone in Hesse. But these reports took time, and as always the passage of time was the hidden enemy of censorship. (Franz Dingelstedt's publisher in Hamburg, Julius Campe, wrote to him in 1842, "Winning time means winning everything!")[20]

Sometimes a Hessian bookman's own records showed that he had traded in writings now banned. Then the police could ask more questions and get more answers. Were there confrontations? Were these visits just formal exercises, following a well-known script read among acquaintances? The records seldom tell.

What is clear from the records is that the results of this policing were very mixed. Its effectiveness varied from year to year, from one banned book to the next, but most of all from one bookseller to another. For example, in 1834, orders went out to the provinces to track down and confiscate the anti-Catholic *Missionary Association*. The results in Fulda and Marburg were very different. The police in Fulda, the center of Hessian Catholicism, confiscated forty-two copies from Euler's bookshop, discovered that he had sold four more, and made him retrieve all of them from his customers. It was the sort of book that even outside Fulda had attracted a lot of interest, and so it was not surprising that at Marburg the dealer Garthe had fourteen copies of it. The police there, without a bishop to encourage them, merely affixed their seal and let Garthe send them back to the publisher. They took a single copy from Marburg's other dealer, Elwert, who had sold seven more, but they were unable to learn anything about them.[21]

For booksellers, the books that were easiest to hide were the ones they had already sold. Exceptionally weak memories about these transactions afflicted many merchants. In Cassel, efforts late in 1841 to find copies of Franz Dingelstedt's *Songs of a Cosmopolitan Night Watchman* led to interviews with three of the principal dealers in town as well as the proprietors of another, lesser shop. Luckhardt had given one copy to the police (for the censors to read, who promptly banned it) and one to the crown prince. A third copy he had sold for cash, he said, to someone he did not know. About a fourth, he just could not recall. Dealer Fischer told also of having sold two copies for cash. The Appel shop had had one copy, but the proprietor said he had already returned it to the publisher. The Messner brothers, who ran an antiquarian bookshop and lending library, reported that they had had one copy and lent it. Altogether, from their visits to Luckhardt, Fischer, Appel, and the Messners, the police knew eight copies of Dingelstedt's poems were in Cassel, but they could get their hands on only two.[22]

Noa Elwert in Marburg often said he had sold things for cash to unknown strangers traveling through town and never seen by him since. Euler in Fulda admitted to many sales but rarely had anything more to say. It was the time delay between distribution and policing, more than anything else, that made these evasions possible.

Euler's detailed recordkeeping in Fulda shows how the race was run between distributors and the police, step by step. On 17 October 1846, in self-defense, Krieger at Cassel submitted to the censors a copy of one of Sylvester Jordan's books, *Wanderungen aus meinem Gefängnis* (Rambles From My Jail). The following day, 18 October, Euler received eight copies of it from the publisher. On 22 October, the fifth day after Krieger had delivered his copy to the police, the Censorship Commission issued its ban. At the beginning of November, ten days after the ban, the police in Fulda came to Euler asking about the book. In the two weeks that had passed since he received his eight copies of it, he told them, he had sold them all.[23]

Much of the confusion—and failure—that surrounded these efforts to police the book trade was a natural by-product of the way the business was conducted. Books and pamphlets often came to dealers unsolicited. Usually these, like the publications they had ordered, were on short-term approval, obliging dealers either to pay for the wares or to return them before long or to forward them to another dealer who might do better with them.

In effect, booksellers had their own private post because along with these shipments of books to each other, they included letters. It was simple that way to learn what books were in demand, and then to get them to each other quickly. So it was that Noa Elwert in

Marburg, when questioned in 1842 about the banned volume, *Gedichte eines Lebendigen* (A Quick Man's Verses), could tell the police that he had gotten one copy from the publisher but another from a bookseller in Gießen, only twenty miles away, yet in another state, the grand duchy of Hesse-Darmstadt. One of Elwert's two copies the police found and confiscated in the reading room of the local Academic Museum, a civic club. The other, as so often happened, he had sold for cash to an unknown stranger who was passing through town.[24]

In 1845, Euler in Fulda, when asked by the police about his handling of yet another tome from the pen of August Boden, *Untersuchungsprozeß gegen Pfarrer Weidig* (The Interrogations of Pastor Weidig), said that he had sold two copies and sent two others to dealers at the nearby towns of Lauterbach and Alterschlirf, both a few miles away across the border into Hesse-Darmstadt.[25] All of this movement, and the natural, close, even familial relations among booksellers in neighboring German states made it difficult for the police in any one state to do their job effectively. Small wonder that they acted more harshly than dealers would have liked on occasions when either copies were at hand or there was evidence that they had been.

The conflicts about reimbursing booksellers for what the police took from them, which became more frequent and more acrimonious during the 1840s, were not a matter just between shopkeepers, police, and the courts. They touched the Hessian Censorship Commission as well. It was the censors, after all, who when they wanted to examine books had the police get them. It was the censors who seemed responsible when a book that the police confiscated, even without the censors asking, was not returned because, meanwhile, they had banned it. If it had been for the censors to decide, booksellers would have been reimbursed for what they lost through police seizure and censor's scrutiny. But in this as in so many other matters, what the censors thought was not what the Hessian government wanted or did.

In September 1844, the Censorship Commission sent three bills to the Interior Ministry for payment, one each from the Krieger, Appel, and Luckhardt shops in Cassel, listing works that the police had taken to the commission and that the commission had banned. In one case, perhaps in the other two, it was the censors who had wanted to see the book but because of the trouble they had gotten into before for anything that looked like "executive action," they let the police be their intermediaries.

One of the books was *Hermine* by Zirndorfer, a work that the censors asked to see because they had heard it "distinguished itself through its impudent immorality." The commission had gotten word of it in May 1844 not long after its publication in Hanau, where the Censorship Deputation had been dissolved four years earlier. Although Hanau's publishers and printers were supposed to forward manuscripts to Cassel for approval, often they did not. In their notes to each other, before obtaining the book, the censors mulled over the cost of buying it, an expense that their modestly funded office could not support. "With regard to the costs arising from the acquisition of this and other books," Christoph von Rommel suggested, "as our budget is already quite limited, now is a fit time to request a special appropriation." But the book came to them, courtesy of the police, before the problem of paying for it could be settled. Four months later Zirndorfer's *Hermine,* now banned, costing one taler and six good groschen, appeared among the censors' bills at the Interior Ministry.[26]

Officials at the ministry were displeased. In answer to the censors' request that the bills be paid for them, the ministerial opinion was that "for works procured only for review, there is no obligation to pay their price." Censor Schubart retorted that whatever men might think at the ministry, one had to cut the pages of a book to read it, and it was common knowledge that no publisher would take it back after that. He continued, with undisguised sarcasm, by wondering whether the booksellers ought to be told to pay themselves for books surrendered for inspection, making presents of them to the government, and then, if they were returned later in unsalable condition, to keep them for their own edification. The best answer, Schubart wrote, was to make the police pay for them because they had taken them.

Four weeks later, the questions whether to pay and which office should pay were settled temporarily when the ministry agreed to cover that year's bills. Why is unclear, although it may have been because Karl Kempf's first suit of 1844 against the government for compensation was still on appeal, and so far Kempf was winning.[27]

A little more than one year later, in January 1846, ministry officials again quizzed the censors about payments to Cassel booksellers that they had asked be covered: eight taler, twenty-two good groschen for Bohné; five taler, fourteen good groschen for Luckhardt. These bills could not be for banned books, the ministry wanted its censors to know, because banned books always had to be confiscated or returned to the publisher, and in either case nothing was due. The censors objected, sounding more like bookmen than policemen, that it was wrong to punish a dealer who was compelled to turn over a book that the government banned later. What justice was there in making one dealer a victim because he cooperated with the police, when other dealers, hearing of the ban, would be able to return their copies quickly to the publisher and suffer no loss?

The police who confiscated books, the censors added, furnished dealers with receipts for them; now the government should honor its receipts. As it had two years before, the ministry acquiesced and paid the new bills. But in 1847 it also issued a new instruction to the Censorship Commission, requiring that from now on booksellers were to deliver books for the censors "ready to read," that is, with the pages already cut, and the censors were not to compensate the dealers for them.[28]

Wanting to be tough and stingy, but often relenting after a struggle in individual cases, the government of Hesse ended up with neither the modicum of goodwill from booksellers that prompt payments might have brought nor the money that refusing payment would have saved it. The truth was that circumstances often extenuated the supposed offense of possessing a book later deemed unsuitable for Hessians to read. In many cases, the censors, sometimes even joined by the police, did not share the ministry's harsh view.

In January 1846, Karl Gutzkow's scandalous novel, *Wally, die Zweiflerin* (Wally, the Skeptic), about a free-thinking woman and her love, received the censors' curse. Police investigation in Hanau revealed that a citizen there named Merz had bought it at Edler's shop. The police went to Merz and took it from him. Merz demanded compensation for the three gulden and eighteen kreuzer (equal to one taler and twenty-one good groschen) that he had paid for it. Here was a case that seemed clearly to involve private property guarded by the constitution. All of the cases until then that had brought the ministry and the censors into conflict, where the ministry cited the instruction to the censors of 1816 to justify its policy of no compensation, were about things taken from bookshops, not private homes. After six weeks the ministry acquiesced, and Merz got his money.[29]

The Interior Ministry also allowed compensation for books by the group of authors labeled "young Germany," which the police took from bookshops in the 1830s. This, too, was easily an exceptional case because the German Confederation, at the insistence of the Austrian delegation, had forbidden in one stroke all of the writings—past, present, and future—of five nationalist authors. In its usual fashion, the government of Hesse-Cassel balked initially at reimbursing proprietors caught holding books that suddenly were contraband, although some of the books were not new at all. In Rinteln, the police took four works by "young Germans," as well as two others, from bookman Osterwald. It was January 1835, the Confederal ban had just appeared, and the Rinteln police told Osterwald to petition the government for reimbursement of the books' retail price as his just compensation.

The following summer, Osterwald went to court, testified that the books had been on his shelves for two or three years, noted that it had been two weeks after they were confiscated before the police even told him about the confederation's ban, and asked for compensation. The ministry, citing the instruction of 1816, refused. A few weeks later, it reversed itself, acknowledged that the books had been lent by Osterwald for years without the police noticing them, and agreed that he was entitled to some compensation for not being allowed to keep them now.[30]

Still there was quibbling. Osterwald wanted thirteen taler and eight good groschen, the retail value of the books. From Cassel came instruction to the administrative council in Rinteln to settle with him for less because he had already recouped part of his cost through lending the books. In the end, Osterwald got almost everything he wanted: twelve taler for the books, plus one taler and three good groschen for the administrative fees he had had to pay while trying to get his money back.[31]

Soon afterward, the ministry ordered the police in Hanau to see that bookman Edler be paid thirty taler, twelve good groschen, and thirteen pence, due him for thirteen volumes of "young German" books taken from his shop. What Edler got, too, was almost equal to full payment of the sixty-one gulden and forty-one kreuzer of south German currency that he had claimed in a bill submitted eight months earlier.[32]

Stingy from start to finish, inconsistent and intrusive, the government of the principality gave booksellers in Hesse ample reason to resent its behavior. In the process it dragged the censors into the middle of yet another controversy in which their sentiments and their duties were at odds. But the tale of how censorship related to the book trade would be incomplete if it ended here, amidst administrative delays and capricious policing, dominated by injuries and insults, with bookmen in and out of the law courts seeking some defense against tyranny. There is more to the story because bookmen, like bureaucrats, were not always as innocent as they pretended to be.

EIGHT

Top Secret
Chasing Conspiracies among Bookmen

On 3 August 1832, Dietrich Albrecht Geeh, a printer in Cassel, sent to the bookseller Friedrich Oehler in Frankfort fifty copies of a play entitled *Der Bürger* (The Citizen), which Geeh had printed clandestinely in his shop. "If the person and place providing these things are kept top secret," Geeh promised Oehler, "then more writings like this will follow soon."[1] Geeh was one of a coterie of bookmen, in Hesse-Cassel and neighboring states, who challenged the censorship system directly by producing, distributing, and marketing forbidden literature, often in collusion with each other.

Geeh was proud of the influence that he as a printer and others as sellers of books and pamphlets were having on political discourse. "Booksellers have played a prominent part in politics lately," he pointed out in another letter during 1832 to a dealer named Kunze in Mainz. "Through their liberal sensibilities, through the distribution of fine writings, they have earned high praise."[2] These letters from Geeh ended up several years later in the hands of the Cassel police, earning him not praise but dates in court and, in the end, jail sentences for the secret, illicit printing he had done.

What Geeh claimed in his correspondence, imprudently as it turned out, was true: bookmen were prominent in liberal German politics of the 1830s and 1840s. Their little conspiracies were one of the motors, although not the only one, that drove opposition to the ruling princes. Bookmen of every sort—printers, dealers, and publicists—who shared Geeh's sentiments, who shared liberal political passions that governments would not tolerate, who shared with each other and their customers writings meant to spread those passions, also shared years of close scrutiny by public authorities. In fact, what they did made the entire book trade suspect.

Authorities sensed many times that local bookmen were spreading dangerous publications, although questions about their activities came more readily than answers. Which bookmen? Conspiring with whom? By what means? Spreading which publications? These things were not easy to discover.

Stealth, deception, and lies met the police when they tried to learn what publications the bookmen were preparing on their presses at night, what messages they communicated to each other in code, what contraband they sneaked along the highways in false compartments of hats or on wagons under other merchandise; what persons they employed as their agents, delivering packets from one town to another, leaving anonymous pamphlets at gates and doorsteps. Police investigations of conspiring bookmen hit their target sometimes but missed it many others.

Catching conspirators called for another sort of policing—investigative, assuming subversive, criminal intentions—alongside the routine policing that followed the censors' bans. Routine policing was only meant to control the comparatively innocent act of selling contraband, for which the usual penalty was confiscation and the worst was a fine, and often the consequences for bookmen were buffered by sympathy and support from the censors. Investigative policing was rougher and led to long jail sentences.

At this point, where men in the book business conspired against their rulers and the rulers' laws, where the police were charged with rooting out conspiracies, censorship was not the censors' business anymore. Of course, even in other things that were their business, the Cassel censors' role had always been limited. In the review of manuscripts and published works, directives from the Interior Ministry constrained them; in the policing of unauthorized book and pamphlet sales, the extent to which local officials cooperated set boundaries on what they could accomplish. But in tracking down and punishing illicit printers, publishers, and distributors, the censors were not just held back, they were irrelevant. Exposing the secrets of conspiratorial bookmen was a task only for police and magistrates.

The historical record is limited by what the police uncovered or stumbled upon, what they learned but often only years after it had happened, what they could surmise, and what informants told them. The record also includes the explanations, admissions, and denials made to the police by bookmen under arrest. Altogether there are many clues but few certainties about what went on.

Among bookmen in Hesse-Cassel during the last two decades of the censorship system, one (Noa Elwert in Marburg) never came under suspicion of criminal acts, although for all that went on in his print shop, he should have. A second (Christian Dietrich Garthe, also in Marburg) suffered under unfriendly police attention, although in all likelihood the source of his undoing was his associations, not his actions. A third (Dietrich Albrecht Geeh in Cassel, writer of the boastful letters) was caught, tried, and jailed for the things he truly had done, about which police and magistrates ended up knowing so much, there could be no dissembling. A fourth (Friedrich König in Hanau) and a fifth (Professor Karl Bayrhoffer in Marburg) had their difficulties with the police and courts too, but they were not so much the instigators of dissent as its communicators. The opinions they published other men had formulated, and other men would spread them whether König and Bayrhoffer were silenced by fines and imprisonment or not. The more police looked into what bookmen did, the more apparent it was that opposition to political life as it was and publicity on behalf of political change had many more promoters and supporters than just bookmen.

Noa Elwert, early nineteenth-century proprietor of a Marburg bookshop that is still doing business today, seemed hardly to have an interest in politics. He cultivated good relations with prominent intellectuals and politicians of Hesse-Cassel, including August Vilmar, the quite conservative headmaster of the Marburg grammar school, and Christoph von Rommel, the cautiously moderate chairman of the Censorship Commission in Cassel. Vilmar and Rommel both relied on Elwert to print and publish their writings; so did professors at the University of Marburg.

Elwert took seriously the honorable appellation, "Bookseller to the University" *(Universitätsbuchhändler),* which he acquired in 1828 along with the bookshop on Wettergasse, a title which to his mind brought with it privileges of an old sort, privileges that neither the Marburg police nor the Cassel censors had any business questioning. In Marburg, the police mostly left Elwert alone. From Cassel the censors tried, now and then, to make him obey the most recent laws on review of manuscripts before publication, but he simply would not.

Was Elwert a political man? Did he know that in his shop during the early 1830s someone was printing revolutionary pamphlets secretly? If he knew, if he was political, he was also very discreet because there is no evidence to link him to the controversial enterprises of the liberal and democratic opposition that went on so close to him.

His discretion or his innocence, whichever it was, allowed him to conduct his business as he liked rather than as the censors would have preferred.

Elwert's supposed innocence is remarkable in view of what was printed in his shop. It was not merely local politicking. Two of the most seminal revolutionary works of the age were given extended lives on the presses at Elwert's in the 1830s. They were the notorious *Hessischer Landbote* (Hessian Courier), Georg Büchner's and Ludwig Weidig's call from the neighboring grand duchy of Hesse-Darmstadt to the common people to revolt, of which the second printing came from Elwert's; and the widely read *Paroles d'un Croyant* (Words of a Believer), the democratic testament of a former French priest, Félicité Lamennais, condemning tyranny and oppression, printed in German translation at Elwert's.[3]

Heinrich Fischer, a bookseller in Wiesbaden and former proprietor of a bookshop in Gießen where Elwert had trained, translated the *Paroles* from French into German under the anagrammatic pseudonym of "Ch. S. Frei." The title page gave "Scheld & Co." of Philadelphia as the publisher, but, in fact, one of Elwert's employees printed it, in a run of one thousand copies, on Elwert's press. The police only discovered these things in the early 1840s, helped by a lead from Christian Dietrich Garthe's account book that listed transactions with Fischer. More remarkable was the fact that the second printing of the *Hessian Courier,* with its incendiary opening, "War on the Palaces! Peace to the Hovels!" also originated at Elwert's and the Hessian authorities never found out.

Efforts to get Elwert to comply with censorship laws were episodic. His responses were consistent, full of references to the law, or some of it anyway. The claims he made were crafty, argumentative, and, most importantly, successful.

In 1841, the police in Marburg questioned him about the circumstances under which his shop had printed a pamphlet *Über die Elemente, die Möglichkeit oder Nothwendigkeit einer konservativen Partei in Deutschland* (Concerning the Principles, the Possibility, or the Necessity of a Conservative Party in Germany) by V. A. H., who was Professor Victor Aimé Huber of the University of Marburg. Elwert had not received any censor's clearance for printing the manuscript, the police pointed out. He did not need it, he answered them, because the professor's dean had approved.

Elwert was referring to an old practice begun long before the age of parliamentary politics, when a scholar's sponsor, usually the dean, was his censor too, something remembered even today etymologically in German in the seemingly separate two meanings of *Zensur,* censorship but also academic grading. This old practice was supposed to have ended for all political writing a decade earlier by decree from Cassel, but professors and bookmen alike in Marburg defied the change. Whoever should have censored what Elwert was printing, he went on to make a greater, more devious claim, that he was not responsible for submitting it to the censors because he was not the publisher, only the printer, working on commission. The police should ask the author, who was his own publisher, how his manuscript had been censored, said Elwert; but the author-publisher, Professor Huber, just happened to be away on a vacation trip and the investigation lapsed.[4]

In June 1842, it was the Censorship Commission's turn to warn Elwert for ignoring censorship regulations, this time in printing without authorization a Whitsuntide sermon by August Vilmar. One month later, Christoph von Rommel wrote to the Marburg police that Elwert would not answer the censors about where he had received permission to print a *Hessisches Historienbüchlein* (Little Book of Hessian History) also by Vilmar. "Not just with this work," Rommel complained, "but with many items from his publishing house, Elwert has wholly bypassed the censors, violating the requirements of the Confederal Assembly and the laws of this land."

Elwert answered these new complaints against him as he had earlier ones, full of self-assurance and a knowledge of the laws. There was nothing political in Vilmar's booklet. It was full of old material previously published. He had done nothing wrong. He had had guarantees, he said, from former Marburg police director Carl Wilhelm Robert [actually the acting director from 1832 to 1834] that he did not have to submit scholarly works to the censors, only political ones.[5] It was a variant of the claim Elwert had made about Professor Huber's writings, and neither time was his recollection quite correct. Anything professors wrote that was not political, their deans censored. Any book or pamphlet that was political, or that someone else wrote, however, should have gone to the Censorship Commission for review. What Huber wrote was political, and Vilmar was not a professor, so Elwert was wrong about both of them. Who would brief the censors though on what the rules were for Marburg? Who would compel Elwert to follow the rules?

Four years later, in 1846, Christian Schubart reminded his fellow censors that since the controversy about the *Little Book,* Noa Elwert had not submitted a single manuscript to them for review. So they wrote him a letter asking for an explanation. His reply is a calligraphic wonder, full of fine lines and swirls, not in the angular German script that everyone used then, not legible either. Censors in that quill-penned era had to read and judge handwritten submissions every day, but only Schubart of the three commission members could see any words at all in what Elwert had sent them.

It seemed, Schubart told Christoph von Rommel and Piderit, that Elwert was still insisting that only university professors censored the scholarly manuscripts of their colleagues. And he had added a new claim that the local Marburg police directorate was responsible for censoring pamphlets, something that certainly was not true. The police censored newspapers assigned to them by the Interior Ministry, but nothing else. Elwert went on to recommend, as best Schubart could decipher it, that if the censors wanted to know what he had published they should ask "through his authority," the Marburg police, and not question him directly. It was a suggestion that the censors could not ignore because they had been reprimanded recently for exceeding their authority by corresponding directly with booksellers.

Among the censors' papers from the mid-1840s is an undated draft report to the Interior Ministry on their dealings with Elwert. As "Bookseller to the University" it related, he claimed the privilege of censorship only by the faculties he served. He had never obeyed the censorship instruction of 14 June 1816, even after 1842 when the police delivered to him his own summary, prepared by the censors, of the laws that he was obliged to follow. But the censors did not send this cataloging of Elwert's offenses on to the ministry, and why should they have, when their counsel was so often ignored.[6]

Even if they had informed the ministry, nothing would have happened to Elwert. Although the government was forever complaining about faulty censorship, its various branches made exceptions to the rules all along. In June 1831, the Censorship Commission—comprised then only of Justus Rommel—had approved a sermon without reading it, noting that he would get to it later.[7] Surely that was harmless when the author was known to him, and he deemed the man's opinions unobjectionable.

A few authors were so much in the good graces of government ministers that they escaped the usual scrutiny. One of them was August Vilmar, spokesman for conservatism in the Hessian legislature, rejuvenator of the Marburg grammar school as its director, and consultant to the Interior Ministry on educational matters. A manuscript by him came to the censors once with Interior Minister Hassenpflug's personal request that they approve it; they did. The same guardianship benefited Victor Aimé Huber, whose appointment as professor at Marburg was credited to Hassenpflug. These protected men of letters, along with Christoph von Rommel, were in Noa Elwert's regular stable of authors.

Elwert was also the publisher, in 1846, of an annotated edition of the Hessian Supreme Court's decision overturning Sylvester Jordan's conviction for abetting treason. The editor was Carl Michael Eggena, loser to Jordan in 1831 when the professor drafted a very different constitution from the royal proposal that Eggena had penned and loser to Jordan again in the appellate court decision. Eggena used this unusual edition to explain his own part in the case. What he wrote was a barely veiled attack on the Supreme Court, an institution with a long, proud history of independence dating back well before the constitutional era. Elwert published Eggena's book without submitting it to the Censorship Commission for review, and soon the censors, having learned about it, were discussing it in their circular notes to each other. Piderit thought it should have been published in the official *Wochenblatt* (Weekly Journal) by the Marburg administration—that was the usual way for fulfilling the constitutional requirement that verdicts be published. Schubart wrote that what Eggena had added to the judges' text was an insult to the court and the Hessian state, and if he had submitted it for censoring, the commission would have required revisions or banned it outright. But neither Elwert nor Eggena got into trouble, because the edition had the blessing of the Ministry of Justice.[8]

Marburg's other full-time bookseller through the 1830s, Christian Dietrich Garthe, came into more conflicts than Elwert over press infractions, with very different results. For Garthe, by every indication a meek man, it was his associations with persons caught up in the alleged conspiracy involving Sylvester Jordan that got him into trouble, made him the subject of long police interrogations, kept him under investigatory arrest for several weeks in 1840, and apparently drove him out of business.

Garthe was a native of Frankenberg, a town about thirty kilometers north of Marburg. Trained in the book trade in Gießen, he had come to Marburg at the age of thirty, in 1822, and opened a new shop. His petition for permission to sell books in the prince-electoral university town succeeded because city officials were displeased about how badly Krieger's (later to be Elwert's) establishment was tending to its responsibilities as Marburg's major book supplier.

The newcomer should have done well. Two years after beginning, he added a lending library to his bookshop. Scolded for not asking permission first, he wrote an apologetic note to the Marburg administration, with the assurance "that I certainly will never include any book that harms the reputation of state or church." His library, although small at first, grew steadily, until by 1839 it contained 3,733 volumes. Seven years later, though, in 1846, Garthe was living at his wife's family home in the nearby village of Rauschenburg, whence a police report came to Marburg saying he was "in needy circumstances," deeply in debt. Marburg officials denied him permission then to turn over his former business to another man, something that usually would have been approved routinely.[9]

Garthe was treated roughly at the hands of the Marburg police in 1840. They had started watching him years before that. As early as 1832 the gendarmerie had noted that the apothecary Döring (that scoundrel whose later statements to the police made possible the entire fantastic case against Sylvester Jordan) and the bookseller Garde [sic], both from Marburg, had been seen at a patriotic festival attended by hundreds of people on the Wollenberg near Wetter. It was another eight years, though, before Garthe's legal difficulties began in earnest.

From March through May 1840, the Marburg police sitting as a court of inquiry questioned Garthe half a dozen times. After one day of interrogation in May, he took ill suddenly with what his physician called a "gastric fever." The police allowed him to rest at home for several days while they combed through his account books. When he next appeared, they arrested him, and the questioning went on until the prisoner's wife complained to the Criminal Senate of Marburg's Superior Court. The court ordered the police to come up with enough evidence of his alleged crimes to justify holding him any longer, but the police could not, so they had to let him go. Nine years later, the Superior Court released Garthe from an oath of silence about the proceedings, and invited him to sue for compensation on account of the official excesses committed against him.[10]

The police inquiries of 1840 did not uncover anything quite conspiratorial that Garthe had done, but they also left little doubt that he sympathized with the political opposition to princes that had been so lively in Hesse-Cassel and neighboring states eight years earlier. The police were able to show that he had sold several pamphlets after Hesse had banned them, but on more serious questions of subversion and incitement to revolt, the evidence was circumstantial and inconclusive. Garthe's own statements kept alive suspicion about what he had done, without making the case against him.

On 11 May, during one of the interrogations, Garthe's answers illustrated the connections between the literature of the day and revolutionary politics:

QUESTION: There was a general expectation ... [in 1832 and 1833] ... here that a common uprising was going to start in Germany. What did you know about that?
ANSWER: Nothing! Unless I got some notion of it from the newspapers and similar sorts of publications. Otherwise I knew nothing about it. Of course, at that time in every public place, in fact in nearly every home, people talked about how a general revolt might well be at hand, and everyone shuddered and trembled. . . . A lot of pamphlets appeared at that time on the subject too, such as the writings of [J. G. A.] Wirth and [Philipp Jakob] Siebenpfeiffer about liberty in Germany, and a similar work by Dr. [Wilhelm] Schulz. These pamphlets were read here, and it may be that I discussed them a lot with others.
QUESTION: It is said too that you received detailed prior information about the plans for a revolution then.
ANSWER: That is absolutely untrue.
QUESTION: Didn't you hear then that in Württemberg and Frankfort a revolt was expected soon?
ANSWER: No! Only what I heard through the newspapers *after* the Frankfort uprising [of 3 April 1833].[11]

These denials, even if true, did not square well with Garthe's dealings during 1832–34 with literature and with people that the authorities considered revolutionary.

It was true, he agreed, that in the summer of 1832 he had collected money at an outdoor tavern for the defense funds of August Wirth and his fellow publicist Philipp Siebenpfeiffer, both then on trial for press crimes in the Bavarian palatinate. The police knew also that Garthe had belonged to a club organized by Döring in 1832 that raised money to honor Sylvester Jordan. And they knew from Garthe's own admission that he had belonged to another private society in the early 1830s that met at the home of a gold lace craftsman named Buch and had been organized, Garthe said, by a bookkeeper named Wagner. Other members were Döring, the local postmaster, and a shoemaker. What was its purpose? Sociability, said Garthe. "We talked politics in our club too, as was common at that time. But I don't remember the details."[12]

The police wanted to tie Garthe with Döring, their informant, to illegal publishing. They tried to draw a line between them and citizens of Hanau jailed for their roles in preparing the *Offene Erklärung kurhessischer Staatsbürger, hervorgerufen durch die Bundestags-Beschlüsse vom 28. Juni 1832* (Public Declaration of Citizens of Hesse-Cassel about the Confederal Assembly Decrees of June 28, 1832). They knew that Garthe had traveled with Döring to Butzbach, south of Marburg near Gießen, in August 1832. There the two men had met with someone. At first Garthe could not remember who it was, but later he volunteered that it might well have been the teacher Merz from Hanau, who had served five months in jail for his role in preparing and distributing the *Public Declaration*.[13] Döring had read the petition aloud at a public gathering in Marburg. But what had Garthe done? Nothing conclusive came from this line of questioning either.

More fruitful, as it turned out, were inquiries into Garthe's dealings in the book trade. From his account books, the police knew that he had received for sale, from the bookseller Ritter in Zweibrücken, many copies of pamphlets by August Wirth, including sixty-six of *Aufruf an die Volksfreunde in Deutschland* (Appeal to the Friends of the People in Germany) in September 1832 and one month later fifty copies of something the police called *Reform der deutschen Verfassung* (Reform of the German Constitution), which might have been any one of several pamphlets with similar titles. Garthe's customers for political pamphlets had included Döring, Sylvester Jordan, and other Marburg citizens who would go on trial with Jordan. Among Garthe's sales were many controversial works, most of them legal, however.

Sylvester Jordan had bought three works by Cornmanns, *Freiheitsblitze* (Freedom's Lights), *Kerkerstimmen* (Voices from Jail), and *Kerkerblumen* (Jail Flowers), as well as two by Harro Harring, *Blutstropfen* (Drops of Blood) and *Die deutschen Völker* (The German Peoples). One of Jordan's later codefendants, Leopold Eichelberg, had bought twelve copies of Lamennais's *Words of a Believer*, more than he needed just to read it himself.[14]

When the police found these entries in Garthe's account books, they asked him about them:

> QUESTION: The *Paroles d'un Croyant*, Wirth's *Appeal to the Germans*, Dr. Cornmanns's *Jail Flowers*, weren't they among the publications banned in Hesse then?
> ANSWER: At that time, when they were published and I sold them, as I remember they were not yet banned in Hesse.[15]

But Garthe remembered badly; two out of these three had been banned when he sold them: Lamennais's pamphlet, in French at least,

135

by the German Confederation three months earlier, and Wirth's *Appeal,* also several months earlier, at Bavaria's urging. The Hessians did not ban Cornmanns's *Jail Flowers* until five months after Garthe sold it. Harring's *Drops of Blood,* though, they had banned two and one-half years before Sylvester Jordan bought it from him.

Although Garthe's sale of Lamennais's pamphlet was three months after the German Confederation had ordered the book banned, it was only eight days after the Hessian censors had added it to their own list of prohibitions. Had Garthe knowingly violated the new ban? If the police in Marburg had not yet informed him of it, was he within the letter of the law, even if outside its spirit? More importantly, where had he gotten so many copies of the book? At the bottom of the police account of who supplied Garthe and who his customers were, his interrogators added a note that nothing had been found yet to connect Garthe's sales of the Lamennais book with Elwert's bookshop in Marburg or Rucker's (formerly Fischer's) in Gießen.

For once the police seemed to have in hand the pieces of a conspiratorial puzzle that only needed to be put together. Fischer, who had trained Garthe in Gießen, was the translator of the banned book, printed at Elwert's, that Garthe had had in large numbers. Friedrich Döring was Garthe's friend; Sylvester Jordan was his customer. Garthe had read and talked about politics a lot. He had traveled out of town to meet men from Hanau who had prepared and printed a pamphlet against the German Confederation. And there was more.

When questioned about the *Words of a Believer,* Garthe admitted that he had received a "large number" of copies of it from the printing at Elwert's, then sold them on commission. It would have been unusual, he told the police, to print fewer than five hundred copies, especially of such a popular work. He knew so much about it, it is hard to imagine that he was not in on the plan to produce and distribute it. But to the suggestion that he had sold something forbidden, Garthe insisted he had not, because notice of the banning came to him afterward. The police called it a secret printing, which to them it was because they had not known about it. Garthe maintained that all he had done, he had done openly.

One more time before they had to let him go, Garthe led the police to the brink of discovering a revolutionary connection, but it too vanished in his ultimate denials. He admitted, with embarrassment the police recorder noted, that in February 1832 he had gotten an anonymous letter offering him a mysterious printing job. The letter read:

Enclosed you will receive the beginning of a little written work that arises out of the requirements of the age. For particular, important reasons, the author has decided not to name himself. Even a thorough look into the matter will bring out absolutely nothing about the name of him whom it concerns. What it really is all about is human welfare. The composition will always stay within the boundaries of truth and moderation, and if you undertake to publish it, the author will reveal himself entirely to you as necessary and in your interest but only with the promise that concerning him you adhere to strictest secrecy.[16]

The letter went on to urge Garthe to put a coded insert in the *Hanau Gazette* telling how much he wanted to be paid for the work. According to the letter writer, the newspaper's publisher, Kittsteiner, was sympathetic with the cause. Garthe and his wife also told of visits to their house by a stranger urging them to take up the same project.

Garthe was no peasant who would have run to the police out of innocent fear and suspicion any time an oddity like this fell into his hands. He knew what sort of enterprise was behind it. But he had refused to have anything to do with it, he said again and again. Understandably, the police for their part wondered who this stranger was at Garthe's door and why the unknown correspondent had made the offer to him. Was this someone like the strangers who passed through town, silently bought controversial literature (at Elwert's mostly) and never were seen again? The mysterious letter to Garthe had been accompanied by the opening passages of the proposed publication, but that fragment is not with it in the archive, so there is no knowing what it was that Garthe so adamantly denied he had printed.

There are few certainties about what went on in the booksellers' establishments in Marburg. At Elwert's shop there was some illicit printing, that is for sure. Yet Noa Elwert himself went through the 1830s and 1840s scarcely troubled by it all. It was his rival in the trade, Garthe, collecting money for liberal causes, joining clubs, selling pamphlets banned or about to be banned, traveling to meet men from Hanau, receiving secret letters and visits but still apparently just on the fringes of the conspiracies then, whom the police troubled a great deal. In Cassel the police hit their mark better because in Cassel there was clear evidence about the criminal doings of one man, the printer Geeh.

Dietrich Albrecht Geeh, whom Garthe admitted to knowing, author of indiscreet letters about indiscreet literary practices, came into conflict repeatedly with the Cassel police during the 1830s and 1840s over the products of his print shop. "Pamphleteering is about the only thing," he wrote in one of his letters to Kunze, his correspondent in Mainz, "that still might have an impact" on public opinion.[17] It could have been Geeh's motto.

Geeh's confrontations with the police were not just legal, they were physical too. He would bar his door, the police would force their way in, and he would end up on the docket in criminal trials where the struggle continued. For a time in court it was a three-sided joust. Geeh on trial did not deny the things the police knew he had done, he only argued that under constitutional law he was entitled to print, publish, and distribute whatever he wanted. The government urged the judges to allow none of this but to punish Geeh for disrespectful, disobedient actions that endangered the established order. The third player, the Hessian judiciary, set limits, at least during 1832 and 1833, on the government's claim to police its subject Geeh on the basis of traditional authority beyond the boundaries established by modern constitutional law.

This triangular battling over what Geeh could print in Cassel typified the efforts of Germans to come to terms with changes in political culture signaled by written constitutions and changes in literary culture signaled by mass literacy and the growth of an inexpensive periodical and pamphlet literature. In the short term, the Hessian courts adhering conservatively to the law helped to keep Geeh free; but inevitably the administration and the judiciary learned to agree and Geeh went to jail. The space that had been created in the triangle—at its corners Geeh who only wanted liberty, a regime that only wanted obedience, and constitution-minded jurists who only wanted lawful conduct—collapsed as the courts went over to the side of the government.

Of all the printers in the principality during the 1830s and 1840s (twenty-five in 1842 operated a total of sixty presses), Geeh was among the busiest and the most ambitious. He became the most notorious. He was a man who always had a new idea, always wanted to start a new enterprise.

This most daring of Hessian bookmen never had a bookshop in Cassel, although he once had sought to establish one. In 1829, he informed local authorities that, in his opinion, because the trade in books was not organized into a guild and because as a printer he belonged already to the community of shopkeepers in Cassel, he was entitled to sell books if he wanted. Like Noa Elwert in Marburg, Geeh knew all about the laws and regulations that governed the book trade; beginning in 1831 he would know just as much about the new constitution; and he meant to use laws, regulations, and the constitution to his advantage. The Interior Ministry rejected Geeh's claim in 1829 to a place in the booksellers' trade, telling him that it was "too important to be left entirely to itself, wholly open to unrestricted competition." So he continued to make his living as a printer.[18]

Geeh became notorious as the editor and sometime printer of the *Friend of the Constitution,* Cassel's voice of the liberal political opposition during 1831–34. Except with that one controversial, short-lived daily newspaper, his efforts during the decade of the thirties to extend his business beyond the print shop halted at bureaucratic roadblocks that the government put in his way. In 1833, he asked for permission to issue a new periodical on behalf of a Popular Federation for Industry, Commerce, and Iron (*Bund der Völker für Gewerbe, Handel und Eisen*), with the purpose, he said, of reporting on economic policies of the German Confederation, informing the public about the progress of railways, and providing news on other sorts of commerce. The government was already having trouble keeping the *Friend of the Constitution* under some control; it was not foolish enough to allow Geeh more publications that could easily turn political, so it denied the request. In 1834, the Interior Ministry reminded Geeh that printing and selling books were not the same thing, and selling books was something he was not allowed to do.[19]

When Geeh's legal troubles began, unlike the sheltered Noa Elwert, he had no high-placed friends, and there were no ambiguities about what he had done of the sort that kept Christian Dietrich Garthe out of jail. Karl Bernhardi, hidden sponsor of the *Friend of the Constitution,* never had the influence in government circles that Elwert's patrons had. For Bernhardi to speak up on Geeh's behalf, anyway, would have been incompatible with the silence he kept about his own influence on the newspaper. In Geeh's long legal troubles, spanning more than ten years, he was on his own.

Geeh's life as a criminal began with fines in police court for censorship infractions during 1832. He had been printing unauthorized items in the *Friend of the Constitution.* In this first round, he appealed a fine of twenty taler to the Hessian Supreme Court, which invalidated it because at the police "trial" of Geeh, only one member of the police commission had been there, interrogated him, and passed sentence. It was a limited victory for the bookman. While forcing the government to observe the rule of law (a concern that the judges shared with Christoph von Rommel on the Censorship Commission, Sylvester Jordan, and many other delegates to the legislative assembly), the court also charged Geeh the court costs, an unusual gesture.[20]

Meanwhile, the Cassel police spotted more violations of censorship regulations in the *Friend of the Constitution* and instituted new proceedings against Geeh. With two commissioners present now at his interrogations (one questioning him, the other sitting across the room tending to other business), they found him guilty again and fined him twenty taler. The Supreme Court upheld this verdict. Still, the judges showed Geeh some sympathy, halving the fine because they thought he honestly believed that he had done what the law required.[21]

Geeh was not chastened or grateful but emboldened. He lithographed sheets with articles and portions of articles from the *Friend of the Constitution* that the censor had stricken, arguing that lithography was not printing and so was not subject to regulation. The police commission disagreed and this time decided to jail him. Again Geeh appealed. Again he lost.

Altogether in three decisions handed down during late January and early February 1833, the Hessian Supreme Court rejected all of Geeh's arguments: that there had to be limitations on censorship, that administration (the police commission) and justice (its sittings as an investigatory court) were not separate as the constitution mandated, that the constitutional guarantee of a free press was valid even without enabling legislation, that a petition to the legislature that he printed had already been signed by more than one thousand Hessians and read aloud in the assembly chamber before he printed it, that lithography was not quite printing. Geeh's sentences, in December 1832 and again in January 1833, to two-month terms in jail withstood all appeals.[22]

By the next summer, Geeh was out of jail and in trouble again. He had a new project for 1833, as compiler of a book, long enough to escape precensorship, on the legislative session that opened that spring. The Interior Ministry, informed about the book and its criticisms of politics in Hesse, insisted that it not be published.

On 4 June 1833, the police appeared at Geeh's house to take from him the entire stock of one thousand copies, printed and ready for sale. He resisted by locking his doors and announcing that he would answer force with force, even if it meant shooting or stabbing officers of the law. The police went away but came back the next day and took the books. The following autumn Geeh was in Cassel Superior

Court seeking remedy for the confiscation. The judges agreed with him that because the book was longer than twenty sheets it was exempt from censorship before publication and the police had to give it back. They did, reluctantly, then waited only one month—while Geeh added more, newly printed, sheets of material updating the book—and confiscated the whole lot again.

Geeh's book, expanded from its original twenty sheets to thirty-five sheets, was made up mostly of reprinted legislative documents. Only fourteen sheets were original materials. Because of unoriginality, the government argued this second time around that he was liable after all for violating the law that publications of fewer than twenty sheets had to be censored before printing. That reasoning suited the Cassel Superior Court, which sentenced Geeh to five months imprisonment, commuted to three months on appeal to the Hessian Supreme Court. These decisions like many court matters took a long time, and came in January and December 1837.[23]

In 1834, what had been local matters, as much about the government's efforts to police censors and legislators as about Geeh and with penalties that were surely unpleasant but still modest, all turned serious when the Confederal Investigatory Bureau established that year at Mainz sent word to Cassel that the printer Geeh had revolutionary connections in other parts of Germany. Information from letters, including Geeh's, in the possession of the Frankfort publicist, Friedrich Oehler, who was under arrest by the confederation, revealed that Geeh and the bookseller König in Hanau were distributing revolutionary literature.

Now more trials followed, ending in harsh sentences. The moderating role that Hesse-Cassel's judiciary had played for two years gave way to a hard line. Judges took months and years to act on Geeh's petitions to reconsider his convictions. Like Sylvester Jordan, he became a captive of interminable proceedings.

Two days after word of Geeh's involvement reached Cassel, the police director ordered a search of his house. At eight o'clock on the morning of 14 October 1834, five police officers arrived. They stayed for seven hours, sorting through Geeh's papers, and when they left in the afternoon, they took with them nearly three dozen pamphlets on German nationalism, politics in Hesse-Cassel, French constitutionalism, and Polish nationalism. Geeh had objected in the morning that this search was illegal and announced that he was leaving to inform his lawyer. The police arrested him. The lawyer arrived, wanting to know the grounds for Geeh's arrest, but was told that he would learn in good time.[24]

From Geeh's papers and from interrogating him, the police confirmed their tip from the confederation. Geeh was conspiring with booksellers in Frankfort and Mainz to distribute illegal pamphlets. One of his letters to Oehler in Frankfort made it apparent that the conspirators feared as early as the summer of 1832 that agents of the law were close to finding them out. "Geeh had just received a frightened communication [in the Investigatory Bureau's paraphrase] from the Metzler bookshop in Stuttgart. As a result, Oehler could have at his disposal one hundred copies of the pamphlet [*Deutschlands Juli Ordonanzen* (Germany's July Ordinances)] that had been sent to the Stuttgart shop. The fifteen taler to the organization, which Oehler would pay for them, should be sent to Geeh immediately." But despite this scare, their secret held well. It would be two more years before the German governments knew that Geeh had been the source of the pamphlet. Too late to prevent its distribution, in 1834, they knew by Geeh's own admission that hundreds of copies of it had gone to booksellers Oehler, Körner, and Meidinger in Frankfort, König in Hanau, Metzler in Stuttgart, Kunze in Mainz, and Oswald in Heidelberg, as well as to book printer Schneider in Frankfort.[25]

Again prosecution of Geeh proceeded very slowly. In November 1838, four years after his arrest, the Cassel Superior Court finally convicted him. For illegally publishing several pamphlets, especially the *July Ordinances* and *Blick auf Kurhessen im Augenblick der Auflösung seines Landtags, am 26. Juli 1832* (A Look at Hesse-Cassel at the Moment of Dissolution of Its Legislature on July 26, 1832), for "founding or at least participating in a secret political organization for the printing and distribution of revolutionary writings in circumvention of the censors," for insulting the German Confederation and the German states, showing disrespect for rulers, and stirring up discontent, Geeh was sentenced to ten months in prison.[26]

Consideration of his appeal took four more years, a delay that inconvenienced the government too. In October 1840, the Justice Ministry was asking that the Hessian Supreme Court return papers that the ministry had furnished a year earlier because it needed them for other investigations. But it was not until June 1842 that the higher court handed down its decision, upholding Geeh's sentence.

In formulating the appeal, Geeh's attorney had denied very little about the charges. Admittedly, there was a "dangerous tendency" in the pamphlets, but what they contained were mere opinions, protected under article thirty-nine of the Hessian constitution. As for the fact that Geeh, in one pamphlet, had labeled the Confederal Assembly a "servant of princes" (*Fürstendiener*), a statement that raised the prosecutor's ire, it was only the truth because the German people had no representation in the Frankfort meetings of the confederation. "Who will deny," Geeh's appellate brief asked the judges, "that the [confederal] decrees [of 28 June 1832] could lead to an unrestricted princely despotism, cripple the independence and effectiveness of the estates assembled in the exercise of their constitutional responsibilities, and infringe upon the people's rights and freedoms that even confederal law recognizes?"

The judges, though, were asking themselves different questions. They were not deciding the case to respect the niceties of constitutional law but to suppress subversion. There had been a secret organization. Geeh had belonged to it. Citing an imperial police ordinance of 1577 that forbade attacks on the government, the court quashed Geeh's appeal.[27]

Did bookmen conspire with each other? Some surely did, as Geeh's papers showed. His contact in Hanau, bookseller Friedrich König, was active in a constitutional society formed during the summer of 1832, the Hanau Society for Maintenance of [sometimes Adherence to] the Constitution (Hanauer Verein zur Aufrechterhaltung [Beobachtung] der Verfassung), whose members wrote and distributed the petition, *Public Declaration of Hessian Citizens*. As a result, thirteen of them, including König, stood trial before the Hanau Superior Court and early in 1834 received prison sentences of between eight days and eight months for incitement to rebellion. König's sentence was five months.

Copies of the petition appeared in Marburg shortly after its publication, one in the hands of the apothecary Döring. It was this connection among others that the police were chasing when they interrogated Garthe. In Garthe's visit with Döring to Butzbach where Garthe said they met the teacher Merz from Hanau, in his receipt of the mysterious request to print things evidently for someone in Hanau, in his dealings with Fischer in Wiesbaden, in his admission that he knew Geeh in Cassel, the police sought one web of ill-minded men. In Cassel, they had found a web and decided that its spider was Geeh.

König of Hanau was not so much a spinner of conspiratorial webs as one of the drones in a busy nest of political hornets, stinging the government in Cassel and the confederation in Frankfort with their liberal politicking. How influential each of them was can be gauged from the lengths of the sentences they received on 1 March 1834 for their uncensored petition. The teacher Merz got five months, a term just as long as König's. Dr. Denhard, whose name would appear repeatedly in police reports about liberal activities, earned six months imprisonment, whereas Administrative Councilor Emmerich got the longest term of all, eight months.

König had other encounters with the law. He enriched the police coffers by twenty taler, the fine he had to pay for accepting from Geeh thirty-nine copies of *Germany's July Ordinances,* all of them lacking the name of the publisher and the place of publication that confederal law required. He was the printer of a *Protestation deutscher Bürger gegen die Preßsklaverei in Deutschland* (Protest by German Citizens Against the Press Slavery in Germany) that appeared at about the same time as the *Public Declaration,* discussed the same concerns, and had some of the same signatories from Hanau, joined this time by inhabitants of neighboring states as well. But there were so many liberals and democrats in Hanau, that even if König had been as well behaved as Noa Elwert in Marburg, the government in Cassel would have had just as much trouble in its most troublesome town.[28]

A man in a like position, helpful but not indispensable to opponents of the government, was Professor Karl Bayrhoffer, who operated a bookshop in Marburg and got into trouble in the 1840s for his publicity on behalf of religious dissenters, a controversy that was as much political as theological. Bayrhoffer lectured on *Das wahre Wesen der gegenwärtigen religiösen Reformation in Deutschland* (The Truth About the Current Religious Reformation in Germany) at the university in 1846, then printed it in his shop as a pamphlet, which he presented free of charge to 124 persons in Marburg. The police went around and confiscated them along with other copies still in the shop, 217 in all. A ban on the work came two weeks later on 23 October 1846. In Fulda, the police got another five copies from the bookseller Henkel.[29] It was a large cache for a single censored publication. Even before the confiscation, Bayrhoffer had been in great trouble.

The government had an easier method for disciplining him than private booksellers because he was a civil servant. It could penalize him without going to criminal court or even police court. In July 1846, for his activities on behalf of dissenting churches of Hesse, the Interior Ministry fined the professor forty taler and ordered him to desist. He ignored the order, attended another meeting of the Protestant Friends of Reform (Protestantische Reformfreunde), and within less than two weeks had earned himself another administrative fine of forty taler.

Bayrhoffer obtained a hearing on these administrative decisions before the Marburg Superior Court, where he objected that the fines were contrary to article sixty of the constitution that "no condition of government employment may require something contrary to the laws." "By no means," he insisted, "have I, in return for my state appointment, forfeited the freedom of the individual guaranteed to everyone through article thirty-one of the constitution." The Interior Ministry's rebuttal was that "service to the state and a public professorship entails a high degree of respect for and an obligation to remain faithful, obedient, and attentive to the government and its will, in one's conduct both within and without the immediate exercise of such an appointment." Once again, the word of law was to bow down before the voice of tradition.

Bayrhoffer wanted the discussion in these civil court hearings to be about the Hessian constitution, just as Geeh wanted in his criminal trials. Bayrhoffer cited articles thirty-nine guaranteeing freedom of opinion, thirty guaranteeing freedom of creed and religion, and thirty-five guaranteeing freedom of petition to no avail. The Marburg court concurred with the ministry. The university allowed for "a broad degree of free movement in scholarly speculations," but Bayrhoffer had gone too far. He was "injuring his academic office" through his public appearances and published writings. The case was left on continuation for more than a year. Then, late in 1847, the judges announced that they would not reconsider their decision. Guarantees in the constitution, especially of religious freedom, they announced, were limited insofar as the constitution "did not authorize the inhabitants of the electoral principality to join together in the exercise of their rights."[30]

By then the courts, the police, and the Interior Ministry all knew very well that Hessians were joining together, bookmen, professors and other men in the professions, civil servants, and tradesmen alike—plotters, schemers, and simple dreamers—trying to exercise their constitutional rights. Bookmen were cooperators and facilitators as often as they were conspirators in these liberal communities. Although the police tried to single them out as culprits in the spread of dangerous ideas, they were not alone. Even in the loneliness of an interrogation room, behind them stood participants in a community, sometimes visible, sometimes deep in the shadows, but always there. Behind Bayrhoffer stood Protestant dissidents; behind Geeh stood sponsors and readers of the *Friend of the Constitution;* behind Garthe stood shadows without names; behind König stood a civic association that included some of the leading men of Hanau. Every effort to harness the bookmen of Hesse only revealed that a broad German-wide sentiment for a new politics was pushing out of kilter the traditional, paternalist system of policing in which censorship had come to play such a large part.

NINE

Friends of a Free Press
The Readers of Banned Writ

Who read the sorts of censorious literature that Dietrich Albrecht Geeh printed and distributed to booksellers, that Christian Garthe sold in quantity, that Noa Elwert may have known everything or nothing about? How did bad writings come into the hands of readers other than through these bookmen? The second question is easier to answer than the first.

Every traveler on the roads of Germany a century and a half ago, every package in transit then, might have harbored the literature of political subversion, moral degeneracy, and religious heresy. The police knew from experience that bad pamphlets could be hand-carried on a stage coach, stowed in a peddler's sack, sent through the mail, hidden among other wares and in hats, shoes, and clothing. Once they turned up in a wagon loaded with leeches bound from Hungary to France; another time they were in a shipment of wine from Philadelphia.

Now and then hidden along with the literature would be a little note telling the recipients what to do with it. "We direct your attention particularly to . . . [this] pamphlet," read one that the police in Fulda found at Euler's bookshop among copies of something called *Scherz und Ernst zur Lust und Lehre in einer trüben Zeit* (Jollity and Gravity to Instruct and Regale You in These Dreary Times). "It is certain to be well received among the free-thinking public. At the same time, we ask, for good reason, that it be distributed AS QUICKLY AS POSSIBLE." That was in 1833. The previous year, also in Fulda, the police had come upon this: "The German Fatherland's Union of Zweibrücken asks that these sheets [something printed, not with the note anymore] not be laid aside and neglected, because they contain important things for honest Germans who are friends of a free press."[1]

The mail would seem an unlikely conveyance for the literary underground, given that throughout Germany the police commonly monitored post offices. Still, some pamphlets came across the border that way. In 1819, Hessian officials tried hard to discover the source of the revolutionary *Little Book of Questions and Answers* by examining postmarks and quizzing local inhabitants who had received it by post, but the investigation led nowhere. Only statements made by the author, Wilhelm Schulz, after his arrest six months later, solved the mystery.[2]

Items that arrived by some other path without postmarks often provided no way to identify their sources. While booksellers told the police that they had sold their wares to unknown strangers passing through town, who paid cash and were never seen again, townspeople talked as if the literature in their hands had appeared mysteriously at their feet. It might as well have fallen out of the sky. Who was to say it had not?

In 1836, a Marburg shoemaker, Georg Reinhardt Pfau, having come upon a pamphlet "in support of the subjects of Nassau" on Barfüßertor, a principal street, brought it to the police, a common reaction of ordinary people to extraordinary writings, particularly in the countryside. Near Marburg in 1836 the gendarmerie reported having found a letter allegedly written by "Adam Frank" in North America urging emigration. In fact, it was the creation of a democratic group in the Odenwald area of the grand duchy of Hesse-Darmstadt. A Marburg gatekeeper in 1846 turned in a small pamphlet that he found, the *Evangelium eines armen Sünders* (Evangel of a Poor Sinner). And the following year at Sterbfritz near Hanau, gendarmes took from a local man an *Allgemeine Beschreibung der Ende und Ihrer Bewohner* (General Description of the Ends and Their Inhabitants). Where had they all come from? No one knew.[3]

These would-be readers had made no effort to conceal what they found from the police. The police did not suspect that any of them wanted to possess or spread bad literature either. In the case of Pfau, police cleared him quickly and moved on to check the guest logs of local inns in a vain attempt to find the responsible person. As so often, they presumed it was some outsider.

There were always travelers underway from somewhere, there always had been, and among them were some who scattered pamphlet literature as they went, some of it dangerous, intellectual seed corn. These travelers were not a single type, though, which complicated trying to spot them. The police in Melsungen near Cassel stopped Johann Georg Weiwadel and his wife, peddlers by trade from

Ehringen in Württemberg, as they passed through in March 1822 selling all sorts of books and pamphlets door-to-door off their backs. They were carrying almost two hundred volumes: twelve popular novels, as many religious dramas, fifteen works of history and geography, eight erotica, and six assorted others—sixty or seventy titles altogether, about three copies of each title. The police confiscated a half-dozen books, including some of each variety.[4]

Another distributor, apparently benign, was apprehended later in the 1820s at Witzenhausen. Michael Baumgarten, a Jew converted to Christianity, was traveling home to Russian Poland from a monastery in the Westfalian town of Wuppertal, where a clergyman, he said when questioned, had given him a large number of "little pietistic printed works," as the police described them. He admitted to having given away some two hundred of them already. The police took the fifty-nine he had left, then sent him on his way.[5]

These sorts of transients, and the sure fact that there were more, may have worried the authorities, but nothing could be done about them. During the 1810s and 1820s came recurring directives about them—recurring because they were ineffective. One from the bailiff of Allendorf in Lower Hesse instructed nearby village leaders, "In the event that peddlers of posters, books, or song sheets appear in your community wishing to sell their wares, you are to take responsibility for ensuring that they are kept out unless they are able to present written permission from this office, and at the expiration of such permit, you are to send them out of your district." Other directives called for reports on whether organ grinders were selling immoral printed song sheets or warned more generally about immoral and irreligious songs, tales, and posters.[6]

In the 1830s, the tenor of these directives to watch for strangers changed. Before, they had been aimed at the strangers themselves, who had always been regarded suspiciously, whatever their reasons for being in Hesse. Now, the directives warned of political trouble imported from abroad. Before, the worry had been about the persons; now, it was about the ideas that came with them printed on paper. One report late in 1834 warned county councilors to watch for commercial travelers, who it said had become primary agents for spreading political pamphlets. In another message five weeks later, the Interior Ministry warned officials in the towns of the principality that "foreign revolutionaries and ambassadors of propaganda, who of late have feared being searched on the German border, are employing doubled tops in their hats and concealing papers in them, and achieving similar effects with the soles of their shoes."[7]

It was always easier to collect these sorts of stories than to snare the men they were about. When the *Six Commandments of the German Confederal Assembly* cropped up at Gelnhausen in 1832 along with flyers by Jakob Förster—three months after a ban on all of Förster's works—police learned that a traveler had distributed them during a coach ride, but they failed to catch up with him. In the same year, authorities at Schmalkalden reported a traveler who had passed out an inflammatory work that read roughly, "the hour had to be seized, and when the revolution broke out it was necessary to drive out the princes and fight for freedom." A search for him was unsuccessful too.

Thirteen years later, in 1845, came the oddest report of another stranger, riding from Fulda to Hersfeld with the post coach, telling toll officers at some stops along the way that he was "Sadlavio, bishop of Cologne," while identifying himself to others as the bishop of Fulda. His behavior was as outrageous as his persona. He refused to pay the tolls, did not tip the postilions, and handed out an (unidentified) printed text to other travelers. As long as a "Sadlavio" could travel the roads of Hesse unimpeded, the task of keeping undesirable writings away from the subjects of the prince-elector was surely out of control.[8]

Keeping banned books out was like keeping water in a sieve. Everywhere, the stuff leaked in. A forbidden text, *Aberglauben, Eigennutz, Kleinmuth: Ein Predigt gehalten zu Niederkirchen am Osterfeste 1832* (Superstition, Selfishness, Cowardice: A Sermon Delivered at Niederkirchen at Easter Mass 1832), by Pastor Karl Juch, spread in Cassel because Dietrich Albrecht Geeh sold it there. It appeared in Fritzlar where a stranger on foot offered it for sale. In Witzenhausen it turned up in the hands of a retired district tax agent and a shopkeeper—no one said how they had gotten it. The gendarmerie in Witzenhausen seemed unconcerned anyway because both men were "good burghers."[9] So often, when police found banned writ in the hands of Hessians, the possessors were good burghers, not strangers paying cash, but the regular customers of local booksellers, people who bought their reading on credit, who were native, known, and reliable, and so the police treated them gently. The old-fashioned excoriation of travelers from abroad as the source of most literary menaces and an equally old-fashioned trust in familiar persons were slow to die. It was a commonplace, and one of the merrier occurrences in this often gloomy story of political and literary repression, to give homegrown readers of forbidden literature good reports that kept them out of trouble, whatever they possessed. Repeatedly, bailiffs and police officers told of good burghers, "above suspicion," found holding bad publications. A favorable word from some local authority, perhaps with reference to their social standing too, was all that it took to protect many men from the suspicion that they might have had anything untoward to do with the literature that was their own.

Moreover, in a society where the educated elite was small, persons of all political points of view were bound to know each other. Often they socialized with each other. They might even tell each other of their literary ambitions, as when the republican poet Hoffmann von Fallersleben on a visit to the conservative grammar school master Vilmar in Marburg told how he hoped to sneak his next volume of poems past the censors and police for a while at least by entitling them *Unpolitical Verses*.[10] Had the Hessian police known this, would they have arrested Vilmar when Hoffmann's collection did appear with that title, was banned, but sold twelve thousand copies in Germany nonetheless? Surely not. Vilmar was the model of a good burgher, regardless of who visited him and what was said.

There was nothing exceptional about hometown trustfulness. It was a part of the same set of hopes and assumptions that allowed Karl Bernhardi to be a censor in the 1830s although as a student a decade earlier he had been active in the forbidden German nationalist cause and, even more remarkably, allowed him to be a censor while he quietly sponsored a newspaper in Cassel, the *Friend of the Constitution,* which was often in trouble for its censorship infractions. The same system allowed Noa Elwert to conduct business unhindered, while his presses, run by his employees if not by him, printed subversive literature. Such frequent lack of suspicion was right not only for men who lived next door to each other in their hometowns but also for a government that clung so long to its paternal point of view, that only slowly and reluctantly abandoned the safe and certain belief that anonymous agents of subversion through literature could only be intruders from without, not traitors from within. Police, administrators, and diplomats who tried to understand the spread of banned literature this way went on and on with investigations aimed at grand conspiracies (there were some, of course), while the culprits operated right under their official noses in communities where everyone, the enforcers and the violators, knew each other.

In the summer of 1832, Hessian customs officers on the border with Frankfort took a large cache of flyers and song sheets, with "contents inciting rebellion," off a produce wagon. They were in one of several packets that the driver had picked up at a Frankfort hostelry for delivery in Gelnhausen, a town close by. "To Mr. Georg Messinger, Master Butcher in Gelnhausen, Printed Matter Enclosed, Free," read the wrapping. Inside was an unsigned letter, three copies of the *Public Declaration of Hessian Citizens,* thirteen of *Der deutsche Mai* (The German May), thirty-two of a song entitled *Das deutsche Treibjagd* (The German Battering Ram), and twenty-five of *The Six Commandments of the German Confederal Assembly.* Only three days earlier police in Marburg had taken the *Public Declaration* from Friedrich Döring. Within one month, all four of the pamphlets and flyers found on the Frankfort-to-Gelnhausen wagon would be banned in Hesse-Cassel.

The next day news came from Gelnhausen that "Mäsinger" [sic], twenty-nine years old and resident there for the past two years, denied any knowledge of the packet. Furthermore, he was "a man above suspicion." The police did nothing more about him, but the Hessian government launched an investigation that included diplomatic inquiries to Frankfort and neighboring Bavaria, on the suspicion that the printing had been done in one of those places. In Hanau, several respectable citizens would end up in jail for their roles in preparing the *Public Declaration.* Nine years later, the matter was still open enough that when Munich police found a copy of the *Six Commandments* among the papers of a medical student, Wilhelm Hofbauer, they went to the trouble of comparing his handwriting with the decade-old letter to Messinger but could not decide whether Hofbauer had written it.[11]

Another confiscation in 1835 followed an equally inconclusive course. At Witzenhausen, customs officials found *Die neuesten Bundesbeschlüsse in Deutschland* (The Newest Confederal Decrees in Germany) as well as copies of an *Amerikanische-Deutsche Zeitung* (American-German Gazette) in a wine shipment from Philadelphia, of all places. The addressee, said officials in rural Saxony where he lived, was an ignorant peasant, but he had a son who had emigrated recently to America. Police cleared the peasant father of any suspicion, but this time too, the investigation went on through diplomatic channels—even the governor of Graz in faraway Austria was warned of "highly inflammatory" literature being smuggled in wine shipments through the electoral principality of Hesse.[12]

One year earlier, Hessian tolltakers on the Frankfort border had found two issues of Philipp Siebenpfeiffer's journal, *Deutschland* (Germany), among clothing going to a journeyman printer working in Erfurt. It turned out that the journeyman, Wilhelm Rode, from a Hessian village near the town of Homberg, had worked for the printer of the journal, who was always giving him complimentary copies of it. Erfurt officials declared that Rode had a good record—his apprentice's passbook *(Wanderbuch)* showed that—so no one pursued the case further.[13]

Again and again, the presumption of the police was that good faith nestled in the hearts of those to whom political literature was addressed. Sometimes the police knew so little about what was going on just because they believed so much of what they were told. In early May 1831, the Marburg police reported to Cassel that they were having no success locating a pamphlet entitled *Der erste Mai* (The First of May), which they knew had circulated in Hesse the previous month. They had tried to get it through local booksellers, but Garthe told them it had not been distributed through bookshops at all. That almost matched the story out of Hanau, where police related, "The bookseller König here . . . insists that the numerous copies he got . . . directly from Strasbourg, he declined to retail." But soon Marburg officials did procure a copy of it from a private citizen whom they chose not to name and who, they assured the Interior Ministry, "is a dignitary and above all suspicion."[14]

At that early date, had the possibility of collusion, even among booksellers, not yet occurred to authorities in Hesse? Perhaps not. They were yet to come across those little pieces of paper that the Fulda police would find in 1832 and 1833 hidden among pamphlets, which in turn might be hidden among other wares, telling the receivers to dispose of the goods quickly—the sorts of discoveries that allowed for no interpretation except that somewhere men were conspiring to spread subversive literature. A law student in Fulda named Kirchner obliged the wish of the anonymous authors of *Jollity and Gravity* "that it be distributed AS QUICKLY AS POSSIBLE," by buying a copy that he sent on to a friend in Marburg. *Deutschlands Juli Ordonanzen* (Germany's July Ordinances) of 1832 also came to Marburg through the post, sent by Dr. Denhard in Hanau, a member of the Association for Maintenance of the Constitution there. Another member of the same association was the bookseller König, who had gotten the pamphlet from Dietrich Geeh in Cassel.[15] Policing such a lot of private traffic in literature was well-nigh impossible.

Across Hesse-Cassel, friends like these were keeping each other informed and supplied with the latest political writings. Kirchner and Denhard, it would seem, were typical private correspondents on the news of the day, typical buyers of controversial books and pamphlets, because they were educated men. Students and graduates, professional persons, exactly the "prominent persons" *(Prominenzen),* whom the police in Marburg and other towns so often wanted to keep above suspicion, were the common carriers of subversion. Denhard of Hanau, a doctor of philosophy then twenty-three years old, involuntarily dropped out of the private network for distributing political literature soon after his mailing to Marburg. As a defendant along with Friedrich König in the *Public Declaration* trial in Hanau, Denhard was sentenced to seven months in prison, longer than all but two of the other Hanau burghers. It was his reward for having written the first draft of the petition.[16]

Just such respectable, educated persons had been the masterminds also of a work entitled *Die neue Welt entdeckt in 1830* (The New World Discovered in 1830), which in sixty-seven pages attacked the prince-elector, his government, and the church. Fulda police confiscated more than fifty copies of it in September 1831 after a local day laborer named Meier brought them six. Meier related how he had been called earlier in the day to the home of a schoolteacher named Wiesen and how two young men there had given him twenty-six copies of the pamphlet with the addresses to which he was to deliver them. But after starting to hand them out, he had become concerned about what was in them, he said, returned some of them to the house where he had gotten them and brought the rest to the police. Meier's employers were Franz Schell, a priest later to be a much-despised, very literate advocate of the rationalist, anti-Roman "German Catholic" movement, and Dr. Gartenhof, the son of a deceased school teacher.

Wiesen, the homeowner, was away. Schell could not be found. The police turned their attention to Gartenhof.

Interviewed by the police, Gartenhof told them that fifteen hundred copies of *The New World*, "his pamphlet" as he called it, had been produced in two printings at Strasbourg and Frankfort. He, the author, had bought only thirty copies of it, he insisted. This claim quickly proved false, as the same day the police took from the widow of the Fulda lyceum's custodian three dozen more copies in a packet that Gartenhof had left with her for safekeeping.

Two days after his arrest, Gartenhof registered a complaint, citing the constitutional guarantee to free opinions and claiming that he had a right to keep the pamphlet because it was his own property. He insisted further that to distribute what he had written himself was not in violation of any Hessian law. The local judiciary had other concerns, though, and Gartenhof got a four-month jail sentence for the attacks on authority in his pamphlet.[17]

Knowing that many copies of a forbidden work had been sold, even knowing who had sold them, allowed the police to put the culprit on trial; still, it left them with the troublesome task of trying to find out who the purchasers were. The effort was rarely successful. The works of Dr. Gartenhof's collaborator Franz Schell, for example, had a very large market in Fulda and sold rather well in other Hessian towns too. Before the censors and police intervened, the bookseller Euler in Fulda sold 117 copies of *Mein Austritt* (My Resignation) and the proprietor of Fulda's other bookshop, Henkel, sold "many" more. *Das alte und neue Hohepriesterthum* (The Old and New High Priesthood) brought eighteen sales for Euler and "many" again for Henkel. Schell's *Offenes Sendschreiben* (Open Letter) totaled twenty-one sales between the two dealers. Yet for all three works, the police only knew of one reader, a merchant named Kalb in the nearby town of Hünfeld.

Euler reported that he sold about two dozen copies of *Neuer Angriff auf das ständische Bewilligungsrecht* (A New Attack Against the Right of Consent by the Estates), an anonymous work of local political interest, two or three weeks before the police visited to tell him that it was banned. But who the buyers were, he did not want to say, and no one made him.[18]

For all of the 1830s and 1840s, there are just four notations in police records about Euler's customers. In 1833, he sold copies of *Jollity and Gravity* to the Hanau publicist Jakob Förster, to Professor Wagner of Marburg, and to the student Kirchner, who, as noted, then sent it to Marburg. Eleven years later, Euler sold a copy of *Württemberg im Jahre 1844* (Württemberg in 1844) to Superior Court Judge König, and Heinrich Heine's *Neue Gedichte* (New Verses) to Privy Councilor Merz, who the following year was also reading another forbidden publication, *Der Grenzbote* (The Frontier Courier), which Merz had borrowed from Euler and then handed to the police.[19] These four eminent citizens—a judge, a professor, a civil servant, and a student—were they typical readers of subversive literature?

It would seem from the scattered hints that there are about readership that they were. Information on readers of all sorts of literature in the first half of the nineteenth century is sparse, and it is a subject better investigated in large German cities, where the concentration of prosperous people has left enough materials to piece together collages of literate culture.[20] In Hesse, there were no such large cities. Still, there are clues, chiefly lists drawn up for subscription publications and lists of members of civic clubs, giving in both cases each person's craft or profession *(Stand)* along with the surname.

The pamphlets . . . *zunächst für die Leser des Teutschen Volksblatts* (. . . most of all for the Readers of the *German National News*) with which Jakob Förster tried to evade the ban on his journal, went to more than eighty subscribers in Fulda, and additional copies appeared in Marburg. The Fulda police drew up a list of recipients, whose occupations were varied but mostly within the range expected in a burgher community. There were three educators, four clergymen, seven other professionals, fifteen government councilors, twelve other civil servants, twelve merchants and shopkeepers, twelve innkeepers and taverners, one manufacturer, six clerks, two trainees, six craftsmen, and four widows. Most were learned men; others were from the middling mercantile classes; few were in the crafts.[21]

The *Volksblatt aus Würzburg* (People's Paper from Würzburg), which succeeded Förster's banned Hessian paper and was published in the more liberal climate of neighboring Bavaria, had three Hessian subscribers: a chief steward named Neumann and an agricultural manager named Wahler, both in Neuhof, and an innkeeper named Hunek in Hünfeld. Among Hessian subscribers to the *Weser Dampfboot* (Weser Steamboat), before it was banned, were an innkeeper named August Propping and a shopkeeper named Heuser in Rinteln. Nineteen persons in Cassel subscribed to the *Leipziger Lokomotive* (Leipzig Locomotive) before its prohibition in 1843, among them two assistants in the Central Post Office, three innkeepers, two shopkeepers, and the Cassel Police Directorate.[22] All but the police conducted businesses where people were likely to gather, read a newspaper that was lying out, and talk about what they read.

When it was announced that Cassel's troublesome printer Geeh would issue the *Travels of a German Free Spirit,* Dr. Gartenhof collected subscriptions in Fulda and its vicinity to guarantee sufficient sales. The list of persons who signed up ended with the Fulda police. It is a long list, with one hundred and eleven names. Only forty-two of them paid anything in advance; a mere nine paid in full. When the book appeared, some denied having subscribed at all. Beside many more names on the list was a simple notation, "does not want it." In the end, only about one-half of the original subscriptions were delivered and paid in full. A good many of those copies soon ended up with the police, for whom the list was very handy.

The *Travels* subscription list, even with its limitations, shows who would have read politics (and in 1833 all politics was controversial) in Hesse. On it are eight academics, six clergymen, three students, sixteen government councilors, fifteen other civil servants, three men in training for the civil service, one military officer, five merchants and shopkeepers, one innkeeper, one manufacturer, fourteen clerks, seven trainees in private employ, two craftsmen, two foresters, and seven others.[23] Most of them were in the government, in the professions, or preparing for them. Far fewer came from the mercantile and craft classes.

Outside Fulda, the closest comparable source of information on literate, political culture in Hesse is the records of clubs. There were a lot of clubs in Hesse-Cassel then, as there were all over Germany. Great spurts in the growth of civic, fraternal, and self-help organizations in central Europe had come in the last third of the eighteenth century, and then again during the 1820s. How big they were, how they functioned, who their members were—all differed from one club to the next. What they had in common was their impact on civic life as settings for reading literature in greater variety than all but a few men could have afforded for themselves. In an age without participatory political institutions, clubs broadened the availability of written works, and through them of political ideas to townspeople.

Some reading clubs in central Germany had very extensive libraries. A society in Würzburg subscribed to fifty-two periodicals in 1812. Another in Frankfort, just before the turn of the century, had had in its reading room seventy-one German periodicals, twelve French, four English, and two Italian.[24] The Casino Society (Casino-Gesellschaft), founded in 1803 in Cassel, spent nearly one-half of the large sum of four hundred taler that it collected in annual dues from its sixty members on journals, newspapers, and "useful writings."

The members of the Cassel Casino around 1820 included a teacher, a cook in the royal household, a chimney sweep, shopkeepers, manufacturers, two officers of the local police commission, and several dozen master craftsmen; its entry fee of eight taler and annual dues of six taler, payable in monthly installments of twelve groschen, were moderate enough that craftsmen could afford them, although not wage laborers. The members elected what to buy with their dues. "A vote shall be taken," read the Casino Society's by-laws of 1803, "to determine which papers, books for amusement and enlightenment, as well as other weekly and monthly publications, annuals, and so forth, shall be subscribed." It continued:

> The Director and Steering Committee will acquire them. The cost of these newspapers books may not exceed _____ [in 1818, 150] taler.
> These newspapers, books, and other written works shall be kept in an orderly fashion in the reading room. Every member shall be entitled to make use of them freely; however, it is expressly forbidden to take any of them home. The newspapers shall be bound in quarterly

volumes and preserved. When expressly requested, everyone shall refrain from reading aloud, so as not to disturb others present. Improper, confiscated, and polemical writings, books, and so forth, are to be kept out altogether.[25]

How revealing it would be to have some hints as well of what the members bought and read in Cassel, but there are none. These Würzburg, Frankfort, and Cassel clubs were establishments of relative literary luxury. It required far less—one sheet of current news, one man who could read it aloud, and interested listeners—to get political discussion going.

It was during the early 1830s, in Hesse as elsewhere in Germany, that clubs proliferated, diversified socially, and became political without losing their literary intentions. From that time, their interests and activities also got more attention from police, censors, and ministers of government.

At the end of 1831, the Marburg police reported to Cassel on the founding of a patriotic club, the Civic Association (Bürgerverein), which, the report went on to assure, did not appear to endanger the state. Two and one-half years later, another report described the same group as once very political but now just another club. Two banned publications had turned up at its meeting place in 1832, Jakob Förster's *National News* and the pamphlet *Germany's July Ordinances*, on which Geeh in Cassel and König in Fulda had collaborated. It was Friedrich Döring who distributed the *July Ordinances* in Marburg; indeed, he was said to have read it aloud at the Civic Association.[26]

Another, more controversial society in Marburg was the Academic Museum, founded in 1832 by and for professors and students of the university. A report of 1845 from Police Director W. H. Wangemann, Sylvester Jordan's interrogator, told that once thirty-three faculty members and eighty-four students had belonged. The prorector of the university wrote of more than three hundred members, half of them students. Either way, in a small university town it was a popular venue. The Academic Museum's home was a three-story building on Barfüßertor in the center of Marburg. Its membership, contrary to the original concept, came to include prominent citizens not affiliated with the university, among them Police Director Wangemann.[27] During his tenure as director in Marburg, from 1842 until the 1848 revolution, disputes over a portrait of Sylvester Jordan that hung in the club and a series of publications lauding the professor that were in the reading room, led finally to a government order that the club be shut down.

This local storm over the club, its reading material, and its political enthusiasms lasted the two years, 1844 and 1845, that Sylvester Jordan's conviction was under appeal to the Hessian Supreme Court. A subscription to the *Sächsische Vaterlandsblätter* (Saxon Fatherland's Report), banned once before in 1841, had to cease in 1844 when dispatches on Jordan's fate led Hessian officials to renewed alarm over the newspaper. The same year, police reported that someone had bought a copy of another periodical out of Saxony, *The Frontier Courier,* with an article about Jordan, and put it in the club's reading room. Lightning struck in 1845. In mid-December that year, nearly two months after the Hessian Supreme Court exonerated Jordan, a police official, acting on Wangemann's order, entered the Academic Museum and confiscated the *Illustrirte Zeitung* (Illustrated Gazette), yet another popular Saxon magazine, it too with a long article on the Jordan case.[28]

Members protested: according to the by-laws nothing was to be removed from the reading room without their approval. At the urging of Jordan himself and Karl Bayrhoffer, both members, both professors on very bad terms with local authorities, the club voted to expel Wangemann. "In its present constitution," the police chief wrote to his superiors in Cassel, "the club threatens to turn genuinely revolutionary." That was enough for the Interior Ministry; within two weeks it ordered the Academic Museum closed. A short time later some of the old members organized a New Museum, with official approval but on the condition that students not be full members.[29]

It was not the first time that there had been confiscations of the sort. In the summer of 1842, the Marburg police had taken Georg Herwegh's banned *Quick Man's Verses* from the Academic Museum. And Friedrich Murhard had written pointedly one decade earlier in his analysis of the Hessian constitution that "according to the unmistakable intent of article 117 [protecting citizens against house searches except with court warrants], it would be . . . absolutely unconstitutional for a police officer to go into a local reading institute and take away a newspaper belonging to the members without the knowledge and approval of the membership or at least of its directors."[30] He could only have been writing from experience.

Most club matters in Hesse were never as exciting as what went on at the Marburg Academic Museum, where the man assigned to enforce local allegiance to the traditional regime, Wangemann, and his nemesis, the most renowned challenger of the old order, Jordan, were members on equal footing. Yet there were organizations like it throughout the principality, in all of its main towns, and increasingly in smaller communities (much like the concurrent spread of lending libraries). Everywhere they encouraged reading that could not help but be political in an age when public life was becoming so thoroughly politicized.

At the village of Besse in the vicinity of Fritzlar during the mid-1830s, the postmaster organized a Farmer's Casino (Bauern-Casino) with twelve members, he by his own appointment being its director and "newspaper reviewer." The club had a target, Village Supervisor Knaust; so at least, Knaust reported. "The postmaster has even made noises in the local police court," Knaust wrote to the county office at Fritzlar, "about this farmers' assembly, but it seems for now insignificant and narrowly based." Even with Knaust's assurances, Fritzlar officials asked the Besse postmaster for a copy of his statutes with the remark that it seemed to them the group's intentions were "less socializing and far more discussion of matters concerning local government and the constitution." Nothing more came of it.[31]

There is scattered evidence of other civic associations that were active during the 1830s and 1840s. A Citizens' Club (Bürgerverein) organized in Cassel in the aftermath of the 1830 revolt. In 1832, a police report told of its members collecting funds to buy proconstitutional publications. At the Evening Club (Abendverein), also in Cassel, a copy of August Boden's *Third Volume* on behalf of Sylvester Jordan turned up in 1845, and the police confiscated it. An anonymous letter had told them that it was there. The bookseller Osterwald was one of the leaders (along with a forester, a court clerk, and an art instructor) of a club at Rinteln in 1834. At Rotenburg, midway between Cassel and Fulda, there was an Evening Society in 1844, known to history only because a local official found Boden's *Nachträge* (Supplement) on Jordan there.[32] At one time or another every sizable town in the principality had a place where residents gathered together, read politics, and talked about what they read.

The Hessian towns with the liveliest civic cultures in addition to Marburg were Fulda, Bockenheim, and Hanau. Cassel, as the seat of government, was a place that people with nationalist and liberal sentiments came to more than came from. Bockenheim was a problem for the government because it was so close to Frankfort with its liberal inhabitants and the conservative Confederal Assembly, together a volatile mix, and remote from Hanau, whence it should have been supervised. The town went pretty much its own way until the 1840s, producing unruly periodicals that caused complaint from Frankfort. The response of the Hessian government was to establish a deputation of the Hanau police directorate right in Bockenheim, a rare act, to exercise more control over local affairs.

An embarrassed report from the Hanau police to the Interior Ministry in May 1834 indicated how far out of hand matters were in Bockenheim. Yes, it admitted, the Press and Fatherland Society (Preß- und Vaterlandsverein), founded in the south German states by the notorious publicist August Wirth and banned throughout Germany, was meeting in Bockenheim. But how was anyone to have known, when the progressives *(Bewegungs-Parthei)* comprised five-sixths of the citizenry and had as their leaders both the mayor and a councilor representing the Cassel government.[33]

There is no reason to think that Hanau's own leaders really worried about the difficulty with Bockenheim; Hanau had its own liberal tradition. Sixty years earlier an unauthorized book fair had operated there, with renegade traders calling publicly for an end to preventive censorship while the organizers of the fair furnished space for the sale of illicit books. Emperor Joseph II suppressed the fair, but the burghers of Hanau continued to be progressive and independent minded. It was in Hanau that the Hessian disturbances of 1830 were most severe, and, after 1830, it was there that the discrepancy remained greatest between what censorship required and what, in fact, was published. It was there also that links were forged with liberals and nationalists in other German states to the south, forming a chain that carried undesirable political literature to other parts of Hesse-Cassel.[34]

The center of Hanau's liberalism was the Society for Maintenance of the Constitution, which met on Saturdays in a beer hall. It was at these weekend sessions, police learned, that the *Public Declaration of Citizens of Hesse-Cassel* had been born. The society's interests were very political. Only one day after a police order in 1832 banned further meetings, the members assembled to hear excerpts from a pro-constitutional journal, *Die Volkshalle* (The People's Chamber), read aloud by Administrative Councilor Emmerich, whose name later headed the list of defendants in the trial about the *Public Declaration*. Reminded that the society's meetings were now prohibited, the beer hall proprietor, Jacob Koch, himself a member, reminded the police that under the constitution such an order was illegal.

Other members of the society were also well versed in the rights to which they felt themselves entitled under the constitution that they had organized to defend. During the week after their first unauthorized meeting, Carl Wilhelm Schehl, a local goldsmith who had been there, cited articles 21, 31, 35, 60, 95, 153, 155, and 160 of the new constitution in his own defense during a police interview.

Dr. Denhard also cited the revered document while denying again and again that he belonged to a forbidden organization. At the next meeting of the society, several days later, Denhard brought along a copy of *Die Völkerstimmen* (The People Speak), which the police called very revolutionary. The society was still meeting in August 1832, three weeks after first being proscribed. Now the members confined themselves to reading from the Bible, but the police objected to that too because it was done merely to evade their order and a misuse of the Holy Book. Only the convictions meted out to thirteen of its leading members in criminal court finally shut down the club.[35]

At Fulda as well, many citizens were involved in proconstitutional activities during the early 1830s, and there, too, reading was central to their meetings. The Society of Fulda Citizens (Gesellschaft Fuldaer Bürger) had 160 members, the police reported to Cassel in 1832, each of them paying monthly dues of six kreuzer, or about one-twentieth of a taler, for the purchase of periodical literature. At that rate, the society had about one hundred taler available yearly, two-thirds as much as the Cassel Civic Casino had spent on its reading a dozen years earlier. But they were also very different organizations. The Cassel club brought together burghers reading quietly to themselves. The Fulda society drew from broader social strata, and, like the contemporary Hanau society, it held large public meetings, settings for reading out loud in a group, rather than silently and individually. Its spirit was political, not recreational.[36]

Two police informants reported on a November 1832 banquet of the Fulda Society, which twenty-three craftsmen attended out of forty-six persons there altogether. Eight merchants and innkeepers, seven men in the learned professions, three trainees including two for the civil service, one clerk, and four persons whose occupations were not identified made up the other half of the group. Its leadership, at least in 1832, was left to its most prominent members. The directors were the editor Jakob Förster, a physician, and the master of the post office horse stalls. Advising them was a committee that included two merchants, two superior court advocates, a physician, a watchmaker, a chandler, and an apothecary. It appears to have been much like a club for the educational improvement of handicraftsmen founded in Gießen in 1831 by two lawyers and a professor, known as Dr. Bansa's Reading Club (Leseklub), in which the organizers read to their political apprentices from *Der Westbote* (The Western Courier), a newspaper soon banned by the German Confederation.[37]

By the winter of 1834, the leadership of the Fulda society had changed. Now the directorate included seven full members and three alternates: a physician, a veterinarian, a tailor, a student of law, a carpenter, a salesman, and a watchmaker; two locksmiths and a typesetter.[38] Fulda's prominent citizens had vanished from the leadership, just as throughout the principality the initial cooperation between burghers and the lesser orders in 1830 and 1831 soon had given way to the formation of civic militias aimed at protecting private property from the rabble. Reading together for a time had been suitable for a club that mixed social groups; much more was not.

Police notes from the 1840s on the membership of a Fulda Reading Museum reinforce the impression that social distinctions were important in civic, literary associations except under the strained circumstances of the early 1830s. The Fulda club's members numbered sixty-five, of whom only five were in the crafts. Civil servants were not numerous either, but they were present, along with many schoolteachers, men in the professions, young employees of local businesses, and the dean of the cathedral chapter. What they read is not known, except that one member, a teacher called Dr. Müller, subscribed to the *Mannheimer Journal* (Mannheim Journal).[39] Hesse banned it in 1846.

Altogether, common men were uncommon participants in civic clubs and reading societies, especially the Hessian popular organizations of the 1830s and 1840s where reading played a role and where the texts chosen often met with official disapproval. Their presence in the Fulda Civic Association and in the Besse Farmer's Casino was as exceptional as Wilhelm Schulz's *Little Book* of 1819 and Georg Büchner's and Ludwig Weidig's *Hessian Courier* of 1834 were, with their appeals to ordinary peasants and craftsmen.

By and large, forbidden literature was addressed to and came into the hands of people with some book learning. After the startling experience of 1830, when Hessians of all social ranks had revolted and when educated men demanded and got a constitution, these knowledgeable burghers learned how to get and read what they liked, regardless of what the government wanted. Through the 1840s, the government continued to use time-tested, now inadequate, methods against these new, self-made citizens, its old subjects. How futile political censorship and literary policing were bound to be, it might have learned two decades earlier from the wise commentaries of Jacob Grimm. But it had not paid him attention then, and by the time of constitutional freedoms, inexpensive literature, and organized opposition, he was long gone.

TEN

The Failure of Censorship

Censorship in all its forms ended in Hesse-Cassel in 1848, at least for a time. Old-style censorship ended for good. That year for the third time in a half-century, a revolution that began in France crossed the Rhine and infected the German states. In March, revolt broke out in Cassel, as it did in Berlin, Vienna, Frankfort, and other German capitals.

The old autocracy just melted away in the "March days" of 1848 like sooty, crusty snow caught by the sun on a late winter's day. Justice Minister Bickell missed the tumult in Cassel by dying only days before it began. Interior Minister Scheffer was ill but recovered enough to flee the country on 6 March, the first day of unrest. The chiefs of the finance, war, and foreign ministries all resigned. It was left to the Cassel police director to countersign a decree by the prince-elector abolishing censorship immediately. In the city hall, drunken celebrants shouted, "Free press! Free press!" to which Police Director Morchutt answered, "Yes, just write, just write; everything you write will be printed!"[1]

The initial image of Heinrich Heine's poem, "Night Thoughts," had been suddenly waking up in the night with thoughts of Germany that made him sob. In a later stanza of the poem, past that rude awakening, Heine's mood had turned more hopeful:

> Deutschland hat ewigen Bestand,
> Es ist ein kerngesundes Land,
> Mit seinen Eichen, seinen Linden,
> Werd' ich es immer wiederfinden.[2]
>
> (Germany will forevermore stand,
> It is a mighty vigorous land,

THE FAILURE OF CENSORSHIP

With its ashes and its lindens,
I will always find it again.)

In 1848, it seemed that Germans who shared Heine's political and literary inclinations, like their country's strong ash and linden trees, having withstood the storm of the previous three decades, were finding their way to the kind of Germany they had only dreamed of earlier. It seemed that censorship was ending for all time.

During the summer of 1848, the Hessian assembly, to which Sylvester Jordan had been elected once again, passed a press law. Mimicking the events of 1831 in Cassel and Jordan's role in them, it was the most radical in all Germany. Under its protection, liberals and democrats of every sort, even German Catholics, published newspapers in Hesse.

As elsewhere in Germany, however, the new freedom of the press lasted only a short time. The princes regained their courage, reasserted their authority, and reappointed conservative ministries during 1849 and 1850. Daniel Ludwig Hassenpflug returned to Cassel in February 1850 and resumed his old duties as minister of justice and the interior. Again, as eighteen years before, under his abrasive guidance, domestic politics polarized quickly in Hesse. The government on one side and the legislature and the press on the other found no common ground.[3]

The history of the 1830s appeared to be repeating itself during the 1850s, but it was not, because the political and cultural circumstances of the earlier decade could not be reproduced. Naive assumptions on all sides that had once exacerbated the sense of injury shared by princes, legislators, censors, readers, and writers were gone now. Censorship had grown from a small institution affecting a circumscribed literate elite into a large issue that concerned a broad array of Germans. Public life was wide awake in the German states, politicking was every literate man's business, much of literature was about politics, and more than any other issue the national question engrossed politics and literature both.

There were national associations for German liberals, national associations for police coordination, national associations of many sorts, even though there was not yet a German nation.[4] German nationalism had awakened from its dreamlike state of the early nineteenth century to be the principal political issue throughout the German lands for the next two decades. Among the earlier, intractable, ever-present, political issues that it overshadowed was censorship.

There were hints already in 1849 and 1850 of how the national question was going to be answered—more decisively than the censorship question ever was—by princely force, not by popular will. King Friedrich Wilhelm IV of Prussia rebuffed the effort of the Frankfort Constituent Assembly, born out of the unrest of 1848, to offer him in one hand an imperial crown for himself and in the other hand a constitution for all Germany. He reminded the bearers of these gifts, when they came to him early in 1849, that there was still no one place called Germany, by his insistence that all German princes agree before he donned the proffered crown. That was impossible. The constitution was discarded with the crown.

Hesse's own renewed constitutional crisis was resolved by force from beyond the borders of the principality, in the fall of 1850, when Bavarian and Prussian armies marched in. They were purportedly there to help quell the disorder of the legislative assembly in Cassel, but, in fact, they were shadowboxing over animosities between south Germans and north Germans about what form a new, united Germany should take. For Hessians, the immediate result was that their newfound freedoms ended.

In 1852, a different sort of constitution replaced the one that Sylvester Jordan had first brought to life in 1831, then helped to resuscitate in 1848. Now the extensive powers that the legislature had had were gone. Press policies conformed with recent enactments of the German Confederation, which imposed a harsh censorship.

In 1862, the constitution of 1831 reappeared in Hesse-Cassel, and with it came a freer press again. By then, however, the issues that filled newspaper pages were wholly different from the leading questions of 1815 or 1832 or 1848. The most daring Hessian newspapers during the 1860s were the ones that stood for independence in the face of increasing Prussian interest in a political union. The year 1866 brought war between Prussia and Austria. Hesse, in its opposition to a Prussian-led German national state, sided with the Austrians. Upon losing the war, it lost its existence as an independent land. Among his first acts, the Prussian military governor of Hesse suppressed the anti-Prussian periodical press.

Censorship, particularly repressive censorship, especially censorship of newspapers, would go on. But it would never again have the novelty that it had had in the first half of the nineteenth century. It would never again elicit the shocked pain of an initial encounter with something unpleasant that it had caused for writers, readers, censors, rulers, bookmen, police, diplomats, magistrates, and burghers only a few decades before, when the institution had first become an issue.

In 1815, Joseph von Görres had written in gentle, conciliatory language about the people coming of age politically and the newspapers becoming their restrained spokesmen. It had still been possible at that time for a publisher such as Johann Cotta to regard censorship as a necessary mechanism for ensuring that political discourse was proper and safe. The language of literature and politics by the 1840s did not have the gentleness of Görres any more, nor was Cotta's moderate point of view any longer imaginable.[5] Writers and publishers did not restrain themselves. They were partisans for a cause. They had been awakened to censorship as a new issue that could be contested, quite different from the old institution that had often been respected, sometimes circumvented.

They had honed their pens during years of mental dueling with the German princes, their police, and their censors. Ludwig Walesrode, a censored popular writer, described the German literati in 1842, in a book that the Hessians banned: "They grow whiskers and moustaches, so that the gendarmes and censors will fear them. Their ink is prepared with crab apples and vitriol; they write with sharp-tipped pens, with which . . . they simultaneously can cut up their literary enemies."[6] When there had been the prospect of literary freedom and the promise of political reform, Görres had counseled governments not to fear the people's writing. But after three decades filled with battles over censorship, Walesrode left no doubt, however humorous his imagery might have been, that the best thing for writers was to be fearsome. It was their surest defense against the fearful censorship that Görres had foreseen but could not forestall.

By 1845, the literary liberty for which Walesrode fought was within sight. Despite Metternich's best efforts to muzzle writers and hobble publishers, censorship in the German states was failing. Austria's legate in Leipzig reported that the press in Saxony was revolutionizing the people. Another agent sent word from Hamburg that the publishing firm of Hoffmann and Campe, on being informed that its entire output might be banned by the German Confederation, responded that that would be welcome because it could only improve business.[7]

"Forbidding the sale of individual publications is almost always illusory," wrote Franz Hugo Hesse, "and at that it frequently serves the spread, rather than the hindrance of a work, something that every bookseller and common sense will confirm."[8] The Cassel censors had confirmed it too, years before anyone relieved them of their role in perpetuating the illusion.

Censors in the German lands in 1815 had been functionaries still, subjects of their local princes doing a necessary task that had long been widely accepted among the educated elite. The setting for censorship was still often collegial or at least fairly anonymous. The task reflected local circumstances and moods. Between 1815 and 1848, the censors were made into a single, undifferentiated object of popular wrath, a nasty caricature of policing and administration, a target at which literary and political warriors aimed their crab apples, vitriol, and sharp-tipped pens.

At the same time, the task became less and less the censors' own. Although their responsibilities came to encompass more and more forms of literature and varieties of opinion, they were allowed less and less authority over their work. Policing literature and opinions, in an era of newfound public opinion filled with opinionated writers and readers, fell to police and magistrates. In Hesse-Cassel as in other German states, policing the press turned out to be a more uniform, more workable enterprise than censoring it. Yet even policing failed by the 1840s to defuse the explosive growth of free-minded political literature.

For all of Hesse's atypicality in its economy, its culture, and its royal family, its censorship experience was very typical. Everywhere in the German states was the "great divergence of interests and opinions" that Christoph von Rommel lamented in 1831. Everywhere, local commercial considerations and local politics of the moment influenced the practice of censorship. What was not permissible in one time or place might well be in another.[9]

Everywhere, foreign ministries were crucial players in censorship policy making and administration because borders were so permeable. What happened in the deliberations of the confederation is deceptively uninformative about censorship everywhere in Germany. A witness to that is the inactivity of the Confederal Assembly as a group from 1836 until 1848, when as a body it only banned two publications while its delegates busily urged their own increasingly frequent bans upon each other, to little good effect. Everywhere in Germany, the things most threatening were not products of the presses at home but imports from abroad.[10]

Everywhere where there were not legislatures, Germans regarded the press as a substitute conveyor of public opinion. Everywhere where there were legislatures, reporting freely on their proceedings became a chief objective of the press, and freeing the press to report became a chief objective of the legislature; they were inevitably, closely allied.[11]

THE FAILURE OF CENSORSHIP

Everywhere, censorship expanded endlessly. Everywhere, it became hopelessly ineffective. The targets had first been students and the press; then they expanded to include liberal states and the press and foreigners and the press; and eventually they encompassed teachers and the press, preachers and the press, civil servants and the press, legislators and the press, and civic associations and the press. Everywhere among educated Germans, as censorship grew, the line between who was censoring and who was censored became more and more murky.[12] Everywhere, "freedom of the press," even more pointedly, "sacred freedom of the press," became a slogan that had the power to bring together people whose interests would otherwise have been very different.[13] Everywhere, what had been an institution became an issue.

The ever-longer lists of publications banned by the 1840s reveal what a vicious cycle of activity there was for and against censorship, a cycle that went on building until 1848. Each action, whether by police and censors or by free-minded writers, bookmen, and readers, provoked the other side's reaction. Because most efforts by governments to make censorship more thorough and more effective were institutional tinkering, they were ineffectual or even injurious to the same governments' interests about censorship as an issue. Public opinion, which censorship had been meant to control, became freer, in fact, as a result of it.[14]

The fairy tales that the Brothers Grimm collected did not always have happy endings, but they did always have lessons. The moral of this story is the more that censors banned, the more that censorship failed.

Appendix
Banned in Hesse-Cassel 1831–1848

The list that follows was compiled from many files in the Hessian State Archive at Marburg. Among the principal ones were

Marburg Administration (File 17)
(folders) g 74 30, 32, 34, 37
   Cassel Administration (File 19)
      h 868–70
   Police (File 24)
      b 153
      d 129, 130, 132, 138
      f 39, 45, 47
      g 485, 725, 730
   Censorship Commission (File 25)
      19–28
   County Councilors (File 180)
      Fritzlar 176
      Fulda 21
      Hünfeld 127
      Kassel 2198
      Marburg 262

These papers were supplemented by four lists of banned publications:

"Verzeichniß der im Jahr 1842 verbotenen Bücher und Schriften" [with supplements through February 1848], in "Geschäftsbuch für die Kurfürstliche Censur-Commission," 25 27
"Verzeichniß der verbotenen Schriften (pp *ohne Berichterstattung von hier)*" and "Verzeichniß derjenigen verbotenen worüber *von hier aus berichtet worden ist*," both in 9 b (Gesandtschaften) IV (Bund) 245
"Verzeichniß der zu unterdrückenden Zeitschriften" [books and pamphlets too], in 180 Hünfeld 127
"Verzeichniß über verbotene Schriften," dated 29 December 1838 in 82 c 771

APPENDIX

Titles and authors named in the archival files and lists were compared with information in bibliographic reference works and secondary sources. Particularly useful in this work of reconstruction were Reinhard Görisch and Thomas Michael Mayer, eds., *Untersuchungsberichte zur republikanischen Bewegung in Hessen 1831–34* (Frankfurt, 1982); Wilhelm Heinsius, *Allgemeines Bücherlexikon* (Leipzig, 1812–94); Michael Holzmann and Hanns Bohatta, *Deutsches Anonymen-Lexikon, 1501–1926* (Weimar, 1902–28); idem, *Deutsches Pseudonymen Lexikon* (Vienna and Leipzig, 1906); Julius Marx, "Liste der beschlagnahmten und mit Schedenverbot belegten Werke: I. Werke in deutscher Sprache," *Die österreichische Zensur im Vormärz* (Vienna, 1959), 97–106; F. Hermann Meyer, "Bücherverbote im Königreiche Preußen von 1834 bis 1882," *Archiv für Geschichte des Deutschen Buchhandels* 14 (1889): 317–49; and Hans-Joachim Ruckhäberle, *Flugschriftenliteratur im historischen Umkreis Georg Büchners* (Kronberg in the Taunus, 1975).

Using these aids, wherever possible titles were corrected and the names of anonymous authors and editors were added, with the purpose of making evident the character and variety of literature that was prohibited in Hesse-Cassel. Even with my emendations, the list contains many signs of its origin in the incomplete information that police, censors, and other officials in Hesse had. It is not a critical, annotated bibliography of censored works as they were known to Hessian authorities, something that would require a volume of its own.

Year

Month
    Office
        Title
            Author

1831

May
    Interior Ministry
        Das Leben der deutschen Jugend
            Anonymous
        Der erste Mai
            Anonymous
        Bitt um's Wort
            Herold

August
    Hesse-Nassau
        Der Haus- und Staatsminister von Nassau, mit sich selbst in Fehde
            Anonymous

APPENDIX

September
>   Fulda
>   > *Die neue Welt entdeckt in 1830*
>   > Dr. Gartenhof

1832

February
>   Confederation
>   > *Das konstitutionelle Deutschland*
>   > Harro Harring

March
>   Interior Ministry
>   > *Blutstropfen*
>   > Harro Harring
>
>   Confederation
>   > *Neue Zeitschwingen*
>   > Gustav Oehler
>   > *Die deutsche Tribüne*
>   > J. G. A. Wirth
>   > *Der Bote aus Westen*
>   > Philipp Jakob Siebenpfeiffer

May
>   Marburg
>   > *Der Hausfreund*
>   > Philipp Jakob Siebenpfeiffer

June
>   Interior Ministry
>   > *Aberglauben, Eigennutz, Kleinmuth . . .*
>   > Karl Juch
>
>   Bavaria
>   > *Aufruf an die Volksfreunde in Deutschland*
>   > J. G. A. Wirth

August
>   Interior Ministry
>   > *Schaumburger Volksblatt*
>   > Osterwald
>   > *Die deutsche Volkshalle*
>   > Johann Friedrich Funck
>   > *Teutsches Volksblatt*
>   > Jakob Förster
>
>   Hanau
>   > *Der deutsche Mai*
>   > Anonymous

APPENDIX

    Das deutsche Treibjagd
      Johann Wilhelm Sauerwein
  Lower Hesse
    Offene Erklärung kurhessischer Staatsbürger . . .
      Anonymous
  Marburg
    Deutschlands Juliordonanzen . . .
      Anonymous
  Confederation
    Allgemeine politische Annalen
      Karl von Rotteck
    Der Volksfreund
      Joseph Meyer
    Deutsche allgemeine Zeitung
      C. A. Mebold
  Bavaria
    Der Freisinnige
      Kandidat Giehen
    Der Wächter am Rhein
      Franz Strohmeyer

October
  Interior Ministry
    Erste Flugschrift . . .
      Jakob Förster
    Zweite Flugschrift . . .
      Jakob Förster
  Marburg
    Die sechs Gebote des deutschen Bundes
      Fleischmann
  Bavaria
    Flugschrift von dem Volkstribun, Nr. 4
      Gottfried Widmann
    Flugschrift von dem Volkstribun, Nr. 5
      Gottfried Widmann

November
  Bavaria
    Das Volksblatt
      Friedrich Theil

December
  Marburg
    Das Recht des deutschen Volkes . . .
      Wilhelm Schulz
    Rhein Main Zeitung
    Deutschland! Wahrheit! Recht! Freiheit! Ehre!
      Harro Harring

APPENDIX

1833

January
    Frankfort/Main
        Der Komet des Jahres 1834 . . . .
        Anonymous

February
    Hanau
        Das Jahr 1831 in seinen Staatsumwälzungen . . .
        Julius Franz Schneller

June
    Interior Ministry
        Loos zu einer Lotterie
            Frauen- und Mädchenverein am Hardtgebirge zur Unterstützung der Familien eingekerkerter oder verbannter s.g. deutscher Patrioten

July
    Hanau
        Scherz und Ernst zur Lust und Lehre . . .
        Anonymous
    Confederation
        Sämmtliche Werke
        Karl von Rotteck
        Sämmtliche Werke
        Philipp Jakob Siebenpfeiffer
    Baden
        Über die badische Kammer
        Karl von Rotteck

September
    Interior Ministry
        Reisen eines deutschen Freigeistes
        Erhard von Haselstein

October
    Interior Ministry
        Aufforderungen zur Auswanderung nach Rußland
        Oekonomiekommissar Schmidt

November
    Foreign Ministry
        Sinnreiche Einfälle in Stunden froher Laune . . .
        Franz Lohmeyer

1834

January
> Confederation
>> *Neckarzeitung*
>>> Heinrich Elsner
>>
>> *Das neue hessische Volksblatt*

February
> Interior Ministry
>> *Blicke auf die deutschen Lande*
>>> Johann Friedrich Funck

March
> Interior Ministry
>> *Bauern-Conversations-Lexicon*
>>> Johann Christoph Freyeisen, Johann Friedrich Funck, Friedrich Sigmund Jucho, and Johann Wilhelm Sauerwein

May
> Confederation
>> *Glaubensbekenntnis eines Geächteten*
>>> Anonymous
>>
>> *Erklärung der Menschen- und Bürgerrechte*
>>> Anonymous

June
> Fulda
>> *Der Missionsverein, oder die Jesuiten in Hessen*
>>> Anonymous

July
> Confederation
>> *Les paroles d'un croyant*
>>> Félicité de Lamennais
>>
>> *Aufruf eines Geächteten an die . . . Volksfreunde . . .*
>>> Anonymous
>>
>> *Vertheidigungsrede*
>>> Degeorge
>>
>> *Vertheidigungsrede*
>>> Vergueur
>>
>> *Unwille eines vom volksthümlichen Geiste beseelten . . .*
>>> Anonymous
>>
>> *De la démission de M. Dupont d'Eure*
>>> Anonymous
>
> Bavaria
>> *Erklärung der Rechte des Menschen*
>>> Anonymous

APPENDIX

October
    Hanau
        Der dreijährige Denunziant, oder Spiegel . . .
            Anonymous
        Herr du Thil mit der Eisenstirn
            Carl Flach and Friedrich Ludwig Weidig
    Confederation
        Der Geächtete
            Jakob Venedey
        Sämtliche Veröffentlichungen
            Schuler in Strasbourg
        Sämtliche Veröffentlichungen
            Silbermann in Strasbourg
        Deutsches Leben, Kunst und Poesie
            Heinrich Joseph Garnier
    Hesse-Darmstadt
        Der Hessische Landbote
            Georg Büchner and Friedrich Ludwig Weidig

1835

January
    Cassel
        Blick auf Kurhessen im Augenblick . . .
            Dietrich Albrecht Geeh

February
    Rinteln
        Kerkerstimmen
            Viktor Amadeus Cornmanns

March
    Interior Ministry
        Darlegung der Hauptresultate . . .
            Anonymous
    Confederation
        Geisterstimmen der Ermordeten
            Anonymous
    Baden
        Die sieben Todtsünden der Liberalen
            Hartwig Hundt-Radowsky
        Das Nordlicht

June
    Foreign Ministry
        Bibliothek der deutschen Klassiker
            Brüder Diedrich

APPENDIX

July
    Confederation
        Authentische Actenstücke aus den Archiven . . .
            Gustav Kombst

October
    Censorship Commission
        Wally, oder die Zweiflerin
            Karl Gutzkow
    Lower Hesse
        Die neuesten Bundesbeschlüsse . . .
            Anonymous

December
    Interior Ministry
        Wanderungen durch den Thierkreis
            Ludolf Wienbarg

1836

January
    Interior Ministry
        Fieschi, ein poetisches Nachtstück
            Ernst Ortlepp
        Erinnerungen aus Paris . . .
            Anonymous
        Die Revolution, . . . Sittengemälde
            August Schäfer
        Das Manifest der Vernunft . . .
            Friedrich Clemens [Gerke]
        Die junge Literatur und der Roman "Wally"
            Gustav Bacherer
        De l'Absolutisme et de la Liberté
            Félicité de Lamennais
    Confederation
        Sämmtliche Werke
            "Junges Deutschland": Heinrich Heine, Ludwig
            Börne, Karl Gutzkow, Theodor Mundt,
            Heinrich Laube

June
    Hanau
        Der deutsche Bundestag, politische Wizze
            Gustav Kombst

APPENDIX

      Rinteln
          Politische Schriften
            Ernst Grosse

July
      Marburg
          Briefe aus Amerika
            Adam Frank

September
      Interior Ministry
          Europäische Geheimnisse eines Mediatisirten
            Leopold Langenschwarz

December
      Interior Ministry
          Gedanken eines Republikaners
            Theodor Schuster
      Lower Hesse
          Die zehn Wirthshausgebote
            Anonymous

1837

April
      Confederation
          Menzel der Franzosenfresser
            Ludwig Börne

May
      Interior Ministry
          Forschungen über die Verfassungen . . .
            Simonde von Sismondi
      Confederation
          Der Mord verübt an Ludwig Lessing
            Anonymous
          Aktenmässige Darstellung . . .
            Joseph Schauberg

June
      Interior Ministry
          Der vollständige Rathgeber . . .
            Dr. Krause
          Die Teufelsschlacht im Dom zu Goslar
            Friedrich Bartels

APPENDIX

        Lelia
            George Sand
    Confederation
        Politisches Rundgemälde auf das Jahr 1835
            Becker

July
    Interior Ministry
        Anatomie des Staats . . .
            Leopold Langenschwarz
    Lower Hesse
        Mittheilungen aus dem Gebiete der . . . Völkerkunde
            Ludwig Börne
        Das junge Europe
            Heinrich Laube
        Ferdinand und Caroline . . .
            Anonymous
        Briefe aus Paris
            Ludwig Börne
        Blumenblätter aus den Gefilden der Phantasie
            Friedrich Karl von Dankelmann
        Blasius Lustig, oder der verliebte Magister
            Anonymous
        Augusta, oder Geständnisse einer Braut . . .
            Friedrich Karl von Dankelmann
        Abendtheuer im Walde bei Vinzennes
            Anonymous

August
    Fulda
        Die Waldenser
            Heinrich König

September
    Cassel
        Foi et avenir
            Giuseppe Mazzini

November
    Interior Ministry
        Wichtige Tage aus dem Leben Napoleons
            Heinrich Elsner
    Fulda
        Privatleben des Marschalls von Richelieu
            Anonymous
    Marburg
        Der Wiener Jakl
            Anonymous

APPENDIX

1838

April
    Fulda
        Die rothe Mütze und die Kaputze
        Karl Gutzkow

August
    Marburg
        Stoff zum Nachdenken . . .
        Anonymous
        Jesus, der Kinderfreund
        Anonymous
        Ernstliche Ermahnungen . . .
        Anonymous
        Die Gottheit Christi
        Anonymous

September
    Fulda
        Der Mönch in der Flucht, oder . . .
        Anonymous

November
    Cassel
        Hännchens Hin- und Herzüge
        Anonymous
    Marburg
        Die zehn Wirthshausregeln
        Anonymous

December
    Confederation
        Die Radical Reform des deutschen . . . Privatrechts
        W. Deutschmann

1839

July
    Confederation
        Was wollen die Republikaner?
        Gustav Kombst
        Die preussische Tendenz
        Anonymous
        Die nordische Allianz
        Anonymous
        An die rheinpreußischen Katholiken
        Anonymous

APPENDIX

        Aufruf an die deutschen Arbeiter
          Anonymous

October
    Confederation
        Preußen und Preußenthum
          Jakob Venedey
        Gutachten der Juristischen Fakultät zu Tübingen
          Friedrich Christoph Dahlmann

November
    Cassel
        Ueber die Vermittelung in Hannover
          Johann Jakob Christien

December
    Hanover
        Aufruf . . . Gesellschaft deutscher Vaterlandsfreunde
          Anonymous

1840

February
    Foreign Ministry
        Die Volkshalle
          Johann Friedrich Funck

August
    Baden
        Caspar Hauser, der Thronerbe Badens
          Sebastian Seiler

1841

February
    Cassel
        Sächsische Vaterlandsblätter
          Cramer

April
    Confederation
        Vier Fragen beantwortet von einem Ostpreußen
          Johann Jacoby

May
    Cassel
        Die Nonne und die Schauspielerin
          George Sand

Fulda
    Ueber Ludwig Börne
        Heinrich Heine

Hanau
    Lebenswirren
        Theodor Mundt
    Leichtfertigkeiten in kleinen Romanen
        Anonymous
    Gefährliche Stunden
        Carl Gottlob Cramer
    Hochverrat und Buhlerei . . .
        Anonymous

Marburg
    Zehn Gebote der Eheherren an ihre Frauen
        Anonymous

Confederation
    Die kölnische Kirche
        Anonymous

Austria
    Bergerliche Haamlichkeite aus der Umgegend . . .
        Leopold Langenschwarz

September
    Lower Hesse
        Geschichte der Herzogin von Portsmouth
            Anonymous
        Die . . . Laterna Magica
            Anonymous

December
    Interior Ministry
        Lieder eines kosmopolitischen Nachtwächters
            Franz Dingelstedt
    Lower Hesse
        Crasinello, der verkappte Dirnenräuber
            Carl Santo
        Eugen Neuland
            Anonymous

1842

January
    Censorship Commission
        Die Pietisten
            Heribert Rau

APPENDIX

	Marburg
	Ein Osterwort aus Hessen
	Franz Dingelstedt
March	Marburg
	Der hinkende Teufel
	Alain René le Sage
	Sämtliche Werke
	Ernst Friedrich Fürst
	Adolf der Schöne . . .
	Anonymous
April	Prussia
	De la Prusse et de sa domination
	Anonymous
June	Marburg
	Gedichte eines Lebendigen
	Georg Herwegh

1843

April	Cassel
	Die wahrhaftige Geschichte vom deutschen Michael . . .
	Wilhelm Schulz
	Fulda
	Der schwache König
	Anonymous
	Lebenswandel . . . eines Frauenzimmers
	Anonymous
	Marburg
	Meyers Universum
	Joseph Meyer
May	Interior Ministry
	Leipziger Lokomotive, Volksblatt
June	Marburg
	Sohn der Zeit
	Ludwig Sanger

APPENDIX

July
>Interior Ministry
>>*Wahrheiten mit und ohne Schleier*
>>>Anonymous
>Lower Hesse
>>*Unsere Zeit*
>>>Aiax

August
>Lower Hesse
>>*Philosophische Abendstunde*
>>>Anonymous
>Marburg
>>*21 Bogen aus der Schweiz*
>>>Georg Herwegh
>Foreign Ministry
>>*Die endlich offenbar gewordene Philosophie* . . .
>>>H. E. G. Paulus

December
>Marburg
>>*Die Selbstverständigung des Professors Jordan*
>>>Sylvester Jordan

1844

January
>Interior Ministry
>>*Nachträge zur Vertheidigung des Professors Jordan* . . .
>>>August Boden
>>*Landständischer Bericht*
>>>Abgeordneter von Waitz
>Cassel
>>*Mefistofeles: Revue der deutschen Gegenwart*
>>>Stein
>Foreign Ministry
>>*Die geheimen Beschlüsse der Wiener Konferenz*
>>>Anonymous

February
>Interior Ministry
>>*Jordan, Vertheidigungsschrift eines deutschen Advokaten*
>>>Ferdinand Fischer
>Foreign Ministry
>>*Deutsches Noths- und Hülfsbüchlein* . . .
>>>Anonymous

APPENDIX

March
    Interior Ministry
        Die Grenzboten, eine deutsche Revue
            Ernst Dronke
        Der Deutsche in Amerika
            Anonymous

April
    Bavaria
        Teutsch-französische Jahrbücher
            Arnold Ruge and Karl Marx

June
    Interior Ministry
        Hermine, oder der Aprilabend zu Frankfurt
            S. Zirndorfer

July
    Interior Ministry
        Dritte Schrift zur Vertheidigung . . . Jordan
            August Boden
    Cassel
        Die Klage des Johann Conrad Kuhl . . .
            Johann Conrad Kuhl
        Die Politik der deutschen Minister . . .
            Anonymous

August
    Interior Ministry
        Die moderne deutsche Konstitution . . .
            Hauptmann Möller
        Die Eisenbahn, ein Unterhaltungsblatt
            Robert Binder
    Lower Hesse
        Weser Dampfboot
    Prussia
        Beleuchtung der Schrift über Fabrikanten . . .
            Hugo Jahn

September
    Cassel
        Der Streit der Kritik mit Kirche und Staat
            Edgar Bauer
    Brunswick
        Denkwürdigkeiten
            Karl von Braunschweig
    Prussia
        Humor auf der Bank der Angeklagten . . .
            Ludwig Walesrode

APPENDIX

October
- Interior Ministry
  - *Censuriana, oder Geheimnisse der Censur*
    - Wilhelm Held
- Hanau
  - *Freuden und Leiden eines Commis Voyeurs*
    - Anonymous
- Prussia
  - *Neue Gedichte*
    - Heinrich Heine

November
- Interior Ministry
  - *Allgemeine Zeitung*
  - *Hildburghauser Dorfzeitung*
    - Joseph Meyer
- Bavaria
  - *Der Gevattersmann, neuer Kalandar*
    - Berthold Auersbach
- Prussia
  - *Die Berliner Gewerbeausstellung*
    - Adolph Glaßbrenner
  - *Der deutsche Handwerksbursche . . .*
    - Ferdinand Adrian
  - *Deutschland, ein Wintermärchen*
    - Heinrich Heine
  - *Glaubensbekenntnisse, Zeitgedichte*
    - Ferdinand Freiligrath
  - *Der Einzige und sein Eigenthum*
    - Max Stirner
  - *Die preußische Bürokratie*
    - Karl Heinzen
- Saxony
  - *Wichtige Urkunden für den Rechtszustand . . .*
    - Karl Theodor Welcker

December
- Interior Ministry
  - *Drei Dombausteine den Rheinländern gewidmet*
    - Anonymous
  - *Deutsche Fürstenlieder*
    - Anonymous
  - *Der dem Kommunismus . . . geworfene Handschuh*
    - Etienne Cabot
  - *Rücklosigkeit der Schrift "Dies Buch gehört"*
    - Lebrecht Fromm

APPENDIX

    Cassel
        Der Preßprozeß Edgar Bauers . . .
           Anonymous
        Württemberg im Jahre 1844
           Johannes Scherr
    Marburg
        Sylvester Jordans Leben und Leiden
           F. Trinks and G. Julius

1845

January
    Interior Ministry
        John Hampden . . . vom gesetzlichen Widerstande
           Jakob Venedey
        Die Grenzboten
           J. Kuranda
    Hanau
        Die Ruinen
           Comte de Volney

February
    Interior Ministry
        Julius Rubner
           Hermann Friedrich Handschuh

March
    Cassel
        Deutsches Taschenbuch
           Hoffmann von Fallersleben

April
    Interior Ministry
        Ueber die Untersuchungsprozeß gegen . . . Weidig
           August Boden
    Marburg
        Mannheimer Abendzeitung
           Friedrich Moritz Hähner
        Stadt Aachener Zeitung
           Louis Lax
        Weser Zeitung
           C. Schünemann
    Prussia
        Ein Steckbrief
           Karl Heinzen
        Von der Tyrannei
           Graf Victor Alfieri

APPENDIX

May
    Prussia
        Der Geheimrath und der geheime Sekretär . . .
            Dr. Scheel

June
    Censorship Commission
        Ueber die sogenannte Religionsgefahr . . .
            Anonymous
        Die Menschheit, wie sie ist und wie sie sein sollte
            Wilhelm Weitling
    Confederation
        Die deutsche Schnellpost
            Eichthal and Bernhard

July
    Cassel
        Geheime Inquisition, Censur und Kabinetsjustiz
            Wilhelm Schulz and Karl Theodor Welcker
    Fulda
        Briefwechsel zwischen . . . Diplomaten
            Gustav von Struve
    Confederation
        Sämtliche Veröffentlichungen
            Literarisches Comptoir in Winterthur

August
    Interior Ministry
        Der Herold
            Karl Biedermann
    Cassel
        Die Kölnische Zeitung
    Prussia
        Das enthüllte Preußen . . .
            Johannes Scherr
    Saxony
        Gedichte aus dem ungedruckten Nachlasse
            Graf August von Platen-Hallermunde
        Deutsche Gassenlieder
            Hoffmann von Fallersleben
        Zwei authentische Aktenstücke . . .
            Anonymous
        Hoffmannische Tropfen
            Hoffmann von Fallersleben

September
    Prussia
        Narrenalmanach für 1846
            Eduard Maria Oettingen

APPENDIX

> *Katechismus eines Republikaners der Zukunft*
> Wilhelm Marr
> *Pillen eigenes Präparat . . .*
> Wilhelm Marr
> *Die Seherin, dramatisches Gedicht*
> Emil Mecklenburg
> *Deutsche Londoner Zeitung*
> Karl von Braunschweig

October
- Censorship Commission
  - *Einfälle und Geschichte . . .*
    - Anonymous
- Prussia
  - *Dankadresse an die Herrn Itzstein und Hecker*
    - Anonymous
  - *Rheinische Jahrbücher zur gesellschaftlichen Reform*
    - Hermann Püttmann
  - *Mehr als 20 Bogen*
    - Karl Heinzen
- Saxony
  - *Leipzigs Todte*
    - Ferdinand Freiligrath

November
- Censorship Commission
  - *Akten Stücke des Grossherzoglichen . . .*
    - Gustav von Struve
- Confederation
  - *Briefwechsel eines Staatsgefangenen . . .*
    - Wilhelm Schulz
- Prussia
  - *Bekannte Geheimnisse*
    - Luise Dittmann
  - *Skizzen und Briefe aus der Gegenwart*
    - Luise Dittmann
  - *Neuer Rheinecke Fuchs*
    - Adolf Glaßbrenner

December
- Cassel
  - *Jordans Bewußtsein über seine Schuld oder Unschuld*
    - Anonymous
- Marburg
  - *Illustrirte Zeitung*
- Confederation
  - *Glaubensbekenntnis und Abschwörungsformular . . .*
    - Anonymous

APPENDIX

Prussia
    Zwei Jahre in Paris, Studien und Erinnerungen
    Arnold Ruge

1846

January
  Cassel
    Das Evangelium des armen Sünders
    Wilhelm Weitling
    Vom grausamen Bürgermeister: Eine Volkspredigt
    Anonymous
  Baden
    Politische Briefe
    Gustav von Struve
  Prussia
    Komischer Volkskalendar für 1846
    Adolph Glaßbrenner
    Europas fünfte Macht
    Anonymous
    Neue Anecdote
    Karl Grün
    Unsere Gegenwart und Zukunft
    Karl Biedermann
  Saxony
    Vierteljahrsschrift

February
  Prussia
    Aktenstücke der Mannheimer Censur und Polizei
    Gustav von Struve

March
  Cassel
    Guerrillaskrieg: Versprengte Lieder
    Anonymous
    Sociale Gedichte
    Hermann Püttmann
  Prussia
    Arme Sünder Stimmen
    Ernst Dronke
  Saxony
    Des Pfarrers Tochter von Taubenhein
    Anonymous

APPENDIX

April
    Interior Ministry
        Briefwechsel zwischen zwei Protestanten
            Anonymous
        Ueberzeugungen eines christlichen Greises
            Christoph Friedrich Wilhelm Ernst
    Cassel
        Polizei-Geschichten
            Ernst Dronke
    Prussia
        Schicksale eines Proletariers, ein Volksbuch
            Ehrenreich Eichholz
        Zur gerichtlichen Vertheidigung . . .
            Karl Theodor Welcker

May
    Interior Ministry
        Die kurhessischen Zustände . . .
            Georg Pflüger
    Prussia
        Brüderschaftslieder eines rheinischen Poeten
            Anonymous
    Saxony
        Einer heilsbegierigen Seele Erfahrungen . . .
            Gustav Dornhard Gebel
        Vorwärts: Volkstaschenbuch für das Jahr 1846
            Robert Blum
        Das Bekenntnis des freien Menschen . . .
            Anonymous

June
    Prussia
        Vertheidigung einer Schrift "Das königliche . . . "
            Johann Jacoby

July
    Interior Ministry
        Staatslexicon
            Karl von Rotteck and Karl Theodor Welcker
    Cassel
        Offenes Sendschreiben an das Ober-Censurgericht . . .
            Adolph Glaßbrenner

August
    Interior Ministry
        Mannheimer Journal

APPENDIX

Cassel
- *Die Opposition*
  - Karl Heinzen
- *Deutsche Zeitung ohne Zensur*
- *Deutsches Bürgerbuch für 1846*
  - Hermann Püttmann

Fulda
- *Mein Austritt aus der römischen Kirche*
  - Franz Jakob Schell
- *Das alte und neue Hohepriesterthum . . .*
  - Franz Jakob Schell

Prussia
- *Briefe über Kirche und Staat*
  - Gustav von Struve

Saxony
- *Dem deutschen Volke*
  - Wilhelm Held
- *Das Zeitalter der Vernunft . . .*
  - Thomas Paine

September

Interior Ministry
- *Das Verhältnis der Lichtfreunde . . .*
  - Anonymous

Cassel
- *Actenstücke der Badischen Censur und Polizei . . .*
  - Gustav von Struve
- *Dorfbarbier*
- *Wanderungen aus meinem Gefängnisse . . .*
  - Sylvester Jordan

Fulda
- *Offenes Sendschreiben an Johannes Czerski . . .*
  - Franz Jakob Schell

Marburg
- *Das wahre Wesen der gegenwärtigen . . . Reformation . . .*
  - Karl Bayrhoffer

Saxony
- *Briefe einer polnischen Dame (1840–1846)*
  - Anonymous
- *Die Epigonen*
  - Karl Immermann
- *Zeitstimmen aus und über Oesterreich*
  - Emanuel Geibel
- *Jetzt! Historisch-politisches Taschenbuch . . .*
  - Bruno Theobald

Dreißig Kriegsartikel der neuern Zeit . . .
    Karl Heinzen

November
  Cassel

Rheinische Jahrbücher . . .
    Hermann Püttmann
Lehrbuch der christlichen Religion . . .
    Franz Jakob Schell

  Foreign Ministry

Denkfreund: Ein Lehr- und Lesebuch . . .
    Johann Ferdinand Schlez

December
  Interior Ministry

Ein neuer Angriff auf das . . . *Bewilligungsrecht* . . .
    Karl Biedermann

  Cassel

Ça ira! Sechs Gedichte
    Ferdinand Freiligrath

  Baden

Der deutsche Tribun
    Karl Heinzen

1847

January
  Interior Ministry

Deutsch Brusseler Zeitung
    Adelbert von Bornstedt

  Cassel

Armin Galoor
    Ludwig Starklof

  Saxony

Politische und unpolitische Gedichte
    Karl Knorren
Schaum: Dichtungen
    Wilhelm Jordan
Das enthüllte Oesterreich
    M. Kubrakiewicz
21 Bogen für Deutschland
    Anonymous

February
  Interior Ministry

Die deutschkatholische Frage in Kurhessen . . .
    Carl Friedrich

APPENDIX

          Fulda

                Der Leuchtthurm: Monatsschrift . . .
                    Ernst Keil

                Denkschriften an Sie und Sie . . .
                    Georg Pflüger
                Ein Wort an die kurhessischen Stände . . .
                    Georg Pflüger
                Actenmässige Beiträge zur Charakteristik . . .
                    Hans Heiling

March
          Cassel
                Dorfbarbier
                    Ferdinand Stolle
          Confederation
                Sämtliche Veröffentlichungen
                    Literarisches Institut in Herisau
                Zur Vorbereitung
                    Karl Heinzen
          Saxony
                Kampf mit Hierarchy und Kirche . . .
                    Johann Horarik

April
          Baden
                Ein deutsches Rechnungs-Exempel
                    Karl Heinzen
          Saxony
                Die Epigonen
                    Karl Immermann
                Erbauliches und Beschauliches . . .
                    Jedediah Semmelziege
                Humoristisch-satyrische Geschichten Deutschlands . . .
                    Theodor Oelckers
                Polen, seiner Revolution und sein Recht
                    Hartwig Hundt-Radowsky
                Was ist jetzt zu thun?
                    Anonymous
                Vorwärts: Volkstaschenbuch für das Jahr 1847
                    Robert Blum
                Bibliothek der deutschen Aufklärer . . .
                    Martin von Geismar

May
          Saxony
                Libertas, Deutsches Volkstaschenbuch . . .
                    J. Bruno

APPENDIX

June
- Hanau
  - *Allgemeine Beschreibung der Ende und ihrer Bewohner*
    - Eduard Theodor Bösche
- Foreign Ministry
  - *Der deutsche Zuschauer*
- Prussia
  - *Plänkler 1846*
    - Hermann Püttmann
  - *Memoiren einer Prostituirten, oder . . .*
    - D. J. Leisig
- Saxony
  - *Königsberger politisches Taschenbuch für 1847*
    - Friedrich Krüger

July
- Interior Ministry
  - *Unsere Gegenwart und Zukunft*
    - Karl Biedermann
- Cassel
  - *Aktenstücke zur Censur, Philosophie . . .*
    - Arnold Ruge
- Prussia
  - *Die deutsche Revolution: Gesammelte Flugschriften*
    - Karl Heinzen
- Saxony
  - BERLIN XV
    - Anonymous
  - *Sociale und politische Zustände Oesterreichs . . .*
    - Anonymous

August
- Confederation
  - *Sämtliche Veröffentlichungen*
    - Schlägersche Buchhandlung in Herisau
- Saxony
  - *Oesterreich und Seine Armee*
    - Fenner von Fenneberg

September
- Bavaria
  - *Revolutions-Aufruf an Deutschland*
    - C. Richter, Bierbrauer
- Prussia
  - *Deutsches Volksliederbuch*
    - Anonymous
  - *Die Föderativ-Republik*
    - Anonymous

APPENDIX

October
- Censorship Commission
  - *Russland und Deutschland*
    - Anonymous
- Interior Ministry
  - *Die deutsche Zeitung*
- Cassel
  - *Die Geheimnisse des christlichen Alterthums*
    - Georg Friedrich Daumer
  - *Gesammelte kleine Schriften*
    - Arnold Ruge
- Württemberg
  - *Ludwig Philipp, König der Franzosen, ist nicht* . . .
    - Anonymous

November
- Censorship Commission
  - *Kassel: Humoristische Schilderungen*
    - K. Puschendorf
- Prussia
  - *Demokratisches Taschenbuch für 1848*
    - Anonymous

December
- Interior Ministry
  - *König und Volk, oder der 11. April* . . .
    - Anonymous
- Cassel
  - *Weder einst noch immerfort*
    - Paul de Kock
- Baden
  - *Meine Ausweisung aus Zürich*
    - Karl Heinzen
- Saxony
  - *Einiges über deutschen Servilismus und Liberalismus*
    - Karl Heinzen

1848

January
- Interior Ministry
  - *Deutsche Zustände*
    - Anonymous
  - *Das Frankfurter Journal*
    - F. A. Hammeran

Fulda
    Das Rheinische Volksblatt
        Theil
Confederation
    Wahrheit ohne Hülle
        Theodor Braklow
Baden
    Verhandlungen der Bundesversammlung . . .
        Anonymous
Saxony
    Die Freiheitsbestrebungen der Deutschen . . .
        Emil Weller
    Geschichte des ersten preußischen Reichstags
        Karl Biedermann

February
  Interior Ministry
    Unsere Zukunft und Gegenwart
        Karl Biedermann
    Thüringische Zeitung
  Fulda
    Europa: Chronik der gebildeten Welt
        Gustav Kühne
  Lower Hesse
    Gruß zum neuen Jahr! An unsere Brüder . . .
        Anonymous
  Confederation
    Ein Wort aus der Schweiz
        Karl Heinzen
    Sämtliche Veröffentlichungen
        Janni, Sohn in Bern
  Saxony
    Volksbuch: Aus dem ungarischen übersetzt
        Michael Stanasius

Notes

KEY TO NOTES FROM THE ARCHIVES

Notes of this sort:

Chief Police Commissioner Wendly to Prince-elector, 19 March 1820, 24 a 85.

refer to documents in the Hessian State Archive at Marburg. In these references to archival sources, the format is

[originating office] [to receiving office—if applicable], [day month year], [file number]

I have used the following short English renditions for the branches of government in the electoral principality of Hesse-Cassel (Kurfürstentum Hessen, or Kurhessen) to which I refer most often:

Interior	Ministerium des Innern
Foreign	Ministerium des kurfürstlichen Hauses und der auswärtigen Angelegenheiten (des Aeußern)
Censors	Zensurkommission/deputation
Police	Provinzialpolizeidirektion
Administration	Regierung
County Office	Landratsamt
Supreme Court	Oberappellationsgericht
Superior Court	Obergericht

1: THE CHALLENGE OF CENSORSHIP

1. Robert Darnton, "What is the History of Books?" in *The Kiss of Lamourette: Reflections in Cultural History* (New York, 1990), 107–10.
2. Robert Darnton, "Reading, Writing, and Publishing," in *The Literary Underground of the Old Regime* (Cambridge, Mass., 1982), 182.
3. Darnton, *Kiss of Lamourette*, 111–13.
4. See Darnton, "The Forgotten Middlemen of Literature," in *Kiss of Lamourette*, 136–53, and "A Spy in Grub Street," in *Literary Underground*, 69–70.
5. See Jack Goody and Ian Watt, "The Consequences of Literacy," in *Literacy in Traditional Societies*, ed. Jack Goody (Cambridge, England, 1968), 55–57.

6. Leslie Bodi, *Tauwetter in Wien: Zur Prosa der österreichischen Aufklärung, 1781–87* (Frankfort on Main, 1977), 43–57, 161–66; James Van Horn Melton, "From Image to Word: Cultural Reform and the Rise of Literate Culture in Eighteenth-Century Austria," *Journal of Modern History* 58 (March 1986): 95–124.

7. Mack Walker, *German Home Towns: Community, State, and General Estate 1648–1871* (Ithaca, 1971), 119–33.

8. There is a succinct description of the emergence of public opinion in early nineteenth-century German political and literary discourse in Daniel Moran, *Toward the Century of Words: Johann Cotta and the Politics of the Public Realm in Germany, 1795–1832* (Berkeley, 1990), 13–14.

9. Cited in Rolf Darmstadt, *Der deutsche Bund in der zeitgenössischen Publizistik* (Bern, 1971), 112.

10. Quote from Chief Police Commissioner Wendly to Prince-elector, 19 March 1820, 24 a 85; H. H. Borcherdt, "Das Schriftstellertum von der Mitte des 18. Jahrhunderts bis zur Gründung des Deutschen Reiches," in *Die geistigen Arbeiter*, ed. Ludwig Sinzheimer (Munich, 1922), 55.

11. Friedrich Murhard, *Die kurhessische Verfassungs-Urkunde, erläutert und beleuchtet nach Maßgabe ihrer einzelnen Paragraphen* (Cassel, 1834–35), 1:29; Franz Schneider, *Pressefreiheit und politische Öffentlichkeit: Studien zur politischen Geschichte Deutschlands bis 1848* (Neuwied a/R, 1966), 186–204; idem, "Presse, Pressefreiheit, Zensur," in *Geschichtliche Grundbegriffe*, ed. Otto Brunner, Werner Conze, and Reinhart Koselleck (Berlin, 1972–84), 4:912.

12. Quoted in Norbert Deuchert, *Vom Hambacher Fest zur badischen Revolution: Politische Presse und Anfänge deutscher Demokratie 1832–1848/49* (Stuttgart, 1983), 31, 80.

13. Wilhelm Held, *Dem deutschen Volke* (Leipzig, 1846), 73–81; Jakob Venedey, *Preußen und Preußenthum* (Mannheim, 1839), 2–3.

14. Deuchert, *Zur badischen Revolution*, 29.

15. Heinrich Heine, *Sämtliche Werke*, ed. Ernst Elster (Leipzig, 1887–90), 1:319.

16. See Arno J. Mayer, *The Persistence of the Old Regime: Europe to the Great War* (New York, 1981).

17. Walker, *Home Towns*, 261.

18. For example, James J. Sheehan, *German History, 1770–1866* (Oxford, 1989), pp. 612–15; although Sheehan is otherwise quite attentive to the issue. The title of his book reminds readers that being German came before being Germany, especially since Gordon A. Craig's companion volume on the period of German unity, which appeared first, is titled *Germany, 1866–1945*.

19. Frank Thomas Hoefer, *Pressepolitik und Polizeistaat Metternichs: Die Überwachung von Presse und politischer Öffentlichkeit in Deutschland und der Nachbarstaaten durch das Mainzer Informationsbüro (1833–1848)*, Dortmunder Beiträge zur Zeitungsforschung 37 (Munich, 1983): 94–109, 168.

20. See illuminating scholarship on caricature in the context of humor and censorship in Berlin, in Mary Lee Townsend, "Language of the Forbidden: Popular Humor in 'Vormärz' Berlin, 1819–1848" (Ph.D. diss., Yale University, 1984).

21. Schneider, *Pressefreiheit*, 171–73, calling it a shift from history to actuality, locates it in the Napoleonic period.

2: A Still Life

1. William Jacob, *A View of the Agriculture, Manufactures, Statistics, and State of Society, of Germany, and Parts of Holland and France, Taken during a Journey through Those*

Countries in 1819 (London, 1820), 379; Frances Trollope, *Belgium and Western Germany in 1833* (London, 1834), 2:212.

2. Arthur Brooke Faulkner, *Visit to Germany and the Low Countries in the Years 1829, 30, and 31* (London, 1833), 1:78; Trollope, *Belgium and Western Germany* 2:212.

3. Faulkner, *Visit to Germany* 1:81; John Russell, *A Tour in Germany, and Some of the Southern Provinces of the Austrian Empire in the Years 1820, 1821, 1822* (Boston, 1825), 191; Jacob, *View of Agriculture*, 379–86.

4. Alfred Tapp, *Hanau im Vormärz und in der Revolution von 1848–49: Ein Beitrag zur Geschichte des Kurfürstentums Hessen* (Hanau, 1976), 41–52, 221–23; Heinrich König, *Ein Stilleben: Erinnerungen und Bekenntnisse* (Leipzig, 1861), 1:345; *Jahresbericht über das Kurfürstliche Gymnasium zu Hanau* (Hanau, 1845), pt. 2, p. 2.

5. Jacob, *View of Agriculture*, 389.

6. Ibid., 380.

7. Hans Mauersberg, *Die Wirtschaft und Gesellschaft Fuldas in neuerer Zeit* (Göttingen, 1969), 128–46.

8. Faulkner, *Visit to Germany* 1:100–102; Karl E. Demandt, *Kassel und Marburg: Ein historischer Städtevergleich* (Marburg, 1975).

9. Demandt, *Kassel und Marburg*, 25–27.

10. [Edwin Spencer], *Sketches of Germany and the Germans* (London, 1836), 1:340–41; Faulkner, *Visit to Germany* 1:57.

11. Faulkner, *Visit to Germany* 1:59; Henry E. Dwight, *Travels in the North of Germany in the Years 1825 and 1826* (New York, 1829), 40–41; Russell, *Tour in Germany*, 192.

12. Trollope, *Belgium and Western Germany* 2:218; Russell, *Tour in Germany*, 191; Jacob, *View of Agriculture*, 390.

13. Philipp Losch, *Kurfürst Wilhelm I. Landgraf von Hessen* (Marburg, 1923).

14. Charles W. Ingrao, *The Hessian Mercenary State: Ideas, Institutions, and Reform under Frederick II, 1760–1785* (Cambridge, England, 1987).

15. Karl E. Demandt, *Geschichte des Landes Hessen*, 2d ed. (Cassel, 1972), 279; "Kurhessen under dem Vater, dem Sohne und dem Enkel," in *Demokratische Studien*, ed. Ludwig Walesrode (Hamburg, 1860), 377–442.

16. Ingeborg Schnack, ed., "Wilhelm II., Kurfürst von Hessen," in *Lebensbilder aus Kurhessen und Waldeck 1830–1930* (Marburg, 1939–58), 2:415–22.

17. Schnack, "Friedrich Wilhelm, Kurfürst von Hessen," in *Lebensbilder* 4:91–106.

18. Philipp Losch, *Geschichte des Kurfürstentums Hessen 1803 bis 1866* (Marburg, 1922), 80–106.

19. Ibid., 118; Albert Lotz, "Die Behördenorganisation im ehemaligen Kurhessen nach der Reform von 1821 und ihre Entwicklung in vorpreußischer Zeit," *Schmollers Jahrbuch* 28 (1904): 1343–69.

20. Losch, *Geschichte*, 124–38; Ernst R. Huber, *Deutsche Verfassungsgeschichte seit 1789* (Stuttgart, 1957–78), 1:3–386.

21. Losch, *Geschichte*, 51–63; Manfred Bullick, *Staat und Gesellschaft im hessischen Vormärz: Wahlrecht, Wahlen und öffentliche Meinung in Kurhessen 1830–1848* (Cologne, 1972), 43–86.

22. *Allgemeine Deutsche Biographie*, 14:513–20; *Biographisches Lexikon des Kaiserreichs Oesterreich* (Vienna, 1856–91), 10:260–65; Günter Kleinknecht, *Sylvester Jordan (1792–1861): Ein deutscher Liberal im Vormärz* (Marburg, 1983).

23. Ernst R. Huber, *Dokumente zur deutschen Verfassungsgeschichte* (Stuttgart, 1961–66), 1:201–23; idem, *Verfassungsgeschichte* 2:62–76.

24. Huber, *Verfassungsgeschichte* 2:68–70; Schneider, *Pressefreiheit*, 234.
25. Kleinknecht, *Jordan*, 51–53.

3: The Police State

1. Interior Ministry to Cassel Administration, 27 August 1832, 17 g 74 13.
2. Franz-Ludwig Knemeyer, "Polizei," in Brunner, Conze, and Koselleck, *Geschichtliche Grundbegriffe* 4:875–97, esp. 891.
3. Prince-elector to Captain Wilkens, chargé d'affaires in Berlin, 29 February 1820, 9 b I 225; Foreign Ministry to Lepel, representative to the Confederal Assembly, 28 January 1822, 9 b IV 36.
4. Police Director von Manger, 7 November 1816, with other reports and Kersting's barely coherent explanation of his activities, 5 13107; Privy Council, 2 March 1818, 24 g 724; and correspondence on the "Mediatisierten," 16 VII 23 21.
5. *Sammlung von Gesetzen, Verordnungen, Ausschreiben und sonstigen allgemeinen Verfügungen für die kurhessischen Staaten* (title varies, Cassel, 1813–48), 10 February 1815 and 14 June 1816.
6. Ibid., 19 June 1821.
7. Huber, *Dokumente* 1:90–95; idem, *Verfassungsgeschichte* 1:732–49; Losch, *Geschichte*, 109.
8. Wolfram Siemann, "Ideenschmuggel: Probleme der Meinungskontrolle und das Los deutscher Zensoren im 19. Jahrhundert," *Historische Zeitschrift* 245 (1987): 85.
9. Huber, *Dokumente* 1:119–22; idem, *Verfassungsgeschichte* 2:152–53, 157–58, 162–63.
10. Huber, *Dokumente* 1:123–35; idem, *Verfassungsgeschichte* 2:177–84.
11. Wilhelm II's proclamation, 2 October 1830, 24 a 129; Bullick, *Staat und Gesellschaft*, 45.
12. Murhard, *Verfassungs-Urkunde* 2:150.
13. Huber, *Dokumente* 1:205; Murhard, *Verfassungs-Urkunde* 1:373.
14. *Lebensbilder* 5:101–21; Losch, *Geschichte*, 182–83; *Allgemeine Deutsche Biographie* 27:141–52.
15. *Allgemeine Deutsche Biographie* 11:1–9.
16. Government to Legislature, 12 December 1831, 73 1 B (1900/33) P 2. The government's proposal and the legislature's counterproposal are reprinted in Heinz-Otto Hitzeroth, *Die politische Presse Kurhessens, von der Einführung der Verfassung von 5. Januar 1831 bis zum Ausgang des Kurstaates 1866* (Marburg, 1935), 146–62.
17. Kleinknecht, *Jordan*, 38; Thomas Sirges and Ingeborg Müller, *Zensur in Marburg 1538–1832: Eine lokalgeschichtliche Studie zum Bücher- und Pressewesen* (Marburg, 1984), 165n. 244.
18. Committee proposal and Jordan's report, 2 April 1832, 73 1 B (1900/33) P 2.
19. Legislature to Legislative Commissioner, 10 May, 30 May, 25 July 1832, 73 1 B (1900/33) P 2; Wolf Erich Kellner, *Verfassungskämpfe und Staatsgerichtshof in Kurhessen* (Marburg, 1965), 52.
20. Interior to Cassel Administration, 27 August 1832, 17 g 74 13.
21. Ibid.
22. Interior to Censors, 31 March 1831, and Censors notes, 25 13.
23. Gerling for the committee, 15 and 25 October 1833, 73 1 B (1900/33) P 2.
24. Kleinknecht, *Jordan*, 107–22.
25. Ibid., 129–48.

26. Ibid., 149–55.
27. *Lebensbilder* 1:240–42; *Allgemeine Deutsche Biographie* 30:676–80.

4: This Hated Office

1. Deuchert, *Zur badischen Revolution*, 166; Karl Obermann, ed., *Einheit und Freiheit* (Berlin, 1950), 98–222, esp. 194; Christian Pelzet, *Die Blütezeit der deutschen politischen Lyrik von 1840–1850* (Munich, 1903), 349; Heinrich Gerstenberg, *Die hamburgische Zensur in den Jahren 1819–1848* (Hamburg, 1908), 15; Margarete Kramer, *Die Zensur in Hamburg 1819 bis 1848* (Hamburg, 1975), 77.
2. H. W. Nordmeyer, "Deutscher Buchhandel und Leipziger Zensur 1831–1848," *Journal of English and Germanic Philology* 15 (1916): 364; H. Sieveking, *Karl Sieveking 1787–1847* (Hamburg, 1928), 743.
3. Losch, *Geschichte*, 187; Christoph von Rommel to Interior, October 1831, 16 VII 23 6.
4. M. Laubert, *Presse und Zensur der Provinz Posen in neupreußischer Zeit 1815–1847* (Posen, 1908), 96–98.
5. A list of the censors in Eckhart G. Franz's preface to the catalog of Bestand 25: Zensurkommission; military censors: 2 November 1838, 25 10; 27 December 1847, 25 11.
6. *Neuer Nekrolog der Deutschen*, vol. 15, pt. 2 (1837): 786–88.
7. *Nekrolog*, vol. 7 pt. 1 (1829): 144–49; *Allgemeine Deutsche Biographie* 40: 233–35; Franz Gundlach, ed., *Catalogus Professorum Academiae Marburgensis* (Marburg, 1927), 329–30; Wilhelm Schoof, ed., *Briefe der Brüder Grimm an Savigny* (Berlin, 1953), 330.
8. Karl W. Justi, *Grundlage zu einer hessischen Gelehrten-, Schriftsteller- und Künstlergeschichte, 1806–1830* (Marburg, 1830) 1:159; *Allgemeine Deutsche Biographie* 9:678–88; Schoof, *Briefe*, esp. 53–55, 325–27.
9. Justus Rommel to Interior, 9 November 1829–9 June 1830, 16 VII 23 6; Interior to Censors, 17 June 1830, 25 10.
10. *Lebensbilder* 6:294–309; Franz Christian Theodor Piderit, *Geschichte der Haupt- und Residenzstadt Kassel*, 2d ed., (Cassel, 1882), 495; *Allgemeine Deutsche Biographie* 29:126–28.
11. Sirges and Müller, *Zensur*, 105
12. *Lebensbilder* 1.23–27; Bernhardi's preface to *Vier Briefe, die Gründung der kurfürstlichen Landesbibliothek betreffend* (Cassel, 1853).
13. Justice to Interior, 24 March 1836; Crown Prince to Interior, 27 March–9 December 1841, 16 VII 23 6.
14. Piderit, *Geschichte*, preface to 2d ed. by Jacob Christoph Carl Hoffmeister (Cassel, 1882); 1st ed. (Cassel, 1844), 146, 331–32.
15. *Allgemeine Deutsche Biographie* 32:600–601.
16. Christoph von Rommel to Interior, 6 March–21 November 1831, 16 VII 23 6.
17. Censors, 28 May 1824, 25 4; Censors to Interior, 2 May 1831, 24–30 December 1835, 23 December 1840–3 January 1841, 25 10.
18. Censors to Interior, 20 January 1843, 25 11; record of payment during 1843, 25 26; Censors, 15 May 1846, 25 11.
19. Losch, *Geschichte*, 166–87; Hitzeroth, *Presse*, 20–21, 107–10.
20. Edmund Stengel, ed., *Private und amtliche Beziehungen der Brüder Grimm zu Hessen* (Marburg, 1866), 2:125–28; Schoof, *Briefe*, 299.

21. Otto Gerland, ed., *Grundlage zu einer hessischen Gelehrten-, Schriftsteller- und Künstlergeschichte von 1831 bis in die neueste Zeit* (Cassel, 1863–68), 1:7–34; Censors to Interior, 20 January 1836, 28 October 1837, 25 10.

22. Censors, 7 November 1847, 25 11.

23. Interior to Censors, 29 November 1844, 25 11.

24. Dean of Philosophical Faculty to Dean of Theological Faculty, 27 October 1796, 307 a 3; also packet 5 16339; Rinteln Administration to Prince-elector, 14 March 1818, 16 VIII 23 11; Hanau Censors to Count, 28 January 1792, 81 E 1 IV d 5; decree of 15 May 1775, 91 707; decree of 1 September 1780, 16 VII 23 6; also Eckhart G. Franz, "Jacob Grimm in der Kasseler Zensurkommission (1816–1829)," *Zeitschrift des Vereins für hessische Geschichte und Landeskunde*, 75 /76 (1964 /65): 455–56; Theodor Bitterauf, "Die Zensur der politischen Zeitungen in Bayern 1779–1825," in *Beiträge zur Bayerischen Geschichte*, ed. Karl Alexander von Müller (Gotha, 1913), 306; Karlheinz Fuchs, *Bürgerliches Räsonnement und Staatsräson: Zensur als Instrument des Despotismus dargestellt am Beispiel des rheinbündischen Württemberg (1806–1813)* (Göppingen, 1975), 50; Rüdiger Busch, *Die Aufsicht über das Bücher- und Pressewesen in den Rheinbundstaaten Berg, Westfalen und Frankfurt* (Karlsruhe, 1970).

25. Franz, "Jacob Grimm," 456–60.

26. Sirges and Müller, *Zensur*, 102–8, 165n. 255.

27. Christoph von Rommel to Interior, 19 June 1830, 25 10; Interior to Marburg Police, 11 August 1832, 24 d 132; article 135 of the 1831 constitution, Huber, *Dokumente* 1:220; Interior, 25 January 1834, *Sammlung* (1834), 4.

28. Rinteln Administration to Prince-elector, 14 March 1818–19 October 1819; Interior to Rinteln Censors, 3 November 1832, May–19 June 1837, 16 VII 23 11; Rinteln Censors to Censors, 17 September 1830, 25 26; Rinteln Administration to Interior, 17 October 1822, 17 g 73 4; Interior to Censors, 27 November 1822, 25 4.

29. Censors, 23 September 1824, 10 May–1 August 1827, 16 VII 23 11; Hanau Administration to Hanau Censors, 7 June 1832–8 September 1833, 25 28; Hanau Administration, 14 May 1832, 82 c 780; Interior to Censors, 20 March 1835, 25 10; Hitzeroth, *Presse*, 110–14.

30. Franz, "Jacob Grimm," 463–66; Interior, 21 September 1832, 180 Marburg 262.

31. "Kurze Uebersicht," Interior to Foreign, 14 March 1843, 9 a 1713. It is reprinted in Hitzeroth *Presse*, 182–84.

32. Christoph von Rommel to Interior, 20 October 1831, 16 VII 23 6.

33. Stengel, *Brüder Grimm* 2:124.

34. Censors, 30 December 1841, 25 11.

35. Casparson and Wigand to Privy Council, 22 December 1797, 16 VII 23 6; Stengel, *Brüder Grimm* 2:123; Christoph von Rommel to Interior, 6 March 1831, 16 VII 23 6; Bernhardi to Interior, 20 January 1836, 25 10.

36. Stengel, *Brüder Grimm* 2:128; Christoph von Rommel to Interior, 20 October 1831, 16 VII 23 6; Censors to Interior, 24 September 1837, 25 19.

37. Stengel, *Brüder Grimm* 2:129; Censors, 15 January 1847, 25 11.

38. Censors to Interior, 21 December 1841, 25 13; Censors, 30 December 1841–24 June 1842, 25 11.

39. Interior to Cassel Administration, 26 July 1839, 180 Kassel 2198; Justice to Supreme Court, Civil Senate, 10 February 1841, 261 10 (1941/8) 67; Christoph von Rommel and Bernhardi to Interior, 30 December 1835–20 January 1836, 25 10; Interior to Censors, 22 May and 9 July 1846, 7 November 1847, 25 11.

40. Interior to Censors, 13 June 1837, 25 19.
41. Censors, 30 November 1844, 25 20; Interior to Censors, 28 July 1845, 25 21.

5: DREADFUL, TIRESOME READING

1. Stengel, *Brüder Grimm*.
2. Matthias Wellnhofer, "Die Anfänge der Leihbibliotheken und Lesegesellschaften in Bayern," *Heimat und Volkstum* 17 (1939): 289–91; Marlies Prüsener, "Lesegesellschaften im 18. Jahrhundert," *Archiv für Geschichte des Buchwesens* 13 (1972): 384; Frolinde Balser, *Die Anfänge der Erwachsenenbildung in Deutschland in der ersten Hälfte des 19. Jahrhunderts* (Stuttgart, 1959), 63–64.
3. *Sammlung* (1816), p. 74, sec. 2; ibid., (1821), p. 51, sec. 88, para. 5; Interior to Marburg Administration, 29 June 1821, 180 Marburg 29.
4. Censors, notes of 3 August 1823, printed in Stengel, *Brüder Grimm* 2:128–33.
5. Interior to Foreign, 18 May 1840, 9 a 2896.
6. *Wochenblatt für Buchhändler* 1 (1819): 2; ibid. 2 (1822): 299, quoting from the *Beobachter am Main und Rhein;* Eduard Berger, "Der deutsche Buchhandel in seiner Entwicklung und in seinen Einrichtungen in den Jahren 1815 bis 1867," *Archiv für Geschichte des deutschen Buchhandels* 2 (1877): 125–234.
7. The numbers are for all libraries known to me during the years 1823–1847. Often there is positive evidence of a library for only several years; in some cases there is only a single reference. See 17 g 74 13 and 34; 24 b 153, 24 d 136, 24 f 45, 25 24 and 25, 82 c 771, 175 1284, 180 Kassel 2198, and 180 Marburg 29.
8. Councilor on Instruction and Dean of the Cathedral Pfaff to Fulda Police, 5 August 1830, 24 g 729.
9. Melsungen County Office to Lower Hessian Administration, 27 April 1837, 17 g 74 13.
10. Letter of 9 January 1845 in Cassel Police to Censors, 25 January 1837, 25 25.
11. 20 and 30 April, 21 May, 7 July 1836, 25 24.
12. 19 March [May?], 3 and 10 June, 1836, 19 h 868; 27 July, 15 and 25 August, 27 September, 7 October 1836, July 1837, 25 24.
13. Malkmus and Klöffler to Marburg Police, 16–19 January 1837, 24 d 136.
14. Malkmus and Schmidt to Marburg Police, 1 December 1837 and 26 February 1838, 24 d 136.
15. Trinthammer to Hanau Police, 17 December 1838, and Hanau Police to Interior, 8 October 1840, 24 f 45; Interior to Censors, 26–30 November 1840, 25 24.
16. Interior, 19 December 1840, 24 f 48; Marburg Administration to Police, 14 December 1840, and Interior, 27 April 1841, 24 d 136.
17. Censors to Interior, 12 February 1841, 25 24, Crown Prince to Interior, 27 March 1841, Rommel to Interior, 5–20 November 1841, 16 VII 23 6.
18. Cassel Police to Censors, 29 November and 5 December 1847, 25 11.
19. Interior to Foreign, 18 June 1840, 9 a 2896.
20. Hitzeroth, *Presse*, 15–19, 133–41; Losch, *Geschichte*, 108, 145–46, 166.
21. 10 December 1818–13 December 1819, 24 f 46; Hitzeroth, *Presse*, 23–25.
22. Hans-Friedrich Meyer, *Zeitungspreise in Deutschland im 19. Jahrhundert und ihre gesellschaftliche Bedeutung,* (Münster, 1969), 23–42, 202; P. Magill, "The German Author and his Public in the Mid-Nineteenth Century," *Modern Language Review* 43 (1948): 494n. 9; *Wochenblatt für Buchhändler* 6 (1826): 391; Rolf Engelsing, "Zeitung und Zeitschrift in Nordwestdeutschland 1800–1850: Leser und Journalisten," *Archiv für Geschichte des Buchwesens* 5 (1962/64): 865.

23. Interior to Cassel Administration, 27 June 1824, 17 g 13 4; Clerk Nordmann to Cassel Police, 16 August 1843, 24 b 210; Hanau Police to editor, 10 December 1818, etc., 24 f 46; idem, 29 September 1832, 24 f 42; Police Councilor Bernhardi to Interior, 25 February 1832, 73 1 B (1900/33) P 2; Fulda Police to Interior, 1 July and 24 October 1832, 24 g 730; Sirges and Müller, 110–12.

24. Interior to Cassel Administration, 27 June 1824, 17 g 13 4; Interior to Censors, 23 January 1846, 25 18; idem, 2 June 1845, 25 11; Privy Council to Censors, 14 December 1819 and Bailiff Walther to Hanau Administration, 4 January 1840, 82 c 432.

25. Office of the Chief Administrator of the Israelites to Cassel Administration, 29 May 1823 and 12 March 1841, 17 g 74 16.

26. Hitzeroth, *Presse*, 107; Censors, a note during 1834, 25 13; censored proof sheets of the *Israelit*, 25 16; Interior to Censors, 12 and 19 December 1843, 25 11; idem, 8 January 1847, 25 18.

27. Interior to Christoph von Rommel and Hanau Police Director Neuhof, 19 May 1831, 24 f 11.

28. Hanau Police Director Neuhof to Representative at the Confederal Assembly, 22 November 1831, 9 b VIII 18; Interior to Hanau Administration, 12 November 1831, 82 c 782.

29. *Protokolle der deutschen Bundesversammlung (1816–1866)*, 1832: 176–77; Bernhardi to Interior, 25 February 1832, 73 1 B (1900/33) P 2.

30. Hanau Administration and Ministry of War to Fulda Police, 17 January–7 March 1832, Fulda Police to Jakob Förster, 16–17 April 1832, Police Director Scheffer to Interior, 1–17 July 1832, Printer Müller to Fulda Police, 24 October 1832, 24 g 730; Jakob Förster to Censors, 7 October 1832, 25 13; Hannes Rieder, "Die ersten politischen Zeitungen in Fulda," *Buchenblätter* (Fulda), 17 (1936): 79–80.

31. Interior, 12 March 1841 (including protocol of 21 September 1832), 19 h 869.

32. Hitzeroth, *Presse*, 110–15.

33. Interior to Foreign, 14 March 1843 (including "Kurze Uebersicht"), 9 a 1713; Interior to editor of *Bote aus Kassel*, 30 November 1839, 41 I 3 66.

34. Hanau police, early 1831?, 24 f 94.

35. Censors, 8 October 1832, 25 28; Hanau police, 1–20 October 1832, 14 March 1834, 2 March 1835, 24 f 41.

36. There is no single compilation of requests. My figures are based on cullings from various files cited in this chapter, and it is very likely that they are incomplete.

37. Garthe to Marburg Administration, 3 September–3 December 1831, 19 h 868; Hanau County Office, 20 October–14 November 1831, 82 e 782; Interior to Fulda Police, 5 April 1831, 12 March–9 April 1832, 24 g 730.

38. Collector Zumber of Frankenberg to Ziegenhain County Office, 23 July 1847, 180 Ziegenhain 2726; Heinrich Hotop to Cassel County Office, 10–11 December 1839, 180 Kassel 2198.

39. Robert Prutz, *Zehn Jahre: Geschichte der neuesten Zeit. 1840–1850* (Leipzig, 1850), 1:535.

40. Georg Sommer, "Die Zensurgeschichte des Königreichs Hannover" (Ph.D. diss., University of Muenster, 1929), 42.

6: The Logic of Censorship

1. On lists kept then and the list compiled now, see the Appendix.

2. 25 7–9 [1817–29] and 25 13–18 [1830–48]. The manuscripts are not preserved. On the 1820s, see Franz, "Jacob Grimm," 464–66.

3. Friedrich Murhard to G. F. Cotta, 28 June 1837, in Herbert Schiller, ed., *Briefe an Cotta* (Stuttgart, 1925–34), 3:395.
4. Losch, *Geschichte*, 114–15, 142–44, 206–10; Justi, *Grundlage;* Gerland, *Grundlage; Foreign Quarterly Review* 25 (1840): 249.
5. Karl Schäfer, "Fulda, das kurhessische Siberien," *Vergangenheit* (Fulda) 4 (1951): nr. 6; Günther Hohmann, *Heinrich König: Leben und Werk des Fuldaer Schriftstellers* . . . (Fulda, 1965).
6. Bailiff Windemuth to Prince-elector, 6 March 1818; Privy Council, 13 March 1818, 16 VII 23 21.
7. Hanau Police to Prince-elector, 31 March 1819, 16 VII 23 21; J. Petmecky, "Karl Bernhardi" (Ph.D. diss., University of Frankfort on Main, 1929); Karl-Ludwig Ay, "Das Frag- und Antwortbüchlein des Darmstädtischen Offiziers Friedrich Wilhelm Schulz," *Zeitschrift für Bayerische Landesgeschichte* 35 (1972): 728–70; Walter Grab, *Ein Mann der Marx Ideen Gab: Wilhelm Schulz, Weggefährte Georg Büchners, Demokrat der Paulskirche* (Düsseldorf, 1979), 34–47.
8. F. Hermann Meyer, "Bücherverbote im Königreiche Preußen von 1834 bis 1882," *Archiv für Geschichte des Deutschen Buchhandels* 14 (1889): 317–49, lists 360 works banned in Prussia between 1835 and 1845. It excludes most bans suggested by the Confederal Assembly and all those aimed at lending libraries. My count for Hesse-Cassel in that decade is 186, including both sorts that Meyer excludes.

For bans of German-language publications in Austria, see Julius Marx, "Liste der beschlagnahmten und mit Schedenverbot belegten Werke: I. Werke in deutscher Sprache," in *Die österreichische Zensur im Vormärz* (Vienna, 1959), 97–106. Because the Austrian system allowed for several degrees of censorship, among them confiscation, which is the one Marx has counted, comparisions of this list with the lists for Prussia and Hesse are yet more difficult.

9. Hans-Joachim Ruckhäberle, *Flugschriftenliteratur im historischen Umkreis Georg Büchners* (Kronberg, 1975), 65.
10. Losch, *Geschichte*, 208–9, 214–15, 224, 239, 337.
11. See Ruckhäberle, *Flugschriftenliteratur*, 11–18, on the difficulty of deciding what was a pamphlet. On prices, ibid., 176; *Wochenblatt für Buchhändler* 7 (1825): 337.
12. Marburg Police, 7 August 1832, 24 d 129; Interior to Marburg Administration, 10 September 1832, 180 Marburg 262; Rinteln Police to Cassel Administration, 9 February 1836, 17 g 74 30; Censors, 19 May 1836, 25 19; Interior to Marburg Administration, 1 June 1836, 180 Marburg 262.
13. Marburg Police to Censors, 6 August 1838, 24 d 130; Marburg County Office, 29 December 1836, 180 Marburg 262; Ziegenhain County Office, 26 June 1837, 19 h 868; Frankenberg County Office, 2 May 1838, 24 d 130.
14. Hoefer, *Pressepolitik und Polizeistaat*.
15. *Kurhessisches Staats- und Adressbuch auf das Jahr 1825* (Cassel, 1825), 102–4; *Kurfürstliches Hessisches Hof- und Staatsadressbuch auf das Jahr 1845* (Cassel, 1845), 102–4.
16. Interior to Censors, 20 October 1837, 25 28; 4 December 1837 and 26 February 1842, 25 11.
17. Foreign to Interior, 4 August 1832, 9 a 1717; Interior to Foreign, 30 November 1833, 9 a 1715; 22 April 1836, 9 a 2895; 18 May 1840, 9 a 2896; 14 March 1843, 9 a 1713.
18. Interior to Foreign, 2 February 1841 [actually 1842], 9 a 1007; delegates Fritsch of grand duchy of Saxony, Steglitz of kingdom of Saxony, and Dornberg of Prussia to Rieß of Hesse-Cassel, 26–29 November 1842, 9 a 1708; Interior to Foreign

and Finance, Foreign to Prussia, 23 September–20 December 1836, 9 a 1705; Rieß in Frankfort to Foreign, 5 April 1844, 9 a 1007.

19. Kocher in Munich to Foreign, 29 March 1833; Hesse-Darmstadt to Foreign, 29 July 1846; Hamburg to Foreign, 6 January 1847, 9 a 1708; Baden to Foreign, 24 September 1847, 9 a 1709.

20. Rieß in Frankfort to Foreign, 31 May 1838 and April 1840; Saxony to Foreign, 12 November 1845; Hamburg to Foreign, 22 June 1846; Denmark to Foreign, 24 September 1846, 9 a 1708.

21. Foreign, 9 April–23 August 1847, 9 a 1709.

22. Rieß in Frankfort to Foreign, 13 July–11 September 1847; Foreign to Rieß, 17 January–22 March 1848, 9 b IV 251; *Protokolle der deutschen Bundesversammlung*, 5th session of 1848 (February), para. 66, pp. 102–3.

23. Foreign, 9 a 1716.

24. Interior to Foreign, 20 July 1844, 9 a 1716; Foreign to Berlin embassy, 1 September 1844, 9 b I 225.

25. Hamburg to Foreign, 22 April 1846, 9 a 1708.

26. Bavaria to Foreign, c. 20 August 1832, 16 VII 17 I; Rieß in Frankfort to Foreign, 29 January 1834, 9 a 1709; Rieß to Foreign, 25 October 1844, 9 a 1706; Interior to Foreign, 3 January 1839, 9 a 1705.

27. Foreign, 9 a 1705 and 9 a 1706; Heinrich H. Houben, *Verbotene Literatur von der klassischen Zeit bis zur Gegenwart* (Berlin, 1924–28), 1:421–22.

28. Richard Walter Franke, "Zensur und Preßaufsicht in Leipzig 1830–1848" (Ph.D. diss., University of Leipzig, 1930), 143–58; Bitterauf, "Zensur," 337–51; Gerstenberg, *Zensur*, passim; Karl Glossy, *Literarische Geheimberichte aus dem Vormärz* (published as *Jahrbuch der Grillparzergesellschaft* 21–23 [1912]), 1:104, 15 February 1837.

29. Marx, *Zensur*, 97–115.

30. Meyer, "Bücherverbote," 321–23, 331.

31. Prutz, *Zehn Jahre* 1:363ff.; Meyer, "Bücherverbote," 327–28; Edmund Silberner, "Johann Jacoby 1843–1846: Beitrag zur Geschichte des Vormärz," *International Review of Social History* 14 (1969): 353–60; F. Falkson, *Die liberale Bewegung in Königsberg 1840–1848* (Breslau, 1888), 43–44.

32. Houben, *Verbotene Literatur* 1:421–22; Censors, 3 November 1844, 19 h 869.

33. Houben, *Verbotene Literatur* 1:213–15; Censors, 4 November 1844, 25 20.

7: Scrutiny before Sale

1. Defendants' petition to the Supreme Court, c. 21 August 1844, 261 6 Kriminalakten II K 310 Kempf; *Deutsche Allgemeine Zeitung*, nr. 305 (31 October 1844), p. 2686, in 9 a 1716.

2. F. Hermann Meyer, "Mittheilungen zur inneren Geschichte des deutschen Buchhandels von 1811–1848," *Archiv für Geschichte des deutschen Buchhandels* 9 (1884): 188; Reinhart Koselleck, *Preußen zwischen Reform und Revolution: Allgemeines Landrecht, Verwaltung und soziale Bewegung von 1791 bis 1848* (Stuttgart, 1975), 429n. 135; 24 g 730.

3. *Wochenblatt für Buchhändler* 6 (1827): 386; Paul Heidelbach, *Aus der Geschichte der C. Vietor'schen Buchhandlung Gustav Romer, Kassel 1837–1937* (Cassel, 1937), 33.

4. Verdict of 6 February 1836, 270 f Kassel II K 25 Kempf.

5. Kempf to the court, 22 June 1843, verdict of 27 March 1844, verdict of 10 December 1845, 270 f Kassel II K 28 Kempf.

NOTES TO PAGES 113-26

6. Verdict, 261 6 Kriminalakten II K 310 Kempf.
7. Fulda Police, 15 July 1844, 24 g 725.
8. Euler to Fulda Police, 17 March–28 August 1848, 24 g 725.
9. Dated signatures of mayors acknowledging receipt of notices sent on 9 January 1839, 21 April 1845, 7 September 1846, 180 Hünfeld 127.
10. Police Headquarters to Lower Hesse Police, 17 June 1824, 24 d 129; county councilors to Lower Hesse Administration, November 1824, 17 g 74 9.
11. Interior to Marburg Administration, 28 December 1821, 180 Marburg 163.
12. Marburg Administration to local officials, 30 April 1841, 180 Ziegenhain 2241.
13. These estimates are based on counts from the files cited in the appendix.
14. Fulda Police, 29 October 1832, 24 g 730; Marburg Police, 5 December 1832, 24 d 129.
15. Interior to Marburg Police, 24 September 1833, 24 d 129; Fulda Police, 29 September 1833 and 14 June 1834, 24 g 725; Marburg Administration, 27 June 1834, 180 Marburg 262.
16. Cassel Police, 7–25 January 1841, 24 b 153; Fulda Police, 22–26 August 1846, 24 g 725.
17. Cassel booksellers to Interior, 24 January 1843, 17 g 74 34; 24 g 730.
18. Exchanges between Hoffmann and Eschwege County Councilor, October 1824 and March 1843, 17 g 74 19; Eschwege County Councilor to Lower Hesse Administration, 5 May 1840, 180 Kassel 2198.
19. Petitions of 4 December 1832, 17 g 74 13; 19 November 1842, 17 g 74 34; 7 June 1843, 175 Kassel 1284; 8 November 1828, 180 Fritzlar 180; 5 December 1844, 24 g 732; January 1844, 180 Fritzlar 180; Heidelbach, *Geschichte,* 23.
20. Cited by Edda Ziegler, *Julius Campe: Heinrich Heines Verleger* (Hamburg, 1976), 297.
21. Fulda Police, 14 June 1834, 24 g 725; Marburg Police, 27 June 1834, 180 Marburg 262.
22. Cassel Police, 22 December 1841, 24 b 153.
23. Krieger's submission, 17 October 1846, 25 27; Interior, 22 October 1846, 19 h 870; Fulda Police, 2 November 1846, 24 g 725.
24. Marburg Police, 25 May 1840, 270 Marburg 3 1 (1875/35) 4 Garthe; 23 June 1842 and 13 June 1843, 24 d 130.
25. Fulda Police, 4 May 1845, 24 g 725.
26. Censors, 31 May–7 June 1844, 25 11; Cassel Police to Censors, 2 September 1844, 25 12.
27. Interior to Censors, 18–28 September 1844, 25 12.
28. Interior to Censors, 15 January–11 February 1846, 4 February 1847, 25 12.
29. Merz to Interior, 31 January 1836, 82 c 771.
30. Osterwald court papers, 14 July 1836, 270 (1903/9) Hanau e 3 62.
31. Interior to Rinteln Administration, 15 August 1836, 17 g 74 30; Interior, 6 September 1836, 16 VII 23 54.
32. Edler's bill, 15 January 1836, 82 c 771; Interior to Hanau Administration, 11 February 1836, 16 VII 23 54.

8: Top Secret

1. Cassel District Court to Cassel Superior Court, 21 October 1834, 16 VII 12 27.

2. Supreme Court, 10 June 1842, 261 Kriminalakten II G 193 Geeh.
3. Eckhart G. Franz, ed., *Der Hessische Landbote* (Marburg, 1973), afterword 1–2, 9–11. See also Reinhard Görisch and Thomas Michael Mayer, eds., *Untersuchungsberichte zur republikanischen Bewegung in Hessen 1831–1834* (Frankfort, 1982), 343–45, 387, on the printing of an extract from the *Words of a Believer* at Elwert's.
4. Marburg Police, 24–25 September 1841, 24 d 132.
5. Censors to Elwert, 26 June, 27 July, 4 August 1842, 25 26; Elwert to Censors, 29 July 1842, 25 11.
6. Censors, 15 June 1846, 25 11.
7. Censors, 18 February–30 June 1831, 25 13.
8. Interior Minister Hassenpflug to Censors, 11 February 1834, 25 13; Censors, 22 May 1846, 25 11.
9. Garthe petitions to open a bookstore, 10 November 1821, through 1846, 19 i 866; he submits the sixteenth addendum of his catalog to Marburg Police, 30 October 1838, 24 d 136.
10. Gendarmerie, 5 July 1832, 16 VII 17 I; Upper Hessian Superior Court to Marburg District Court, 27 May 1840, 270 Marburg e 1 (1875/35) 4 Garthe.
11. 11 May 1840, 270 Marburg e 1 (1875/35) 4 Garthe.
12. Ibid., 29 May 1840.
13. The meeting had actually been with Ludwig Weidig, co-author with Georg Büchner of the *Hessian Courier*. See Görisch and Mayer, *Untersuchungsberichte*, 362.
14. 14 May 1840, 270 Marburg e 1 (1875/35) 4 Garthe.
15. Ibid., 21 May 1840.
16. Ibid.
17. Geeh to Supreme Court, 4 January 1842, 261 Kriminalakten II G 193 Geeh.
18. Geeh to Interior, 11 November 1829–6 January 1830, 17 g 74 13.
19. Geeh to Cassel County Office, 14 February 1833, 180 Kassel 2198; Interior to Cassel Administration, 25 February 1834, 17 g 74 13.
20. Geeh to Supreme Court, 28 April 1832, and the court's decision, 22 August 1832, 261 Kriminalakten 1822–36 G 54 Geeh.
21. Geeh to Supreme Court, 8 December 1832, and the court's decision, 24 January 1833, 261 Kriminalakten 1822–36 G 59 Geeh.
22. Supreme Court decisions, 24 January 1833, 25 January 1833, 17 February 1833, 261 Kriminalakten 1822–36 G 59, G 60, and G 75 Geeh.
23. Cassel Superior Court, 31 May–3 June 1833, 270 f Kassel II G 5 Geeh; Geeh to Cassel Superior Court, 24 April 1835, Public Prosecutor to Cassel Superior Court, 14 November 1835, Supreme Court decision, 8 April 1839, 270 f Kassel II G 6 Geeh; Cassel Superior Court and Supreme Court decisions, 31 January 1837 and 23 December 1837, 261 6 II 146 Geeh.
24. Justice to Interior, 11 October 1834, Cassel Police, 13–14 October 1834, 16 VII 12 27.
25. Cassel District Court to Cassel Superior Court, Criminal Senate, 21 October 1834, 16 VII 12 27.
26. Cassel Superior Court to Supreme Court, 18 January 1839, 261 Kriminalakten II G 193 Geeh.
27. Justice to Supreme Court, 12 October 1840, and the court's decision, 10 June 1842, 261 Kriminalakten II G 193 Geeh.
28. Tapp, *Hanau im Vormärz*, 140–88.
29. Marburg Police, 11–13 October 1846, 24 d 7; Interior, 23 October 1846, 19 h 870; Fulda Police, 5 November 1846, 24 d 7.

30. Bayrhoffer to Marburg Superior Court, 30 July 1846–1 October 1847, 270 Marburg g 2 (1882/60) 9 B 4 Bayrhoffer.

9: Friends of a Free Press

1. Fulda Police, 24 July 1833, and undated during 1832, 24 g 485.

2. Franz Stix, "Zur Geschichte und Organisation der Wiener Geheimen Ziffernkanzlei (von ihrem Anfang bis zum Jahre 1848)," *Mitteilungen des österreichischen Instituts für Geschichte* 51 (1937): 138–41; Gustav Heinrich Schneider, "Der Preß- oder Vaterlandsverein 1832-33: Ein Beitrag zur Geschichte des Frankfurter Attentats" (Ph.D. diss., University of Heidelberg, 1897), 98–99; Houben, *Verbotene Literatur* 1:132; Gelnhausen County Office, 12 March 1824, 180 Gelnhausen 7217; Ay, "Frag- und Antwortbüchlein," 728–35; Grab, *Ein Mann*, 47–50.

3. Marburg Police, 16 October 1832, 24 d 129; Gendarmerie to Marburg County Office, 3 July 1836, 180 Marburg 262; Marburg Police, 22 April 1846, 24 d 138; Censors, 11 June 1847, 25 23.

4. Melsungen Administration to Lower Hessian Police, 23 March 1822, 17 g 74 9.

5. Witzenhausen County Office, 2 August 1828, 180 Witzenhausen 542.

6. Bailiff Eichendorf at Allendorf to Schultheiße, 7 March 1818, 16 VII 23 21; Lower Hessian Administration to Fritzlar County Office, 5 July 1823 and 6 November 1824, 180 Fritzlar 469.

7. Marburg Police to Marburg County Office, 22 November 1834, 180 Marburg 262; Interior, 29 December 1834, 330 Treysa 936.

8. Gelnhausen County Office, 24 July 1832, 180 Gelnhausen 7217; Schmalkalden Gendarmerie to Fulda County Office, 4 September 1832, 180 Fulda 21; Fulda Police, 29 September 1845, 24 g 725.

9. Censors, 20 June 1832, 25/19; Fritzlar and Witzenhausen County Offices to Cassel Administration, 7 July 1832, 17 g 74 32.

10. Wilhelm Hopf, *August Vilmar: Ein Lebens- und Zeitbild* (Marburg, 1913), 2:454–55.

11. Hanau Police, 10 August 1832, and a Munich court to Hanau Police, 1 June 1841, 24 f 47.

12. Witzenhausen County Office to Lower Hessian Police, 15 October 1835, and Eisenach police report, 21 October 1835, 24 c 85; Friedrich Wilhelm Kosch, "Das Grazer Bücherrevisionsamt 1781-1848," *Zeitschrift des Historischen Vereins für Steiermark* 60 (1969): 69.

13. Heiligenstock Customs Office to Hanau Police, 2 August 1834, and Erfurt police report, 19 August 1834, 24 f 32.

14. Hanau Police and Marburg Police to Interior, 30 April–7 May 1831, 16 VII 23 15.

15. Marburg Police, 4 August 1832, 24 d 129.

16. Walter M. Fraeb, *Der Buchhandel in Hanau und der Buchhändler Friedrich König* (Hanau, 1931), 95.

17. Fulda Police to Interior, 22 September 1831, 24 g 773, and 24 September 1831, 16 VII 23 15.

18. Fulda Police, 22–26 August and 17 December 1846, 24 g 725; Hünfeld County Office, 10 September 1846, 180 Hünfeld 127.

19. Fulda Police, 24 July 1833, 24 g 485; Fulda Police, 7 February–31 December 1844, 24 g 725.

20. Rudolf Schenda, *Volk ohne Buch: Studien zur Sozialgeschichte der populären Lesestoffe 1770–1910* (Frankfort on Main, 1970), and idem, *Die Lesestoffe der kleinen Leute: Studien zur populären Literatur im 19. und 20. Jahrhundert* (Munich, 1976).

21. Fulda Police, 28 October 1832, 24 g 730.

22. Fulda Post Office to Fulda Police, 19 November 1832, 24 g 489; Fulda County Office, 14 December 1832, 180 Fulda 21; Hünfeld County Office, 2 December 1832, 180 Hünfeld 127; Central Post Office and Rinteln Police to Interior, 22 May and 7 September 1844, 17 g 74 37.

23. Undated subscription list accompanying Fulda Police, 29 September 1833, 24 g 485.

24. Helmuth Janson, *45 Lesegesellschaften um 1800 bis heute* (Bonn, 1963), 19, 33–38, 47.

25. Cassel Police, 1 October–20 December 1815 and 1 September 1821, 24 b 143.

26. Marburg Police to Interior, 1 December 1831 and 28 May 1834, 16 VII 12 43 1; Marburg Police, 28 July–7 August and 28 November 1832, 24 d 129.

27. Documents on the founding of the Academic Museum, 7 August 1832; Marburg Police and University Prorector to Interior, 19–21 December 1845, 16 VII 12 48.

28. Marburg Police, November–December 1845, 24 d 138.

29. Wangemann to Interior, 19 December 1845–2 January 1846, 16 VII 12 48; New Museum to University Library, 10 January 1846, 308 (1937/106) 34; Interior to Marburg Police, 1 October 1847, 16 VII 12 48.

30. Murhard, *Verfassungs-Urkunde* 2:197–98.

31. Fritzlar County Office, 12 April–11 May 1835, 180 Fritzlar 165.

32. Losch, *Geschichte*, 136n. 1; Interior, 2 November 1832, and Rinteln Police to Interior, 2 February 1844, 16 VII 12 43 1; Rotenburg County Office, 17 February 1844, 17 g 74 34.

33. Interior, 29 March 1832, 19 h 868; Hanau Police to Interior, 25 May 1834, 16 VII 12 43 1.

34. Ulrich Eisenhardt, *Die kaiserliche Aufsicht über Buchdruck, Buchhandel und Presse im Heiligen Römischen Reich Deutscher Nation (1496–1806)* (Karlsruhe, 1970), 137–39; Tapp, *Hanau im Vormärz*.

35. Hanau Police to Interior, 16 August 1832, 16 VII 12 43 1.

36. Fulda Police to Interior, 25 September 1832, 16 VII 12 43 1.

37. Fulda Administration to Interior, 25 September–26 November 1832, 16 VII 12 43 1; Paul Krüger, " 'Hochverräterische Unternehmungen' in Studentenschaft und Bürgertum des Vormärz in Oberhessen (bis 1838)," *Mitteilungen des oberhessischen Geschichtsvereins* 49/50 (1965): 97.

38. Fulda Police to Interior, 16 February 1834, 16 VII 12 43 1.

39. Fulda Police, 15 August 1846, 24 g 725; Fulda Police to Interior, 2 November 1846, 16 VII 12 43 1.

10: The Failure of Censorship

1. Losch, *Geschichte*, 235–36.

2. Heine, *Sämtliche Werke* 1:320.

3. On politics and the press in Hesse from 1848 to 1860: Losch, *Geschichte*, 245–91; Hitzeroth, *Presse*, 115–32.

4. James J. Sheehan, *German Liberalism in the Nineteenth Century* (Chicago, 1979), 77–78, 96–97; Wolfram Siemann, *"Deutschlands Ruhe, Sicherheit und Ordnung": Die Anfänge der politischen Polizei 1806–1866* (Tübingen, 1985), 242–304.

5. Moran, *Century of Words*, 17–18, 270–71.
6. Ludwig Walesrode, *Der Humor auf der Bank der Angeklagten* . . . (Mannheim, 1844), 51.
7. Glossy, *Geheimberichte*, 1:lxiii, ciii.
8. Quoted in Willy Klawitter, *Geschichte der Zensur in Schlesien*, Deutschkundliche Arbeiten, B—Schlesische Reihe 2 (Breslau, 1934), 165–66.
9. Moran, *Century of Words*, 204–7; Deuchert, *Zur Badischen Revolution*, 73–74; Ziegler, *Julius Campe*, 37–49; Manfred Treml, *Bayerns Pressepolitik zwischen Verfassungstreue und Bundespflicht (1815–1837): Ein Beitrag zum bayerischen Souveränitätsverständnis und Konstitutionalismus im Vormärz* (Berlin, 1977), 42, 46–50.
10. Koselleck, *Reform und Revolution*, 415; Treml, *Pressepolitik*, 49, 95, 255–60; Schneider, *Pressefreiheit*, 266–67.
11. Deuchert, *Zur Badischen Revolution*, 78–81; Treml, *Pressepolitik*, 145–49; Schneider, *Pressefreiheit*, 171, 222–24.
12. Koselleck, *Reform und Revolution*, 404–16.
13. Schneider, *Pressefreiheit*, 232–40.
14. Koselleck, *Reform und Revolution*, 403–4, 417–18.

Select Bibliography

Archival Sources
(in the Hessian State Archive at Marburg)

File 5 Hessischer Geheimer Rat (16 Jh.-1821)
     6 Polizei
     9 Ministerium des kurfürstlichen Hauses und der auswärtigen Angelegenheiten; auswärtige Vertretungen
       a Ministerium
       b Gesandtschaften
          I Berlin
          IV Bundestag
    16 Ministerium des Innern
    17 Regierung Kassel
    19 Regierung Marburg
    24 Polizeibehörden des 19. Jahrhunderts
    25 Zensurkommission Kassel
    73 Hessische Landstände
    82 Regierung Hanau, in der Hauptsache nach 1821
    86 Hanauer Nachträge
    91 Fulda, Weltliche Regierung
  175 Polizeipräsidium Kassel
  180 Landratsämter
      Fritzlar, Fulda, Gelnhausen, Hanau, Hünfeld, Kassel, Marburg, Witzenhausen, Ziegenhain
  261 Oberappellationsgericht Kassel Kriminalakten 1822–1848
  270 Mittlere Gerichte und Staatsanwaltschaften
  307 Universität Marburg, Fakultäten
      a Theologische Fakultät
  308 Universitätsbibliothek Marburg
  330 Stadtarchive
      Homberg, Treysa, Ziegenhain

SELECT BIBLIOGRAPHY

Published Sources

Allgemeine Deutsche Biographie. 56 vols. Leipzig, 1875–1912.
Ay, Karl-Ludwig. "Das Frag- und Antwortbüchlein des Darmstädtischen Offiziers Friedrich Wilhelm Schulz." *Zeitschrift für Bayerische Landesgeschichte* 35 (1972): 728–70.
Berger, Eduard. "Der deutsche Buchhandel in seiner Entwicklung und in seinen Einrichtungen in den Jahren 1815 bis 1867." *Archiv für Geschichte des deutschen Buchhandels* 2 (1877): 125–234.
Bodi, Leslie. *Tauwetter in Wien: Zur Prosa der österreichischen Aufklärung, 1781–87.* Frankfort on Main, 1977.
Brunner, Otto, Werner Conze, and Reinhart Koselleck, eds. *Geschichtliche Grundbegriffe.* 5 vols. Berlin, 1972–84.
Busch, Rüdiger. *Die Aufsicht über das Bücher- und Preßwesen in den Rheinbundstaaten Berg, Westfalen und Frankfurt.* Karlsruhe, 1970.
Darmstadt, Rolf. *Der deutsche Bund in der zeitgenössischen Publizistik.* Bern, 1971.
Darnton, Robert. *The Literary Underground of the Old Regime.* Cambridge, Mass., 1982.
———. *The Kiss of Lamourette: Reflections in Cultural History.* New York, 1990.
Demandt, Karl E. *Geschichte des Landes Hessen.* 2d ed. Cassel, 1972.
———. *Kassel und Marburg: Ein historischer Städtevergleich.* Marburg, 1975.
Deuchert, Norbert. *Vom Hambacher Fest zur badischen Revolution: Politische Presse und Anfänge deutscher Demokratie 1832–1848/49.* Stuttgart, 1983.
Dwight, Henry E. *Travels in the North of Germany in the Years 1825 and 1826.* New York, 1829.
Eisenhardt, Ulrich. *Die kaiserliche Aufsicht über Buchdruck, Buchhandel und Presse im Heiligen Römischen Reich Deutscher Nation (1496–1806).* Karlsruhe, 1970.
Engelsing, Rolf. "Zeitung und Zeitschrift in Nordwestdeutschland 1800–1850: Leser und Journalisten." *Archiv für Geschichte des Buchwesens* 5 (1962/64): 850–955.
———. *Analphabetentum und Lektüre: Zur Sozialgeschichte des Lesens in Deutschland zwischen feudaler und industrieller Gesellschaft.* Stuttgart, 1973.
Faulkner, Arthur Brooke. *Visit to Germany and the Low Countries in the Years 1829, 30, and 31.* 2 vols. London, 1833.
Fraeb, Walter M. *Der Buchhandel in Hanau und der Buchhändler Friedrich König.* Hanau, 1931.
Franz, Eckhart G. "Jakob Grimm in der Kasseler Zensurkommission (1816–1829)," *Zeitschrift des Vereins für hessische Geschichte und Landeskunde* 75/76 (1964/65): 455–75.
Fuchs, Karlheinz. *Bürgerliches Räsonnement und Staatsräson: Zensur als Instrument des Despotismus dargestellt am Beispiel des rheinbündischen Württemberg (1806–1813).* Göppingen, 1975.

Gerland, Otto, ed. *Grundlage zu einer hessischen Gelehrten-, Schriftsteller- und Künstlergeschichte von 1831 bis in die neueste Zeit.* 2 vols. Cassel, 1863–68.
Gerstenberg, Heinrich. *Die hamburgische Zensur in den Jahren 1819–1848.* Hamburg, 1908.
Glossy, Karl. *Literarische Geheimberichte aus dem Vormärz.* Published as *Jahrbuch der Grillparzergesellschaft* 21–23 (1912).
Goody, Jack, and Ian Watt. "The Consequences of Literacy." In *Literacy in Traditional Societies*, 27–68, ed. Jack Goody. Cambridge, Eng., 1968.
Heine, Heinrich. *Sämtliche Werke*, ed. Ernst Elster. 9 vols. Leipzig, 1887–90.
Heinsius, Wilhelm. *Allgemeines Bücherlexikon.* 19 vols. Leipzig, 1812–94.
Held, Wilhelm. *Dem deutschen Volke.* Leipzig, 1846.
Hitzeroth, Heinz-Otto. *Die politische Presse Kurhessens, von der Einführung der Verfassung von 5. Januar 1831 bis zum Ausgang des Kurstaates 1866.* Marburg, 1935.
Hoefer, Frank Thomas. *Pressepolitik und Polizeistaat Metternichs: Die Überwachung von Presse und politischer Öffentlichkeit in Deutschland und der Nachbarstaaten durch das Mainzer Informationsbüro (1833–1848).* Dortmunder Beiträge zur Zeitungsforschung 37. Munich, 1983.
Hohmann, Günther. *Heinrich König: Leben und Werk des Fuldaer Schriftstellers (1790–1869) mit besonderer Berücksichtigung seines historischen Romans "Die Clubisten in Mainz."* Fulda, 1965.
Holzmann, Michael, and Hanns Bohatta. *Deutsches Anonymen-Lexikon, 1501–1926.* 7 vols. Weimar, 1902–28.
———. *Deutsches Pseudonymen Lexikon.* Vienna and Leipzig, 1906.
Hopf, Wilhelm. *August Vilmar: Ein Lebens- und Zeitbild.* 2 vols. Marburg, 1913.
Houben, Heinrich H. *Verbotene Literatur von der klassischen Zeit bis zur Gegenwart.* 2 vols. Berlin, 1924–28.
Huber, Ernst R. *Deutsche Verfassungsgeschichte seit 1789.* 5 vols. 2d ed. Stuttgart, 1957–78.
———. *Dokumente zur deutschen Verfassungsgeschichte.* 3 vols. Stuttgart, 1961–66.
Ingrao, Charles W. *The Hessian Mercenary State: Ideas, Institutions, and Reform under Frederick II, 1760–1785.* Cambridge, Eng., 1987.
Jacob, William. *A View of the Agriculture, Manufactures, Statistics, and State of Society, of Germany, and Parts of Holland and France, Taken during a Journey through Those Countries in 1819.* London, 1820.
Justi, Karl W. *Grundlage zu einer hessischen Gelehrten-, Schriftsteller- und Künstlergeschichte, 1806–1830.* 6 vols. Marburg, 1830.
Kellner, Wolf Erich. *Verfassungskämpfe und Staatsgerichtshof in Kurhessen.* Marburg, 1965.
Kleinknecht, Günter. *Sylvester Jordan (1792–1861): Ein deutscher Liberal im Vormärz.* Marburg, 1983.
König, Heinrich. *Auch eine Jugend: Erinnerungen und Bekenntnisse.* 2 vols. Leipzig, 1861.

———. *Ein Stilleben: Erinnerungen und Bekenntnisse.* 2 vols. Leipzig, 1861.

Koselleck, Reinhart. *Preußen zwischen Reform und Revolution: Allgemeines Landrecht, Verwaltung und soziale Bewegung von 1791 bis 1848.* 2d ed. Stuttgart, 1975.

Kramer, Margarete. *Die Zensur in Hamburg 1819 bis 1848.* Hamburg, 1975.

Krüger, Paul. " 'Hochverräterische Unternehmungen' in Studentenschaft und Bürgertum des Vormärz in Oberhessen (bis 1838)." *Mitteilungen des oberhessischen Geschichtsvereins* 49/50 (1965): 73–136.

Laubert, M. *Presse und Zensur der Provinz Posen in neupreußischer Zeit 1815–1847.* Posen, 1908.

Losch, Philipp. *Geschichte des Kurfürstentums Hessen 1803 bis 1866.* Marburg, 1922.

———. *Kurfürst Wilhelm I. Landgraf von Hessen.* Marburg, 1923.

Lotz, Albert. "Die Behördenorganisation im ehemaligen Kurhessen nach der Reform von 1821 und ihre Entwicklung in vorpreußischer Zeit." *Schmollers Jahrbuch* 28 (1904): 1343–69.

Marx, Julius. *Die österreichische Zensur im Vormärz.* Vienna, 1959.

Melton, James Van Horn. "From Image to Word: Cultural Reform and the Rise of Literate Culture in Eighteenth-Century Austria." *Journal of Modern History* 58 (March 1986): 95–124.

Meyer, F. Hermann. "Mittheilungen zur inneren Geschichte des deutschen Buchhandels von 1811–1848." *Archiv für Geschichte des deutschen Buchhandels* 8 (1883): 164–285; 9 (1884): 177–237.

———. "Bücherverbote im Königreiche Preußen von 1834 bis 1882." *Archiv für Geschichte des Deutschen Buchhandels* 14 (1889): 317–49.

Meyer, Hans-Friedrich. *Zeitungspreise in Deutschland im 19. Jahrhundert und ihre gesellschaftliche Bedeutung.* Münster, 1969.

Moran, Daniel. *Toward the Century of Words: Johann Cotta and the Politics of the Public Realm in Germany, 1795–1832.* Berkeley, 1990.

Murhard, Friedrich. *Die kurhessische Verfassungs-Urkunde, erläutert und beleuchtet nach Maßgabe ihrer einzelnen Paragraphen.* 2 vols. Cassel, 1834–35.

Neuer Nekrolog der Deutschen. 60 vols. Weimar, 1823–52.

Pelzet, Christian. *Die Blütezeit der deutschen politischen Lyrik von 1840–1850.* Munich, 1903.

Petmecky, J. "Karl Bernhardi." Ph.D. diss., University of Frankfort on Main, 1929.

Protokolle der deutschen Bundesversammlung. Frankfort on Main, 1816–1866.

Prutz, Robert. *Zehn Jahre: Geschichte der neuesten Zeit. 1840–1850.* 2 vols. Leipzig, 1850.

Ruckhäberle, Hans-Joachim. *Flugschriftenliteratur im historischen Umkreis Georg Büchners.* Kronberg in the Taunus, 1975.

Russell, John. *A Tour in Germany, and Some of the Southern Provinces of the Austrian Empire in the Years 1820, 1821, 1822.* Boston, 1825.

Sammlung von Gesetzen, Verordnungen, Ausschreiben und sonstigen allgemeinen Verfügungen für die kurhessischen Staaten. (Title varies.) Cassel, 1813–48.

Schenda, Rudolf. *Volk ohne Buch: Studien zur Sozialgeschichte der populären Lesestoffe, 1770–1910.* Frankfort on Main, 1970.
———. *Die Lesestoffe der kleinen Leute: Studien zur populären Literatur im 19. und 20. Jahrhundert.* Munich, 1976.
Schiller, Herbert, ed. *Briefe an Cotta.* 3 vols. Stuttgart, 1925–34.
Schnack, Ingeborg, ed. *Lebensbilder aus Kurhessen und Waldeck 1830–1930.* 6 vols. Marburg, 1939–58.
Schneider, Franz. *Pressefreiheit und politische Öffentlichkeit: Studien zur politischen Geschichte Deutschlands bis 1848.* Neuwied-on-the-Rhine, 1966.
Schoof, Wilhelm, ed. *Briefe der Brüder Grimm an Savigny.* Berlin, 1953.
Sheehan, James J. *German Liberalism in the Nineteenth Century.* Chicago, 1979.
———. *German History, 1770–1866.* Oxford, 1989.
Siemann, Wolfram. "Ideenschmuggel: Probleme der Meinungskontrolle und das Los deutscher Zensoren im 19. Jahrhundert." *Historische Zeitschrift* 245 (1987): 71–106.
Sinzheimer, Ludwig, ed. *Die geistigen Arbeiter.* Munich, 1922.
Sirges, Thomas and Ingeborg Müller. *Zensur in Marburg 1538–1832: Eine lokalgeschichtliche Studie zum Bücher- und Pressewesen.* Marburg, 1984.
[Spencer, Edwin]. *Sketches of Germany and the Germans.* 2 vols. London, 1836.
Stengel, Edmund, ed. *Private und amtliche Beziehungen der Brüder Grimm zu Hessen.* 3 vols. Marburg, 1895–1910.
Tapp, Alfred. *Hanau im Vormärz und in der Revolution von 1848–49: Ein Beitrag zur Geschichte des Kurfürstentums Hessen.* Hanau, 1976.
Treml, Manfred. *Bayerns Pressepolitik zwischen Verfassungstreue und Bundespflicht (1815–1837): Ein Beitrag zum bayerischen Souveränitätsverständnis und Konstitutionalismus im Vormärz.* Berlin, 1977.
Trollope, Frances. *Belgium and Western Germany in 1833.* 2 vols. London, 1834.
Venedey, Jakob. *Preußen und Preußenthum.* Mannheim, 1839.
Walesrode, Ludwig, ed. *Demokratische Studien.* Hamburg, 1860.
Walker, Mack. *German Home Towns: Community, State, and General Estate 1648–1871.* Ithaca, 1971.
Wochenblatt für Buchhändler. 15 vols. Marburg, 1819–33.
Ziegler, Edda. *Julius Campe: Heinrich Heines Verleger.* Hamburg, 1976.

Index

Aachener Zeitung, 104
Academic Museum, Marburg, 3, 122, 158–59
Allendorf, 149
Anhalt-Bamberg, Duchess of, 30
Apostolic Chancellery and Penance Assessment, 98
Appel bookshop, 118, 121, 122
Arnold, Chief Judge, 92–93
Auguste, Princess of Hesse, 20, 38, 53
Austria, 101, 152; censorship in, 7, 62; censorship, and diplomacy in, 105–6, 107; war with Prussia, 21, 166

Baden, 26, 79, 101; censorship in, 34, 41, 43, 61; censorship, and diplomacy in, 103; press freedom in, 8
Battle of Leipzig, 6
Baumgarten, Michael, 149
Bavaria, 26, 107, 152, 156; censorship in, 61; censorship, and diplomacy in, 102, 107
Bayrhoffer, Karl, 118, 119, 128, 144–45, 159
Berliner Gewerbe-Ausstellung (Glaßbrenner), 107
Bernhardi, Karl, 95, 151; attitude toward censorship, 60; as censor, 55, 57, 58–59, 60, 65, 67, 78, 96; and Geeh, 139; life and work of, 54–55, 56, 92
Besse, 160
Blätter für Geist und Herz, 81, 83

Blum, Robert, 98
Bockenheim, 81, 160–61
Boden, August, 97, 104, 109, 110, 113, 114, 122, 160
Bohné bookshop, 118, 123
Book Censorship Commission, 31, 61, 71
Book trade, Hesse-Cassel, 2; announcement of bans to, 115–17; banned books in, 117–19, 120–22; growth of, 74; investigation of Elwert, 128–31; investigation of Garthe, 132–37; petition to enter, 119; and police confiscations, 110, 111–15; profitability of, 110–11; prosecution of Geeh, 137–43; prosecution of König, 143–44; reimbursement for confiscated books, 122–25
Börne, Ludwig, 7, 98
Bote aus Kassel, 81
Bremen, 107
Büchner, Georg, 129, 163
Bückeburg, 107

Campe, Julius, 120
Carlsbad Conference, 33
Caroline, Princess of Hesse, 19
Cassel, 14, 34, 63; censorship in, 49, 51, 71; censorship and book trade in, 109–10, 111–13, 114–15, 118, 121, 122; censorship and lending libraries in, 71, 74; censorship and newspapers in, 79, 81, 85, 86–87; clubs in, 157–58, 160; described,

INDEX

Cassel (cont.)
17–18; Piderit's history of, 36; prosecution of Geeh in, 137–43; Revolution of 1848, 164. *See also* Censorship Commission, Cassel
Catholicism, 15, 46, 98, 154; and censorship, 63, 75, 120
Censorship Commission, Cassel, 2, 42, 46, 105, 109, 113, 118; and confiscation of banned books, 122–23, 124; duties of, 32; and Elwert, 62–63, 130–31; establishment of, 31; and lending library censorship, 72, 75, 77, 78; membership of, 51, 53–69; and newspaper censorship, 80–81; and political censorship, 90, 91, 93, 94, 96, 97
Charivari, 103
Christliche Kirche, 82
Chronik des 19ten Jahrhunderts, 94
Clubs, 157–63
Collman (school inspector), 75
Congress of Vienna, 22
Constitution of 1831, 3, 9, 12, 24, 25–27, 37–38, 50, 80, 89, 166
Conversationsfreund, 85
Cornmanns, Viktor Amadeus, 135, 136
Cotta, Johann, 167
Courts. *See* Superior Court; Supreme Court

Darnton, Robert, 4
Darstellung des politischen Zustandes von Deutschland, 94
Demandt, Karl, 19
Denhard, Dr., 153, 154, 162, 143
Denk- und Sittensprüche, 91
Denmark, 102, 107
Deutschen Volke, Dem (Held), 98
Deutscher Beobachter, 103
Deutscher Zuschauer, 103
Deutschlands Juli Ordonanzen, 142, 144, 153, 158
Diedrich, Pastor, 119
Dingelstedt, Franz, 91, 92, 93, 98, 120, 121
Dorfbarbier, 103
Döring, Friedrich, 44–45, 99, 133, 134, 135, 136, 143, 152, 158

Dritte Schrift zur Vertheidigung Sylvester Jordans (Boden), 109, 110, 113, 114, 160
Dwight, Henry, 18

Edler bookshop, 85, 118, 124, 125
Eggena, Carl Michael, 25, 38, 132
Eichelberg, Leopold, 135
Elwert, Noa Gottfried: bookshop of, 2, 119, 120, 121–22, 136; and Censorship Commission, 62–63, 130–31; lending library of, 76; as printer, 2, 56, 62–63; as printer of subversive works, 128–32, 137, 151
Emmerich (councilor), 144, 161
Ernst Augustus, King of Hanover, 53
Eschwege, 76, 119
Euler bookshop, 113, 114–15, 119, 120, 121, 122, 147, 155
Evangelical church, in lending library censorship, 75–77

Faulkner, Arthur Brooke, 17–18
Fichte, Johann Gottlieb, 11
Fiedler, J. H., 85
Fischer, Heinrich, 121, 129, 136
Förster, Jakob, 83, 86, 118, 150, 155, 156, 158, 162
Frag- und Antwortbüchlein, 95, 97, 148
Frankfort, 14, 63, 107; clubs in, 157, 158; Constituent Assembly, 45, 166; diplomacy and censorship in, 102, 104; distribution of banned works in, 151–52. *See also* German Confederation, Frankfort Assembly
Frankfurter Journal, 102
French Revolution, 5, 8, 51
Friedrich II, Count of Hesse, 18–19
Friedrich II, King of Prussia, 5, 19
Friedrich Wilhelm IV, King of Prussia, 38, 166
Friedrich William, Prince-Elector of Hesse-Cassel, 47, 55; administrative organization under, 24; authoritarianism of, 38, 39; and censorship, 77–78, 90; and constitution of 1831, 26, 27, 36–37; dismissal of Piderit, 56; life and reign of, 20–21

222

INDEX

Fulda, 92, 110; annexed by Hesse-Cassel, 14–15; censorship and book trade in, 110, 113, 114, 117, 118, 119, 120, 121, 122, 144; censorship and lending libraries in, 74, 76; censorship and newspapers in, 81, 83, 84; censorship and press laws in, 61, 63, 76, 77, 81; clubs in, 162–63; described, 14, 15; distribution of banned works in, 153, 154–55, 156
Fuldaer Zeitung, 81
Funck, Johann Friedrich, 98

Gartenhof, Dr., 154–55, 156
Garthe, Christian Dietrich: bookshop of, 119, 120, 132, 153; lending library of, 76, 132–33; newspaper of, 81, 86; police investigation of, 128, 129, 132–37; and Sylvester Jordan, 40, 44, 132
Geeh, Dietrich Albrecht, 84, 105, 118, 126, 153, 158; as printer of subversive work, 126, 128, 137–43, 150
Gelnhausen, 150, 152
Gerke, Friedrich Clemens, 49
German Confederation, 11, 31; Carlsbad Conference, 33; Central Investigatory Bureau of, 11, 44, 45, 103, 141, 142; decline in 1830s, 35; "Sixty Articles," 35
German Confederation, Frankfort Assembly: ban on nationalist displays and works, 35, 124–25; censorship decrees of, 34, 35, 43, 101; influence on Hessian censorship, 32–33, 34, 43, 89, 90, 101–2; and newspaper censorship, 83; powers under press laws, 33–34; press law of 1819, 32–34, 59, 80, 82; "Six Articles," 34, 43
Gewerbeblätter für Kurhessen, 85
Glaßbrenner, Adolph, 49, 106
Goldschmidt, Moses, 119
Görres, Joseph, 6, 9, 167
Göttingen, 53
Göttingen, University of, 3, 17, 38
Grabbe, Christian Dietrich, 2
Grenzbote, 159

Grimm, Jacob, 1, 3, 8, 20, 38, 39, 54, 92; as censor, 52–53, 57, 58, 59, 64, 65; on censorship, 59, 66–67, 70; on censorship of lending libraries, 72–73; life and work of, 53–54
Grimm, Wilhelm, 1, 3, 8, 20, 38, 39, 51, 53, 54, 57, 92
Grosse, Ernst, 100
Gutzkow, Karl, 69, 98, 124

Hambach, 41
Hamburg, 49, 102, 107, 167
Hanau: censorship in, 61, 63–64; censorship, and book trade in, 118, 124, 125; censorship, and lending libraries in, 74, 76–77; censorship, and newspapers in, 79, 81, 83, 84; described, 14; distribution of banned works in, 153, 154; liberal tradition in, 161–62; prosecution of König in, 143–44
Hanauer Zeitung, 79–80, 81, 84, 102, 137
Hanover, 23, 53, 107
Harring, Harro, 98, 135, 136
Hassenpflug, Ludwig: and censorship, 42, 131; impeachment attempt on, 42; mentor of Scheffer, 46; in prosecution of Sylvester Jordan, 44; and press law proposal, 41, 43; resignation and departure from Hesse, 43, 46, 69; return to power, 165; rise to power, 38, 39
Hauff, Wilhelm, 2
Heine, Heinrich, 2, 98, 107, 155; "Night Thoughts," 8–9, 164–65
Heinzen, Karl, 97
Held, Wilhelm, 8, 98, 105
Henkel bookshop, 144, 155
Henze (wood engraver), 119
Hermine (Zirndorfer), 123
Hersfeld, 76, 86
Herwegh, Georg, 49, 98, 159
Hesse, Franz Hugo, 167
Hesse-Cassel: archive of, 3; censorship and press laws in, 7, 8, 11–12, 26, 27, 28, 29, 30–33, 34, 35–36, 38–47, 64–65, 83–85, 89, 165 (*See also* Book trade; Censorship Commis-

223

INDEX

Hesse-Cassel (cont.)
sion; Lending libraries; Periodicals and newspapers); clubs in, 157–63; constitution of 1831 in, 3, 9, 12, 24, 25–27, 37–38, 50, 80, 89, 166; described, 13–18; diplomatic requests for censorship, 102–7; French occupation of, 22, 31, 52; paternal rule in, 29, 31, 36; police in (*See* Police); prince-electors of, 18–25; religion in (*See* Religion); Reorganization Edict of 1821, 24, 25, 32, 59; scholarship in, 92. *See also names of towns*
Hesse-Darmstadt, 14, 63, 107, 122, 129
Hessian Historical Association, 56
Hessicher Landbote, 129, 163
Hildburghauser Dorfzeitung, 95
Hildebrand, Bruno, 92
Hofbauer, Wilhelm, 152
Hoffman and Campe, 93, 167
Hoffmann, Carl Friedrich, 119
Hoffmann von Fallersleben, 151
Horn, Johann von, 94
Hornthal, Adolph, 119
Hotop, Heinrich, 85, 86–87
Huber, Victor Aimé, 129, 130
Hundt-Radowsky, Hartwig, 98
Hünfeld, 115, 155

Illustrirte Zeitung, 87
Intelligenzblatt, 86
Israelit, Der, 82

Jacob, William, 13, 15, 18
Jacoby, Johann, 98, 106, 117
Jerome Bonaparte, King of Westphalia, 30, 31, 52
Jews, 15, 40, 82, 119
Jordan, Sylvester, 91, 97, 98; and Academic Museum, 158–59; background and education of, 25; ban on works by, 121; on censorship, 40; censorship of supporters, 103–4, 105, 109, 110; and constitution of 1831, 3, 9, 25; customer of Garthe, 135, 136; distribution of banned works on prosecution of, 118; election to Frankfort Constituent Assembly, 45; and press law proposal, 40–41; prosecution for treason, 43–45, 47, 93, 132, 133, 134, 135, 159
Juch, Karl, 150
Jungklaus bookshop, 111

Kassel'sche Allgemeine Zeitung, 79
Kasselsches Schulblatt, 81
Kempf, Karl, 111, 112–13
Kersting (merchant), 30, 31
Kirchner (student), 153, 155
Kittsteiner (printer), 63, 137
Klöffler, Pastor, 76
Koch, Jacob, 161
König, Friedrich, 118, 128, 141, 143–44, 153, 154
König, Heinrich, 14, 92, 158
Kraushaar, Pastor, 81
Krieger bookshop, 62, 107, 111, 118, 121, 122

Lamennais, Félicité, 129, 135–36
Lehmann, Gertrude Falkenstein (Baroness of Schaumburg), 20, 21
Leipziger Lokomotive, 156
Lending libraries: censorship of, 64, 65, 72–79, 90; of Garthe, 76; numbers of, 74; origins of, in Germany, 71
Leo X, Pope, 98
Libraries. *See* Lending libraries; Royal Library
Lieder eines kosmopolitischen Nachtwächters (Dingelstedt), 91, 92, 93, 121
Lippe, 107
Lübeck, 107
Luckhardt bookshop, 91, 121, 122, 123
Luther, Martin, 2, 3
Lutherans, 15

Macrocensorship, 109
Malkmus, Dr., 76
Manger, Ludwig von, 31, 81
Manifest der Vernunft (Gerke), 49

224

INDEX

Mannheimer Abendzeitung, 103
Manuscript censorship, 91, 92, 93
Marburg: Academic Museum in, 3, 122, 158–59; castle in, 3, 45; censorship in, 62–63; censorship, and book trade in, 2, 110–11, 117, 118–19, 120, 121–22, 128–37, 144; censorship, and lending libraries in, 74, 76; censorship, and newspapers in, 81; clubs in, 158–59; described, 2, 15, 17; distribution of banned works in, 148, 153, 155, 156; political dissent in book trade of, 128–37; prosecution of Sylvester Jordan in, 44–45, 47, 93, 132, 133, 134, 135; setting of, 1–2
Marburg, University of, 2, 3, 15, 17, 25, 40, 44, 54, 92; censors from, 61, 62; student political activities at, 95
Marburger Zeitung, 81, 86
Mazzini, Giuseppe, 49
Mecklinburg-Strelitz, 107
Meier (laborer), 154
Melsungen, 74, 148–49
Merz (Privy Councilor), 155
Merz (teacher), 135, 143
Messinger, Georg, 152
Messner bookshop, 121
Metternich, Clemens von, 4, 7, 11, 52, 167
Metzler bookshop, 142
Microcensorship, 109–10
Mohl, Robert von, 7
Monatliche Berichte der Deutsch-Chinesischen Stiftung, 82
Moniteur Westfalien, 52, 79
Morchutt, Wilhelm, 103, 164
Moritz, Karl, 74
Müller, Carl, 110, 119
Munich, 152
Murhard, Friedrich, 7, 37, 52, 159
Musikalische Zeitschrift für Kirche und Schule, 81

Napoleon Bonaparte, 6, 31, 38, 52, 94
Nationalism: and censorship, 98, 99–100, 124–25, 165–66; suppression by German Confederation, 35, 124–25

Neue Zeitschwingen, 84
Newspapers. *See* Periodicals and newspapers
North German Customs Union, 96

Oehler, Friedrich, 126, 141, 142
Offene Erklärung kurhessischer Bürger, 99, 144, 152, 154, 161
Oldenburg, 107
Ortlöpp, Emilie (Countess of Reichenbach), 20, 21
Osterwald bookshop, 99–100, 125, 160

Pamphlets: confiscation of banned works, 111–12, 151–52, 154–55; distribution of banned works, 99, 147–51, 153–54, 155–56, 158; policing of, 99–100
Paroles d'un Croyant, 129, 136
Periodicals and newspapers: censorship of, 65, 79–87; censorship of, diplomacy and, 102–7; numbers of, 79, 80
Pfaff, Karl Hermann: as censor, 51, 54, 78; on lending library censorship, 75, 76
Pfau, Georg Reinhardt, 148
Philipp the Magnanimous, 3, 62
Piderit, Franz Carl Theodor, 55, 56, 68, 69, 131, 132
Pinhas, Jacob, 79
Police: and censorship, 29, 30, 31, 64, 78, 81, 89–90, 94–95; confiscation of banned works, 110, 111–15, 127; investigation of Elwert, 128–31; investigation of Garth, 132–37; paternal spirit of, 28–29; prosecution of Geeh, 137–43; prosecution of Jordan, 45
Politische Schriften (Grosse), 100
Press and Fatherland Society, 41, 43, 97, 161
Press freedom: constitutional guarantees of, 7, 26, 27, 37–38, 89; as political issue, 7–8
Press law: Baden (1831), 34, 41, 43; German Confederation (1819), 59, 80, 82; Hesse-Cassel, 31, 34, 39–40, 43, 39–43, 165

225

Prussia: admired and imitated by prince-electors, 19, 23, 39; censorship in, 6–7, 50, 87; censorship in, diplomacy and, 104, 105, 106–7; newspapers and periodicals in, 6, 87; rule of Hesse-Cassel, 21, 166

Radowitz, Joseph Maria von, 38, 39
Reden an die deutsche Nation (Fichte), 11
Reformed Church, 15, 50, 55, 61
Reisen eines deutschen Freigeistes, 156–57
Religion: conservative/liberal quarrels, 46; dissenters, 144; diversity of, in Hesse-Cassel, 15; and lending library censorship, 75–77. *See also* Catholicism
Reorganization Edict of 1821, 24, 25, 32, 59
Revolutions of 1848, 9, 98, 164–65
Rheinischer Merkur, 6–7
Rinteln, 61, 63, 64, 77, 99, 125, 160
Ritter bookshop, 135
Robert, Carl Wilhelm, 103, 130
Rode, Wilhelm, 152–53
Rollet, Hermann, 105–6
Rommel, Christoph von: as censor, 49–50, 53, 54–55, 56, 57, 58, 66, 67, 68, 82–83, 96, 107, 123, 130, 140; and Elwert, 128, 130; *Geschichte von Hessen*, 2, 54; as librarian, 52, 54; life and work of, 53–54; and newspaper censorship, 82–83
Rommel, Justus, 31, 51, 53, 56, 57, 58, 131
Rotenburg, 160
Rotteck, Karl von, 8, 97
Royal Library: Christoph von Rommel as director of, 52, 54; as source of censors, 50–51, 55, 59; Völkel as director of, 51, 52
Rucker bookshop, 136
Ruge, Arnold, 98
Russell, John, 18

Sächische Vaterlandsblätter, 118, 159
Sauerwein, Johann Wilhelm, 98
Savigny, Friedrich Karl von, 52, 59

Saxony, 87, 97, 101, 159, 167; diplomacy and censorship in, 102, 103, 104, 105, 107
Saxony-Weimar, 107
Scheffer, Friedrich, 164; in religious quarrels, 46; removal of, 47; rise to power, 46
Schehl, Wilhelm, 161
Schell, Franz, 98, 118, 154, 155
Schlotheim, Caroline von, 19
Schmalkalden, 76
Schubart, J. H. Christian: as censor, 55, 56–57, 58–59, 60, 65, 68, 123, 130, 131; on censorship, 60, 66; life and work of, 56
Schulz, Wilhelm, 95, 97, 148, 163
Schwerin, 107
Sechs Gebote des Deutschen Bundes, Die, 99, 150, 152
Siebenpfeiffer, Phillipp Jakob, 97, 134, 152
Spazier, Otto (pseud.), 69
Strasbourg, 97
Struve, Gustav von, 98
Superior Court, Cassel: Geeh case in, 140–41, 142; Kempf case in, 111
Superior Court, Hanau, 143
Superior Court, Marburg: Bayrhoffer case in, 145; Garthe case in, 133
Supreme Court, Hessian, 39; Geeh case in, 139–40; Jordan case in, 45, 132, 159; Kempf case in, 111, 112–13

Teutsches Volksblatt, 81, 83, 84, 86, 118
Treis an der Lumda, 94
Treysa, 46
Trinthammer, Pastor, 76–77
Trollope, Mrs., 13, 18
21 Bogen aus der Schweiz (Herwegh), 98
21 Bogen für Deutschland, 98

Venedey, Jakob, 8, 98
Verfassungsfreund, 3, 55, 58, 81, 82, 83, 84, 95, 139, 140, 151

INDEX

Vier Fragen beantwortet von einem Ostpreussen (Jacoby), 106, 117
Vilmar, August, 92, 151, 128, 130, 131
Völkel, Johann Ludwig, 51, 52, 58
Völkerstimmen, Die, 162
Völksblatt aus Würzburg, 156
Volks-und Anzeigeblatt für Mitteldeutschland, 83
Vossische Zeitung, 104

Wagner, Professor, 155
Waldeck, 107
Walesrode, Ludwig, 167
Walker, Mack, 5–6
Wally, die Zweiflerin (Gutzkow), 69, 124
Wangemann, W. H., 45, 158, 159
Weidig, Ludwig, 129, 163
Weitling, Wilhelm, 98
Weiwadel, Johann Georg, 148–49
Welcker, Karl Theodor, 97
Weser Dampfboot, 156
Westphalia, Kingdom of, 22, 52
Wilhelm I, Prince-Elector of Hesse-Cassel: attitude toward France, 5, 19; and censorship, 30–31, 33, 61–62; life and reign of, 18, 19, 20, 22–23; opposes Carlsbad decrees, 33; paternal rule of, 29, 31; return from exile, 22, 30, 31; ridiculed in press, 29–30; voids edicts of French occupation, 22, 47
Wilhelm II, Prince-Elector of Hesse-Cassel: administrative reorganization of, 23–24, 32, 52; blames foreign influences for unrest, 36; and book trade, 111; and censorship, 32, 37, 90; and constitution of 1831, 24–25, 37; exile in Frankfort, 24; life and reign of, 18, 19–20; paternal rule of, 29
Wilhelm VIII, Count of Hesse, 19
Wirth, Johann Georg August, 8, 41, 97, 134, 135, 161
Witzenhausen, 76, 77, 149, 150, 152
Wuppertal, 149
Württemberg, 26, 107
Würzburg, 157, 158

"Young Germany," 98, 99–100, 124–25

Zeitbilder, 83
Zeitschrift für Alterthumswissenschaft, 82
Zeitschwingen, 83
Ziegenhain, 86, 117
Zirndorfer, S., 123
Zurich, 97
Zwingli, Huldrych, 3

Germany's Rude Awakening
was composed in 10½-point Bembo and leaded a point and a half
on a Xyvision system with Linotron 202 output
by BookMasters, Inc.;
printed by sheet-fed offset
on 55-pound Glatfelter Natural acid-free paper,
Smyth sewn and bound over 88′ binder's boards
in Holliston Roxite B-grade cloth,
and wrapped with dustjackets printed on 80-pound
enamel paper in two colors and film laminated
by Braun-Brumfield, Inc.;
designed by Diana Gordy;
and published by
The Kent State University Press
KENT, OHIO 44242